International Migration and Social Theory

Karen O'Reilly

Professor of Sociology, Loughborough University

palgrave
macmillan

First published 2012 by
PALGRAVE MACMILLAN

Palgrave Macmillan in the UK is an imprint of Macmillan Publishers Limited, registered in England, company number 785998, of Houndmills, Basingstoke, Hampshire RG21 6XS.

Palgrave Macmillan in the US is a division of St Martin's Press LLC, 175 Fifth Avenue, New York, NY 10010.

Palgrave Macmillan is the global academic imprint of the above companies and has companies and representatives throughout the world.

Palgrave® and Macmillan® are registered trademarks in the United States, the United Kingdom, Europe and other countries.

ISBN 978–0–230–22130–7 hardback
ISBN 978–0–230–22131–4 paperback

This book is printed on paper suitable for recycling and made from fully managed and sustained forest sources. Logging, pulping and manufacturing processes are expected to conform to the environmental regulations of the country of origin.

A catalogue record for this book is available from the British Library.

A catalog record for this book is available from the Library of Congress.

10 9 8 7 6 5 4 3 2 1
21 20 19 18 17 16 15 14 13 12

Printed and bound in Great Britain by
CPI Antony Rowe, Chippenham and Eastbourne

THEMES IN SOCIAL THEORY

This series explores how cutting-edge research within the social sciences relies on combinations of social theory and empirical evidence. Different books examine how this relationship works in particular subject areas, from technology and health to politics and human rights. Giving the reader a brief overview of the major theoretical approaches used in an area, the books then describe their application in a range of empirical projects. Each text looks at contemporary and classical theories, provides a map of primary research carried out in the subject area and highlights advances in the field. The series is a companion to the Traditions in Social Theory series, founded by Ian Craib and edited by Rob Stones.

Published

HEALTH AND SOCIAL THEORY
Fernando De Maio

TECHNOLOGY AND SOCIAL THEORY
Steve Matthewman

INTERNATIONAL MIGRATION AND SOCIAL THEORY
Karen O'Reilly

Forthcoming

CRIME AND SOCIAL THEORY
Eammon Carrabine

POLITICS AND SOCIAL THEORY
Will Leggett

HUMAN RIGHTS AND SOCIAL THEORY
Lydia Morris

ENVIRONMENT, NATURE AND SOCIAL THEORY
Damian White, Alan Rudy and Brian Gareau

Further titles in preparation

TRADITIONS IN SOCIAL THEORY

Founding Editor: Ian Craib
Series Editor: Rob Stones

This series offers a selection of concise introductions to particular traditions in sociological thought. It aims to deepen the reader's knowledge of particular theoretical approaches and at the same time to enhance their wider understanding of sociological theorizing. Each book will offer: a history of the chosen approach and the debates that have driven it forward; a discussion of the current state of the debates within the approach (or debates with other approaches); and an argument for the distinctive contribution of the approach and its likely future value. The series is a companion to the *Themes in Social Theory* series, edited by Rob Stones.

Published

PHILOSOPHY OF SOCIAL SCIENCE (*Second Edition*)
Ted Benton and Ian Craib

CRITICAL THEORY
Alan How

STRUCTURATION THEORY
Rob Stones

MARXISM AND SOCIAL THEORY
Jonathon Joseph

MICRO SOCIAL THEORY
Brian Roberts

Forthcoming

POST-STRUCTURALISM AND AFTER
David Howarth

Contents

Series Foreword

A simple aim lies at the heart of this series. This is to deepen understanding of the role of social theory in the creation and validation of the most valuable empirical research in the social sciences. The series rests upon a commitment to explore the vast terrain upon which theory and the empirical meet, and extends an invitation to readers to share in this exploration. Each book takes on a specialized substantive area of research such as health, international migration, crime, politics, technology, human rights, and the environment, and excavates the character of the theory-empirical interplay in relation to key themes within the specialized area.

The authors of the volumes all write clearly and accessibly even when the material they are dealing with is intrinsically difficult. They have a close knowledge of the relevant field, an enthusiasm for the kind of theoretically informed empirical research that has been produced within it, and have themselves a flair for theoretical analysis. Within the general rubric of the series each author (or team of authors) has her or his own style and approach and a distinctive authorial voice. This should translate into a sense of pluralism within the series as a whole, meaning that the investigation of the theory-empirical terrain will take on the broad and varied character required to push forward our understanding in the most open and constructive manner possible.

Each book in the series aims to bring together in one volume some of the most significant theoretically informed empirical work in that subfield. The opening chapters of each book will outline the main theoretical approaches associated with substantive research in the area, and subsequent chapters will bring out how these approaches have been important in facilitating a range of key empirical studies. It will become apparent that a researcher's focus on a particular empirical case has often led her/him to draw on more than one theoretical approach, and then to creatively combine them in a form appropriate to the empirical case. The value of the substantive findings and arguments produced by each highlighted study is paramount, and will be clearly indicated.

It is hoped that the books from the series will play their part in helping to bridge the harmful gap between theory and the empirical that is still too often present within the social sciences, and that they will not only be used on second and third year undergraduate courses, to train and sensitize the next generation of social analysts, but will also be helpful to researchers at all levels. The books will demonstrate that there is already a large existing literature in each sub-field that has indeed combined theory and the empirical, and they will clarify the descriptive, explanatory and critical power produced by such combinations.

The notion of 'themes' referred to in the series title in fact signals two kinds of themes. The *first* kind is *substantive* and refers to the overall theme of the respective volume – health, environment, human rights, and so on – and, more subtly, to the sub-types of thematic content to be found within each of the different clusters of studies highlighted in each volume and indicated through the titles of the more substantive chapters. The *second* type of theme is *methodological*, and refers to the ways in which theory and the empirical are brought together within each of the studies highlighted. I prefer to refer to this set of themes under the label of 'conceptual methodology', rather than just 'methodology', in order to emphasize the ways in which particular theoretical ideas or concepts (and combinations of these) guide more formal methods such as observation, documentary analysis, surveys, interviews and so on, towards certain types of empirical data. Concepts and theories, here, are seen to have identifiable methodological and empirical consequences.

It is relatively self-evident that the *key substantive themes* that emerge in, for example, Fernando de Maio's volume on health – such as those around health inequalities and demographics, the functioning of the sick role, or the practices of pharmaceutical companies – will be distinct from those in other volumes such as Karen O'Reilly's on international migration or Steve Matthewman's on technology. This is not to say that there couldn't be fruitful overlap; it is very easy to envisage research projects looking at the health implications of international migration or at the use of technology in health care. However, it is to say that one might expect a series of distinctive thematic concerns to emerge from a focus on studies that have health as their primary concern. It is probable that the lessons to be learnt from the *conceptual methodological themes* will be more general. Here, more commonality is likely to emerge across sub-fields in the ways that theory and the empirical are combined together, notwithstanding their different subject matters.

All the authors in the series take it for granted that particular ways of seeing, hearing, interpreting and understanding – to name just some of the ways we apprehend the world – are involved every time a so-called empirical fact is given that status by somebody. That somebody, in turn, may be any kind of everyday participant within society, deploying their own cultural and social standpoint on the world, whether they are a political power broker, a homeless migrant, an environmental activist or an academic researcher. Whoever it is who does the apprehending, all empirical facts – and the stories and arguments through which they are joined together into an account of the social world – are already infused with their ideas and ways of seeing associated, in turn, with the particular cultures and subcultures they belong to. Embedded within these cultures are concepts, presuppositions and categorizations that can range from a mixture of the simply inherited and/or confused at one end of the spectrum to a mixture of the systematically reflected upon and/or analytically lucid at the other end of the spectrum. Social theory attempts to produce ways of seeing and apprehending the social world, including the empirical evidence that social analysts draw on to give weight to their claims, are nearer to the latter end of the spectrum than the former.

The degree of rigour and intellectual seriousness implied by these standards, brought into close liaison with the imaginative ways of seeing that good social science seeks constantly to renew, are what should make the activities and claims of social science stand out. Our claim should be that the accounts we produce add something further to public and civic culture, and to political life, than say news journalism or the everyday understandings of ordinary people. Social science has its own generic standards: standards that we constantly need to explore, reflect upon and improve, not least with respect to the relationship between social theory and substantive studies. It is only by doing this that we can genuinely carry forward the ambitious aspirations of a public social science that can play its rightful and much needed part in a thorough and continuing interrogation of the social.

Rob Stones

Acknowledgements

This book has taken a few years to write and it has sometimes been a painful process. It has also been an enlightening and (finally) satisfying one, and for that I thank all those great minds and conscientious personalities that together contributed the body of work without which this would be nothing. As with all such projects, there are numerous individuals I need to thank and I am bound to forget to mention someone who has been vital to my intellectual or personal sanity. So, you know who you are and I thank you! I would especially like to thank Michaela Benson, who provides me with fun and laughter as well as intellectual sustenance. Thanks also go to Maggie O'Neill for her recommendations for Chapter 7. Even though I have not been able to include much discussion of her book, *Asylum, Migration and Community*, I nevertheless highly recommend it to readers, especially because she says: 'processes of integration, belonging and community formation are complex and include structural, agentic, relational, and psychosocial aspects'. Iris Wigger and Daniel Chernilo helped me without even realizing it, because they are both colleagues and scholars of nations and nationalism. I have truly benefitted from working with such a great Sociology team at Loughborough. Other migration scholars I have had the pleasure to work with or meet at conferences have contributed in various ways, mainly by being enthusiastic and intelligent people who enjoy sharing ideas. I particularly mention Caroline Oliver, Mari Korpela, Catherine Trundle, Joaquin Rodes, Klaus Schriewer, Vicente Rodriguez and other members of the lifestyle migration hub. The four anonymous academic reviewers of the first draft were incredibly thorough and generous of their time and energies. The editorial team at Palgrave has been exceptionally patient and I especially thank Anna Reeve for commenting on drafts with such enthusiasm and vigilance. Thanks to the ESRC for funding a number of my own migration research projects, and to the many individuals who let me into their lives to do research on migration. The book owes massive thanks to Rob Stones for his help, support, kindness, and especially his intellectual insights. Finally, my family continues to show me endless patience, and I love the way they all humour me when I get totally absorbed in what they probably think is a complete waste of time. The book is dedicated, as always, to Trevor.

1

Introduction: International Migration and Social Theory

Introduction

International migration affects millions of people across the globe every day, as migrants and as non-migrants. It can arise as a result of rupture in people's lives, it can cause upheavals within communities, and it can reunite families. It can provide much-needed resources for sending and receiving countries, or it can put great strain on destinations or shatter the economies and daily lives when migrants leave. It can lead to emotional, individual, media and policy responses. It can be framed with the rhetoric of floods, tides, and influxes, or it can be warmly welcomed. Migration cuts to the very heart of who 'we' and 'they' are, and to notions of identity, home and belonging.

This book is about *the study of international migration*, the social theories that are being, and might be, employed in the understanding of a phenomenon, and the wonderful breadth of empirical work that has been (and continues to be) undertaken in this diverse field. By referring to 'international migration', I am excluding domestic or internal migration, but I recognize that processes of internal migration may often be interlinked with international migration in ways it is not possible to consider here (see King and Skeldon, 2010). This book is concerned with a phenomenon of increasing importance in recent decades: the movement of individuals and groups from one country, state or nation to another, to reside elsewhere at least on a temporary basis, often more permanently, the purpose being more than a visit or tourism. In particular, this book examines the ways in which the phenomenon of international migration has been studied, conceptualized and theorized by scholars, and suggests a theoretical framework that can provide coherence for the existing mass of disparate

1

works already undertaken and that can inform future data collection and analysis.

Migration is by no means a new phenomenon. Humans have moved as individuals and groups since they first populated the earth, perhaps because mobility, as John Urry (2007) has eloquently demonstrated, is inherent to the nature of all social entities, whether the movement itself is actual or potential. However, there is little doubt that international migration has been increasing, especially in the past 30 years; most academic books on the subject begin with some such statement. Bommes and Morawska (2005: 1) suggest that there was an 'enormous expansion of international population flows' beginning in the 1980s, with numbers of international migrants increasing by about two to four million a year throughout the 1990s. Koser (2007a: 1) says '[t]here are more international migrants today than ever before, and their number is certain to increase for the foreseeable future'. According to the International Organization for Migration (IOM, 2008 – see King and Skeldon, 2010) the number has recently reached two million, though it is worth remembering this still only equates to about three per cent of the world's total population. Faist (2000: 3) made the observation that 'if merged into a single country, this "nation of migrants" would be the world's tenth largest nation-state'. Brettell and Hollifield (2008: 1) suggest that, at the beginning of the twenty-first century, the immigrant population of the US stood 'at a historic high of 36 million' and that 'Europe has experienced a similar influx of foreigners'. Migration now affects every corner of the globe not just the previously recognized countries of net immigration; as Bommes and Morawska (2005) note, migration has become a normal feature of contemporary societies.

Migration has become a vast topic for scholars, and literature on it is abundant and growing every day. As international migration has grown in numbers, and, in extent, has spread to every corner of the globe, and has become increasingly diverse and fluid, so academic interest in the phenomenon of migration has almost reached fever-pitch, with 'analyses from every conceivable point pouring out' (Skeldon, 1997: ix). Migration is a central dynamic in the process of globalization (Skeldon, 1997), that is inextricably linked with other important global issues, including development, poverty, and human rights (Koser, 2007a: 1). We witness increased concern on the part of governments and international organizations to control (permit or stifle) flows, which are seen variously as dangerous influxes that lead to clashes of culture, as the source of valuable remittances, or as challenging the sovereignty of states through increased levels of irregularity and transnationalism (Castles and Miller, 2009: 3; Joly, 2004). Migration researchers discuss the challenges it poses, and its history, draw attention to its increased feminization, and propose various typologies. Reading about international migration, one might typically hear the following being distinguished, *inter alia*: labour migrants, and skilled or professional migrants, students, retirement migrants, nomads, refugees, or asylum seekers, forced migration, or return migration. There are countries of emigration and countries of immigration (a distinction being undermined by contemporary fluid, return, virtual and indeterminate flows); there are South to North and East to West migrations (one hears of flows in the opposite direction to these much less often). And there are migration *systems*, principally North America, Western Europe, the Gulf, Asia and the Pacific, and the Southern Cone of South America (Massey et al., 1998).

Research on migration has drawn the attention of a host of disciplines, including sociology and anthropology, human geography and demography, politics, history and international relations, and even cultural studies and the arts. International migration is analysed in terms of any or all of the following and more besides:

- geographical areas, historical trends, and issues of security, and minorities and politics (e.g. Castles and Miller, 2009);
- globalization, development, irregular migration, refugees, and migrants in society (e.g. Koser, 2007a, 2007b);
- citizenship, social exclusion, the division of labour, and cosmopolitanism (e.g. Cohen, 2006);
- demographics, assimilation, networks and identities, place, politics, and law (e.g. Brettell and Hollifield, 2008);
- ethnicity and nationalism (e.g. Eriksen, 2002);
- entrepreneurship, incorporation, and assimilation (e.g. Portes and Rumbaut, 2006);
- experiences, associations, culture, politics, and effects of migration (e.g. Morawska, 2009).

It has become something of a sub-discipline in its own right, albeit with somewhat differential treatment depending on the disciplinary perspective being employed. This has led to a 'tremendous amount of empirical knowledge' (Bommes and Morawska, 2005: 2), certainly more than one book could hope to capture and summarize.

This book introduces students to the key theories and concepts that have been used to understand migration. It examines how these have been used to understand actual cases, and it offers a more general, sociological, theory of how all of social life unfolds through the practice of daily life as a way of framing, evaluating and understanding this breadth of empirical and theoretical work.

Migration Theories and Social Theory

Migration has been theorized using a host of perspectives and concepts, some developed specifically for migration studies (substantive theories) and others more generally applicable to a range of social processes. It is possible to identify a number of mainstream approaches, as discussed fully in Chapter 3. *Economic theories* are often employed by sociologists, geographers, and anthropologists as well as economists for understanding migration. These attempt to explain, at an individual (or *micro*) level, which economic factors impel migrants to leave some places and which attract them to others; alternatively they outline, at a broader (or macro) level, those forces that create the economic differences between places that lead to migration. These theoretical perspectives are often based on wider social theories that assume individuals act on conscious and rational choices, so they therefore give migrants a lot of agency, or free will. On the other hand, those that explain migration in terms of global relations of power suggest that migrants have no free will at all. In what is known as the *new economic theories*, economic explanations are combined with sociological theories to include social processes – the role of families and networks, for example – in understanding migration. But they still assume migrants are free agents driven especially by a fundamental desire for economic gain. *Migration systems and networks* theory is more sociological. It argues that all migration needs to be understood within the wider context of the system (the social and economic relationships between different countries in different regions), and with attention paid to the role families, friends and other contacts play in assisting or resisting migrants, helping them settle, maintaining their links to home, and so on. This approach is informed (but only implicitly) by a general theory of how social life unfolds. Other substantive theories, such as *segmented assimilation* theory, and *globalization* theory, have been used in migration research to understand the settlement of migrants, especially issues of integration. Earlier approaches tended to see migration as one-off moves, by men, to new places where they would settle indefinitely. More recently, it has become clear that migration is more fluid and complex than that. Contemporary approaches therefore theorize such things as gender and migration, transnationalism (or the to-and-fro of ideas, people and things across borders), and multi-locality, translocality and flows.

While there are a lot of substantive migration theories there is something of a vacuum when it comes to a single theoretical framework providing coherence. There have been attempts to integrate or to synthesize migration theories. In *Worlds in Motion*, Douglas Massey (1998) and his colleagues review the body of knowledge on, and diverse disciplinary and interdisciplinary approaches to, the study of international migration.[1] They explicate the various theoretical perspectives, examine the extent to which they are complementary, and then explore their application to the empirical study of the world's principal migration systems. They conclude that, while certain theories seem to function more effectively in certain systems, nevertheless a synthesis of theoretical approaches can provide an integrated theoretical approach to the study of international migration as a whole. The problem is that a synthesis only brings together existing theories, and continues to overlook aspects that have already been overlooked by those theories (such as culture and politics, as Morawska, 2001, notes). It does not add anything. As Douglas Massey and his colleagues have adequately demonstrated, the range of concepts and approaches used in migration studies are not to be discarded, since each is often useful for understanding a certain part of the story. But a synthesis no more provides a framework for the study of social processes than do the approaches when separately employed. Instead of a synthesis, what is required is a more general-level theory that can offer insights into the fundamental social processes that frame migration and that provides a sociological framework within which to understand the various substantive (migration) theories.

Oliver Bakewell (2010: 1703) begins to provide some of the building blocks of a potential framework for migration studies. Beginning with the premise that migration is a universal phenomenon, Bakewell (2010) looks for some explanation for the patterns and processes which shape it. He believes migration studies needs to address the fact they have never dealt adequately with the problem of structure and agency, which is crucial because agents shape migration and its responses (and, I would add, its outcomes). Drawing on various theories for different applications fails to offer 'any basis for developing robust concepts and hypotheses concerning the interaction of these concepts' (2010: 1692). Instead he proposes a version of critical realist theory (as in the work of Roy Bhaskar, 1989) might inform a more sophisticated analysis of the roles of structure and agency in migration. Bakewell has yet to demonstrate how this helps to deal with the problem of the eclectic mix of theories available to a migration researcher; but he appears to be attempting to at least inform a coherent theory for migration: 'The aim here is to provide an outline of a theoretical foundation which can allow the development of a coherent body of theory to address questions such as: Who moves from A to B and why? Why these people and not others? Why do they move to B rather than C? Why now or then?' (2010: 1703).

Maggie O'Neill (2010: 18) also employs critical theory, 'particularly the principle that analysis of specific social phenomena requires awareness of the connectedness and embeddedness of small-scale phenomena in the broader totality' to understand the interaction of migration, asylum and community (rather than a narrow focus on integration). For Stephen Castles (2010: 1565) 'a general theory of migration is neither possible nor desirable' and both he and Alejandro Portes (2010) suggest it is better for migration researchers to restrict themselves to mid-range theories. However, Castles (2010: 1570) does believe there is a 'failure to understand the historical character, false assumptions of one-way causality, and an inability to understand the overall dynamics of migratory processes and their embeddedness in processes of societal change'. His own solution to this is the social transformations approach, discussed more in Chapter 3. But, as Hein de Haas (2010) suggests, migration theory would benefit from drawing on more general social theory and concepts, in order to address what Nicholas Van Hear (2010: 1535) calls the 'continuing apparent isolation of the field from wider social science concerns'.

One clear attempt to provide a social science framework for migration is the work of Ewa Morawska (2009), who makes a strong case for analysing migration in the context of Giddens' structuration theory (see Chapter 2). The process of migration connects wider and narrower issues such as globalization, transnationalism, and multiculturalism, and in order to understand it we need a theory that can explain the interaction of macro and micro processes, of individual actions and social forms. Structuration theory, which is a theory about the recursive nature of social practices and the ways in which these are ordered across space and time (Giddens, 1984: 2), is able to do just that. Morawska insists that, using structuration, analyses of migration should bring the process full cycle and consider the impact of migrants on society. International migration has expanded, she argues, and has led to global interconnections, policies, laws, and consequences for all countries involved. It also leads to settlement, to heterogeneity, and to glocalization (to use the term popularized by Robertson, 1992), but also to micro transnational networks and relationships, and meso structures; it thus (re)shapes cultures and (re)produces structures. Her book examines eight specific immigrant groups on which there is a good amount of ethnographic and statistical data. The empirical focus is on American immigration and involves a rather broad-brush and ambitious approach examining, for each migration trend, the impacts of resettlement, assimilation trajectories, and transnational involvements at home, in an attempt to 'encourage immigration researchers to undertake investigations of the transformative effects of immigration activities on the society they are embedded in' (Morawska, 2009: 6). Her work thus tends to emulate the traditional approach to understanding what triggers a migration, settlement, assimilation, transnationalism, and second generation experiences (see Chapter 3). But, as Morawska demonstrates, structuration theory does have a lot to offer migration theory, especially when we use the theory critically and address the body of criticism directed towards it (Bakewell, 2010).

What Does This Book Do?

There is apparently some consensus that migration studies would benefit from drawing on broad social theory, and from being linked to wider social science concerns, and some form of structuration or practice theory seems to be the best way forward. This book begins by drawing on Giddens' structuration theory and other forms of practice theory to illustrate how social life is an ongoing process that unfolds through the embodied acting out of daily life, in communities. Practice theory builds on the body of work in social theory, work from Marx and Durkheim, and from Weber and Simmel, from objectivists (who understand social change as mainly driven by the role of social structures) and subjectivists (who emphasize the role of individual agency in social life). But rather than perpetuate this distinction between structure and agency, practice theory perceives social life as the outcome of the interaction of structures (of constraints and opportunity) and actions (of individuals and groups who embody, shape and form these structures) in the practice of daily life. Practice theory, as illustrated in Chapter 2, can also offer concepts through which, empirically, such broad processes can be examined in detail and in depth. Practice theory is thus a meta-theoretical framework, a way of viewing how the world works that underpins, but does not replace, other theories and approaches. Other more substantive theories can be drawn on, evaluated, developed and/or discarded if they are reviewed within this wider framework. Using the framework of practice theory, students can understand various migration trends by piecing together coherent practice stories about them. A practice story understands a series of linked events as a process. It is a complex, sociologically-informed way of understanding phenomena that avoids one-dimensional, static, or narrow explanations.

This book therefore functions on several levels. It makes the case for practice theory to be employed as a meta-theoretical framework for all migration studies. A meta-theory is a theory that frames the use of other theories. It is not an integrated migration theory, but a framework informed by broad social theory. Using it does not preclude the use of other theories, rather it allows for the eclectic (but careful and critical) use of theories within the framework that understands the social processes that are continually involved in the *constitution of social life* (see Cohen, 1989: 12). Migration scholars are already using various concepts and approaches to draw attention to migration as a structured and structuring process, and to acknowledge the role of culture. Such approaches include the migration systems and networks approaches, discussed in Chapter 3, that draw attention to meso level structures that link people and societies both local and global. Transnationalism, also discussed in Chapter 3, is a concept specifically employed to draw attention to activities that extend beyond and between people and places and into differently conceived and constructed social spaces. However, it is still unusual for people to fully deal with the interaction of macro, micro and meso levels, and much more common for them to simply recognize them and/or to separate them out (e.g. Lutz, 2010). This book suggests a way this interaction can be understood.

On a different level, the book provides a map of the study of international migration in the social sciences, critically presenting a wide range of theories, perspectives and concepts that have typically been used, as well as some substantive studies that define the field. Bringing key studies and theoretical perspectives together for the first time in this way provides a companion to theoretical and substantive works that currently only appear separately. The book then synthesizes substantive and theoretical material in such a way as to illuminate specific migration flows, or in other words, to start to tell practice stories about migration. This is not an attempt to provide coverage of the wide range of migration movements occurring globally, nor an historical account of migration trends and processes, causes and outcomes. This has been attempted quite successfully already by, for example, Stephen Castles and Mark Miller (2009), Douglas Massey and colleagues (1998), and Ewa Morawska (2009). Instead, in each of the following substantive chapters a selection from the vast range of diverse (and often very rich) empirical studies on a given process or trend are drawn together within the framework, and employing the concepts, of practice theory. Like Morawska's, the present book is also rather ambitious. But this is because it begins to illustrate how studies and theoretical approaches can be brought together as composite studies of the ongoing (and endless) practice of migration for several different trends.

The Chapters That Follow

Chapter 2 draws from several threads in practice theory to establish a set of useful concepts that can be applied empirically when employing the theory as a framework for migration. This framework especially builds on Anthony Giddens' structuration theory and Pierre Bourdieu's theory of practice (1977), and on the stronger version of structuration theory that has been proposed by Rob Stones (2005) in response to criticisms of Giddens. These traditions are supplemented with insights from the work of Jean Lave and Etienne Wenger (1991), where they describe communities of practice and situated learning, and the elaboration of the concept of agency as proposed by Mustafa Emirbayer and Ann Mische (1998). Key concepts that are elaborated in this chapter, and that are central to the employment of practice theory for migration, include: the duality of structure and agency; the notion of practice; the structuration cycle; external structures that can be both distant and more proximate, hard and more malleable; internal structures, including habitus and conjuncturally-specific internal structures; communities of practice, with conjuncturally-specific external structures; active agency; the ability of the agent to desire and project; and outcomes, that can be any of the above. Practice theory, as used here, is a definite tool for understanding and framing the ongoing process of social life, not (just) a broad abstract theory about general processes. It is thus an approach to research and explanation. The chapter also sets out implications of this approach for methodology and for the role of other theories, perspectives and concepts commonly used in migration studies.

Chapter 3 critically examines key theories that have been used to understand migration. These include economic, structural and network theories as discussed above. It also outlines key perspectives in migration, such as nationalism, transnationalism and globalization. These perspectives to some extent understand, and try to theorize, migration but to some extent they are methodological, drawing attention to specific aspects or stages of the migration process. Acknowledging that migration has tended to be examined as an event (to migrate) or an outcome (settlement) the chapter also examines key theories of settlement such as acculturation, assimilation, and ethnicity. The chapter also illustrates the contribution a given theory or approach can make to the analysis of an empirical case in the context of practice stories. For example, using practice theory, researchers can employ the concept of assimilation to analyse the extent to which there is an ideology of assimilation (and on the part of whom), and the extent to which this ideology is inscribed in policy and actual activities. The outcomes of these assumptions and policies will be visible as a set of surface appearances to explain. Or students can enquire as to whether the information available about meso level networks and relationships (intermediary institutions, or family ties, perhaps) helps us understand the migrants' various communities of practice, within which they adapt their habitus and develop conjuncturally-specific internal structures.

Chapters 4 to 7 draw on substantive, empirical studies in a given field in order to illustrate to students what are the key themes in the broad interdisciplinary programme of migration studies. Theoretical approaches covered in these chapters therefore include assimilation, incorporation, transnationalism, mobility, push and pull theories, globalization, neoliberal critique, postcolonialism, and migration systems theory. Various types of mobility are covered, including circular moves, temporary and more permanent moves, and moves with more or less agency involved. Chapter 4 is about the relatively understudied phenomenon of 'lifestyle migration' – the migration of affluent, elite, privileged or leisured individuals. Migration has tended to be characterized as either labour migration or the migration of refugees and asylum seekers (forced migration). Chapter 5 examines labour migration. Attention has increasingly been drawn to the migration of women, and so Chapter 6 examines domestic labour migration. Chapter 7 looks specifically at forced migration.

The goal in these four chapters is to begin to tell coherent stories about the practice of migration for a selection of specific migration trends, using practice theory as a framework, or background, general theory informing other theories. A selection of studies are therefore brought together as they each make a contribution to our broader understanding of the given process. The chapters thus show how existing theories and studies can illuminate the structuration processes involved, and identify what else is needed (to be located or empirically studied) in order to make a better study of the ongoing practice of everyday life. *Practice theory enables students to seek and recognize coherence in explanations.* We find that researchers appear often to be employing a structuration or practice perspective without necessarily acknowledging it. Many are already keen to draw attention to the ongoing interaction of structures and agency. Other studies concentrate on either phenomenology or the perspective of the actor, or alternatively on the wider structural forms and shifts that shape migration, but pay less attention to the interaction of the two. Practice theory can be used to 'order and inform processes of inquiry into social life' (Giddens, 1984: preface, np). Using practice theory as a framework to identify gaps in the stories, or to locate evidence in order to begin to fill these gaps avoids the rather narrow, restricted, or static perspective that studies that look at only one side of the dualism (of structure and agency) tend to yield. This is especially important where policy might be based on research findings; policies work best if the ongoing (structuration) processes involved in the practice of daily life are fully understood.

Chapter 4 draws together some key studies in the field of British migration to Spain's coastal areas as an illustration of lifestyle migration. What is particularly of note here is that external structures are both constraining and enabling. The chapter demonstrates how broad scale changes that are more easily described using theories of contemporary society, and concepts such as globalization, risk society, network society, liquid modernity, and mobility, are interpreted, enacted, and embodied by agents in practice. But more than that, the chapter illustrates the ways in which such broad changes are negotiated in the context of the agents' own internal structures, habits, desires, needs, goals, and the habits, expectations, norms, rules, and practices of the agents in their communities.

Chapter 5 starts to compile a composite study of Mexican labour migration to the US. In reviewing this work I place what is already known from a few key studies in the framework of practice theory. I review and evaluate the work in terms of what they can tell us about the external structures constraining and enabling the migration, the habitus of the agents (the migrants), the conjuncturally-specific internal structures that develop as migration proceeds and migrants learn how to go on in their new setting, the communities of practice and conjuncturally-specific external structures that are relevant to their daily practice, and the outcomes in terms of subsequent migration, habitus, and other internal and external structures. Practice theory reveals the ways in which what we discover from our reading can be understood in a wider theoretical framework. In the process we learn quite a bit about a specific labour migration trend that shares some patterns with other labour migrations (Morawska, 2009). It is therefore an illustration of a type of migration of great concern to migration scholars, policy makers, and analysts. The main focus of the work reviewed here is on what we might term 'incorporation' and on the work of Alejandro Portes (Professor of Sociology and director of the Center for Migration and Development at Princeton University) and his colleagues, who have been especially driven to try to understand the extent to which Mexican migrants can be considered incorporated into North American society. They have applied a variety of surveys and other research methods in order to examine the precise nature of this incorporation and what factors aid or impede it. This work has often been driven by a desire to address (or allay) concerns in US society about the extent of immigration, and the challenges it brings. This chapter, then, introduces a labour migration, with a specific focus on incorporation, and uses a few key studies to begin to tell a practice story.

Chapter 6 recognizes the role of women in migration, with attention to one particular trend: Filipina domestic labour migration to Hong Kong. Reviewing work in this area is an enlightening task. Push and pull theoretical perspectives draw attention to economic inequalities between the two countries (external structures) that might lead migrants to seek better conditions elsewhere; and historical overviews describe developing cultural schemas (more proximate external structures) whereby Hong Kong women readily consider hiring domestic labour and Filipina women readily consider leaving their families and homes to become domestic workers. Much of the work in this field has been qualitative and has been concerned with demonstrating the experiences of migration for the migrants, especially their lives in Hong Kong. The chapter demonstrates how composite studies (bringing together existing work) can really start to reveal the complex structuration processes, the interaction of structure and agency, over time, in practice, for both migrants and their hosts. An especially revealing aspect is the analysis of the role of intermediary-level employment agencies, especially in the ways in which domestic labour becomes inscribed into the habitus (the bodies, practices, attitudes and expectations) of the migrants as well as in those of the employers (the expectation that migrants will be subservient and grateful, for example).

Chapter 7 examines studies of the settlement experiences of refugees (especially children) in the United Kingdom. The chapter is therefore an illustration of a body of work in forced migration and how structuration processes can be revealed in existing work. Here I have compared studies of broad scope, that attempt to understand the causes and outcomes of forced migration in the context of historical, global change and persistent global inequalities, with very rich, small-scale studies of educational progress of refugee children. It is revealed that such small-scale studies are better at revealing structuration processes in practice than studies with a broader scope. However, using the concepts outlined in Chapter 2 reveals several gaps in understanding of the practice of daily life for refugee children. This chapter acknowledges the important role of the enactment of policy, and the close attention that needs to be paid to agents' communities of practice. For children of refugees this means analysing the daily life and interaction of children in families, with friends, at school, and with social workers and other support services.

The conclusion, Chapter 8, spends some time summarizing some of the mass of detail in Chapter 2, so readers might find it useful to refer to that from time to time. It then discusses the role of theory for migration within the context of a theory of practice. I then draw out the conclusions of Chapters 4 to 7 and their implications for employing practice theory for composite or individual and new migration studies. Together the studies examined illustrate that in order to understand the processes involved we need both studies of broad scope (macro, historical studies) and close, intimate studies of daily life. But more than that, the chapters illustrate that these approaches need to work together. Studies of broad scope are meaningless without the analysis of the role of structures in practice. Close, intimate studies of practice, preferably using ethnographic methods and in-depth interviews, (see O'Reilly, 2011), can reveal who and what are the communities of practice, the habitus of the agent, the emerging conjuncturally-specific external and internal structures, and can put these in a wider context using both what the agents can describe and what researchers perceive for themselves. However, close, intimate studies of daily life need to locate their work in wider themes. Finally, I conclude that a theory of practice for migration requires an attention to time and space, to history and to the present moment of action. This can best be achieved by single researchers undertaking small-scale studies explicitly within the context of a structuration framework (by overtly linking work to that of others), or by composite studies in which researchers actively work together to underpin existing and new work with a theory of practice. Students of international migration will be able to understand a range of contexts in more sociological depth if they are able to critically examine theoretical and empirical studies within this broader framework.

2

Practice Theory: A Framework for International Migration Research

Introduction

This chapter outlines a general, sociologically-informed theory about the way social life proceeds in a recursive manner that underpins the substantive theories about international migration that I will outline in Chapter 3. The diverse migration theories, concepts and perspectives in Chapter 3 each address aspects of the migration process from outlining at a very broad level the social transformations which lead to, or are affected by, international migration through to explanations for migratory moves, to explanations for the behaviour of migrants and non-migrants and ways in which we might understand the consequences (intended or otherwise) of migration for people and places. In each case, the theory, concept or perspective applied to the problem at hand, depends very much on the prior definition of that problem. What international migration researchers want to know varies from researcher to researcher, project to project, and situation to situation. Sometimes, the problem to be explained is actually predetermined by the concept or perspective chosen as the explanatory framework: those examining transnationalism find networks, associations, and ties which cross borders; those examining mobility find fluidity, flux and flow. But if students of migration begin with social world observations that they wish to explain, then concepts such as mobility, transnationalism, and diasporas enable the perception of aspects that might otherwise have been overlooked, without those frames or windows onto the world. The sorts of things we might wish to explain in migration studies will vary, and will include why migrants move, what they experience when they have moved, how states and local individuals react towards migrants, how migrants shape societies, and so on, but these always remain partial stories helping us to understand international migration as a process.

This chapter outlines a more general, sociologically-informed theory about the way social life proceeds in a recursive manner that underpins the substantive theories about international migration. Practice theory can 'order and inform processes of inquiry into social life' (Giddens, 1984: preface, np) and can be employed by students to seek or recognize coherence in explanations. Particular stories or cases of migration can be illuminated by a contribution of substantive theories underpinned by the more general theory about how people interact with their social environment. In order to illustrate the contribution practice theory can make to the study of international migration, I draw on ideas from Anthony Giddens' structuration theory, Pierre Bourdieu's theory of practice, Mustafa Emirbayer's and Ann Mische's analysis of the components of agency, Ewa Morawska's version of structuration theory, Etienne Wenger's and Jean Lave's studies of communities of practice and situated learning, and, especially, from Rob Stones' elaboration of Giddens' work into a stronger version of structuration.[1] One of the great strengths of Stones' version of strong structuration is the concepts, or tools, that can be applied, analytically, at the substantive level. Practice here is understood as:

> synonymous with the *constitution of social life*, i.e. the manner in which all aspects, elements and dimensions of social life, from instances of conduct in themselves to the most complicated and extensive types of collectivities, are generated in and through the performance of social conduct, the consequences which ensue, and the social relations which are thereby established and maintained.
>
> (Cohen, 1989: 12)

Agency and Structure in Social Theory

At the heart of a great deal of sociological theory is what we might term an agency/structure dualism; that is, a tendency to perceive the agency of individual human actors as distinct and separate from social structures. This dualism goes hand in hand with an ongoing debate over the extent to which humans have free will and can act according to their wishes, and the extent, on the other hand, to which humans are constrained by social 'things', society or social institutions for example. The debate is often labelled the agency/structure debate. During the first part of the last century there had been a dominance of approaches that sought to portray sociology as a positive science of society that could equal the natural sciences in identifying causes and making predictions (*positivism*). There was a concern to illustrate, following Durkheim, Parsons and others, how certain social patterns or formations remain stable over time, and sociologists wanted to understand how this happened (*functionalism*). These approaches tended to emphasize the role of social structures in enabling and constraining the agency of individuals. Social structures here are conceived in a similar way to physical structures, like walls, buildings, and even bodies. In the work of Durkheim, for example, 'social facts' such as laws, religion, education, and other more relational aspects such as norms, were depicted as having a force of their own on societies, independently of the individuals and their actions. In Marx's work, socio-economic forces worked independently to shape human societies. Even in studies of language use, discourses (such as a racist discourse, for example) could be seen as existing prior to, or outside of, individual use of specific phrases and terms. Both Giddens and Bourdieu label this approach 'objectivism', in which those concerned with emphasizing the primacy of social structure draw attention to the power of social norms, rules, regulations and practices.

This approach was gradually challenged by a variety of schools of thought we might call 'subjectivism', including symbolic interactionism, ethnomethodology, phenomenological sociology, social constructionism, and hermeneutics. These approaches, in their different ways, all rejected 'the tendency of the orthodox consensus to see human behaviour as the result of forces that actors neither control nor comprehend' (Giddens, 1984: xvi) and instead emphasized the creative, reflexive and dynamic aspects of social life. These were especially influenced by a set of philosophical ideas known as interpretivism. For interpretivists, it is essential to see humans as actors in the social world rather than as *re-acting* like objects in the natural world. Human agents can understand the conditions they find themselves in, can try to make sense of these, and act accordingly. They have reasons for what they do. In order to understand the social world it is therefore necessary to get inside the individuals' heads, to understand their meanings about what they are doing. For Weber, drawing on Kant, everything that is known or understood is interpreted by the human mind. Therefore, a social scientist should study meaningful rational action: that is action taken to achieve an end (instrumental action), that has meaning for the actor, and which is directed towards, or involves, other people. The study of rational action involved interpretive understanding (or *verstehen*); in other words in order to make sense of it the social scientist needed to interpret what the action meant for the actor and to understand his or her intentions. For Schutz, humans make sense of what we receive through our senses, the constant stream of stimuli we see, hear, smell, feel and taste, by splitting up the world around us into categories and sub-categories and things associated with these. In other words we identify things through a process of typification. When we do this to the social world we end up with types of people of whom we expect types of behaviour, and whom we distinguish from other types, and this understanding of the social world directs our own actions towards other people. The ideas have informed later work by Garfinkel (1984) and ethnomethodology, and social constructionist arguments such as that of Berger and Luckmann (1975). Hermeneutics is an attempt to understand groups within the context of their (and our) wider cultures; in other words it involves the interpretation of cultures. Influenced by Gadamer (1989), a hermeneutic approach is hostile to the manipulative and instrumental nature of the natural sciences and to conventional notions of objectivity. It involves a merging of horizons with the group being studied through which the researcher begins to think like them. In these developments, a central role has been accorded to the role of language as an intermediary between thought and action, culture and individual.

Gradually the proliferation of approaches above led to something of a 'war of the paradigms' (Mouzelis, 1991), to an impasse characterized by constant critique, excessive emphasis on one or other side of the great divide, and either an obsession with laws and generalizations, or the abandonment of the attempt to seek any. 'By attacking objectivism – and structural sociology – those influenced by hermeneutics or by phenomenology were able to lay bare major shortcomings of those views. But they in turn veered sharply towards subjectivism. The conceptual divide between subject and object yawned as widely as ever' (Giddens, 1984: xx). We have now reached something of a silent (unacknowledged) consensus, in which it is impossible to ignore all that has been learned on either side and scholars are seeking ways to understand the ongoing interaction of structure and agency (Stones, 2006). This is certainly in evidence in migration research, as we shall see in Chapter 3 (and see, for example, O'Neill, 2010). At the same time there has been more attention drawn to people's communities and networks (as in studies of transnational networks, and the role of the family and intermediaries in migration). This looks at the smaller groups within which actors act and relate, and the patterns that emerge and are reproduced in such groups, that in turn are a form of (constantly shaped) social structure. Finally, 'It is very generally accepted among sociologists and other social scientists that neither the holy trinity of Marx, Durkheim and Weber, nor additions to the sainthood like Simmel, provided satisfactory ways of connecting micro- and macro-analysis of agency and structure' (Bryant and Jary, 2003: 6). Giddens' structuration theory and other theories of practice attempt to address this impasse.

Practice Theories and the Duality of Structure and Agency

Practice theories attempt to understand the interaction and interconnection of structure and agency, first by opposing the notion of a strict ontological dualism. Structuration is a social theory put forward by Anthony Giddens via various publications (especially 1976, 1979, and 1984). It is an attempt to understand the historical processes of society without resorting to either objectivism or subjectivism, which Giddens refers to as 'empire building endeavours' (1984: 2). Its key proposition is that neither agent nor structure is determining in the final instance; structures are both the limits to and outcomes of agency. Structuration theory thus theorizes the relationship between agents as a 'duality of structure'. In a duality of structure, agents and structures do not exist ontologically as two distinct entities, as in a dualism, but are always interdependent and interrelated: 'structures are constituted through action and ... action is constituted structurally' (Giddens, 1976: 161). This interdependency is linked via phenomenology (the way people understand and perceive their world), hermeneutics (shared understandings), and practice (daily, lived experiences and actions). Social structures are the outcomes of agency, and are perceived, understood and practised by agents, while agents embody or include social structures in the form of perceptions, roles, norms and other phenomenological and hermeneutic phenomena. The connection between what is out there (in institutions, constraints, limitations, rules and norms) and what is in here (in minds, bodies, perceptions and understandings) is complex because structure is part and parcel of the agent and the agent is part and parcel of the structure. Thus social structure exists as an intermingling of both agent and structure. Social processes take place through an ongoing cycle, or constant interaction, between external structures (what is out there), internalized structures in agents (what is in here), practices (actions), and outcomes (with intended and unintended consequences). But this cycle of structuration should not be perceived as a sequence of discrete moments: both structures and agency are at all times involved in social processes. If, for example, a specific migration policy appears as a constraint entirely distinct from an agent, nevertheless the agent's actions will depend on her understanding and interpretation of that policy and the outcome will to some extent depend on the malleability of that constraint. Giddens wants to ensure that we do not resort to an understanding of social facts as inanimate things, objects over which agents have no control, or to a reduction of human action to the motivations of agents.[2] Giddens seems to have enthusiastically approached his structuration project for about 15 years, producing books and edited collections, but to have more or less abandoned it since the late 1980s. He thus responded a little, but not adequately, to the range of criticisms, elaborations and applications of his ideas (Stones, 2005: 3).

Bourdieu (whose social theory, Giddens, 1979: 217 appears to acknowledge is somewhat similar to his thesis on structuration) also opposes objectivism and subjectivism. These tend to separate as entirely distinct structural constraints, on the one hand, and things such as preferences

and tastes, on the other. Objectivism (and hence structuralism) in sociology, is based uncritically, Bourdieu argues, on Saussure's separation
of langue (language, grammar) and parole (speech), in which all speech
it seems can be understood in terms of its underlying structure, or its
grammar. These ideas have been incorporated into sociology wholesale,
reducing subjects and actions to the mere outcomes of structures, reducing
history to a process without a subject (Bourdieu, 1990: 41). But, structures are not merely the essence of existence, from which all subsequent
action unproblematically emerges; in fact structures are themselves 'meaningful products of the accumulation of innumerable historical actions'
(1990: 41). Bourdieu describes objectivism as 'a fetishism of social laws'
(ibid: 41) as if 'model and execution, essence and existence' can be
separated (ibid: 32). Subjectivism, alternatively (or voluntarism, as he
sometimes calls it), views agents as free-floating subjects. For subjectivists,
actors can aspire to something, can imagine how others might react if they
act in certain ways, and then make choices with those imaginations in
mind; this makes sense, but subjectivists tend to explain outcomes *solely*
in terms of 'expectations of future profits' (ibid: 46). Invoking Sartre as
the archetypal subjectivist, Bourdieu says he 'makes each action a kind of
antecedent-less confrontation between the object and the world' (ibid: 42).

Bourdieu's work (e.g. 1977, 1984, 1985, 1990, and Bourdieu and
Passeron, 1977) rests on a few key concepts: habitus, field and capital
being the main ones. Habitus is the dispositions, habits, ways of doing
things, ways of thinking, and ways of seeing the world that we each, indi-
vidually and in groups, acquire as we travel through life. The habitus thus
incorporates prejudices and expectations (based on past experiences and
adjusted in light of changing conditions). It is the 'incorporated product of
historical practice' (1990: 52). Habitus is/are fairly fixed but transposable
(changeable, can be developed, slightly altered, in light of changing circumstances). Habitus is discussed more fully below. The field, for Bourdieu,
is the given set of circumstances within which an agent is currently living, experiencing and acting. Each field contains its own cultural logic,
and its own power structure, power struggles, formal structures of control
(1985). The concept of field is somewhat problematic as it can refer to
both metaphorical constructs or real relations of power (Lane, 2000); in
the case of international migration these frame and constrain decisions to
move and opportunities to settle. Capital might be thought of as resources.
Migrants, their various networks and communities, and the diverse groups
with whom they come into contact, each have differing and changeable
amounts of economic, human, social, and symbolic forms of capital.

For Bourdieu, economic factors (such as those often identified to explain
migration, see Chapter 3) have a logic in terms of their impacts on outcomes, but they do not work through rational calculation, nor as structural
determinations, but are enacted in rational practice: 'the practice most

appropriate to achieve the objectives inscribed in the logic of a particular field at the lowest cost' (1990: 50). Practices, he says, are *reasonable* rather than rational calculations, because they are adjusted to the future, but this does not imply they are necessarily the product of an identifiable plan. Certain rules, norms and routines tend to get followed unconsciously and habitually where conditions have not changed much since the dispositions were formed. Sociologists tend to conclude that people are straightforwardly following rules, but they may instead be acting out something of a migration habitus, a tendency towards migration that developed over generations and through socialization. Habitus is what transforms rules into practice. People are always in practical relations to the world: 'the habitus is constituted in practice and is always oriented to practical functions' (1990: 52). The focus of empirical work, then, should not rest with an analysis of rules (structures, norms, laws) and how people respond, nor economic factors and how they 'drive' people, but instead should explore the ways in which people work things through in practice. Practice theory (in the work of Bourdieu and Giddens) draws attention to the ways in which the social world emerges out of an ongoing interrelationship between structures and the way they are interpreted and enacted. Empirical research on international migration thus needs to pay attention to both the structural and hermeneutic 'moments' of this ongoing interrelationship and to the meso level of their interaction.

Elaborating a Practice Theory for Migration

Giddens' structuration theory can be applied both in an overly deterministic way, and in an overly voluntaristic way (thus putting off anyone on the other side of the camp). Thus critical theorists end up unhappy about the emphasis on agency, while phenomenologists remain unhappy about the emphasis (less overt in my opinion) on structure.[3] One of the key criticisms of Giddens' structuration theory, is that it does appear to favour an emphasis on agency over structure, or, to put it another way, it has a tendency towards voluntarism (Bakewell, 2010). As such it could be described not so much as a social theory as a political position – a normative argument to *celebrate* agency as much as to acknowledge it. While Giddens' structuration theory does not necessarily imply that structure is more often reproduced or more often transformed, nevertheless it does rest on the contention that the reflexive individual has the power to change things in the last instance. For Giddens, agents should always be able to act otherwise; even the most oppressive circumstances have a 'dialectic of control' with relations of autonomy and dependence built in (Stones, 2005: 29). It is always possible to say no, or to refuse to comply. Derek Layder (1994) believes that Giddens actually rejects structural analysis and suggests that meanings and motivations should be the core of analysis. I cannot agree, given his constant insistence that we should not reduce explanation to motives, but I concur with Cohen (1989), that in distancing himself from structuralism Giddens remains unclear as to what structures consist of (see below). This all seems more evident in retrospect, as his work developed: certainly, in his later work on reflexive modernity, there is an overemphasis on self-fashioning (Adkins, 2004, see Giddens, 1991a and 1992). The emphasis on agency is also evident in many of the ways the theory has been applied to substantive studies (King and Calasanti, 2009).

Bourdieu, on the other hand, lacks a coherent theory of social change; 'too much emphasis is placed on conformity to a perceived state of affairs in which a similar or predictable future is implicated' (Jenkins, 2000: 159). In migration research this is problematic indeed. For the most part Bourdieu considers habitus and field to be compatible or synchronous. This is because agents retain a *doxic* relation to the world, a pre-reflexive orientation, a practical sense of what is objectively possible, or an unconscious awareness of the horizon of possibilities (Bourdieu, 1984). We thus internalize and embody the objective chances of success in achieving our goals in a given field into the habitus. Although habitus is supposedly transposable, there remains an inertia, or cultural lag, or what Bourdieu terms a hysteresis, of the habitus. As Jeremy F. Lane (2000: 196) observes, because the objective chances of success in a field are embodied and practised, rather than merely informing actions (as in the notion of ideology, for example), then the theory does tend towards the pessimistic and deterministic. Bourdieu suggests that changes in wider structures, or fields of action, can lead to an 'awakening of consciousness' but fails to elaborate on the conditions of this awakening (Adkins, 2004). Bourdieu's theory does not, then, adequately invoke a critically reflexive self. To conclude, practice theory does not need to favour any one side of the duality; it is possible to include aspects of agency that are truly creative and reflexive as well as a clear sense of continually-reproduced structures.

Giddens has complained that researchers employing *his* theory in substantive work often applied his concepts too rigorously, whereas actually it is all but impossible to apply them systematically because they are too vague, general, and abstract (Gregson, 1989). The theory has been applied in a whole host of substantive fields, as was recognized by Bryant and Jary (2001) and, despite some decreasing interest, this is still the case. I found it used in studies of sport, health, and organization, as well as international migration (e.g. Kruythoff, 2008; Cooky, 2009; Kidder, 2009). But rarely do people define the concepts rigorously, usually simply referring very loosely to the duality of structure, to rules and resources, or by merely acknowledging the roles of both structure and agency (Bakewell, 2010). Ewa Morawska's (2009) work is, of course, an exception. Giddens (1991b) himself uses the concepts for very broad-ranging analyses of wide sweeps of history, and acknowledges that he prefers his concepts to be used as sensitizing devices, rather than in an applied manner. Bourdieu's work, alternatively, has had much more success in being applied. However, application tends to take the shape of studies of *aspects* of the theory, or alternatively his concepts are applied without attention to the overall structuration framework (Reay, 2004; e.g. Erel, 2010). There is also a tendency when using Bourdieu to examine (or invoke) social structural reproduction, especially of social class and in the field of education (Adkins, 2004; e.g. Oliver and O'Reilly, 2010; Reay et al., 2009). Despite these criticisms, it is possible, following the work of Rob Stones and Ewa Morawska to provide concepts through which practice theory can be directed towards the particular, in all its complexity:

> The full potential of structuration theory cannot be fulfilled whilst it remains only in the clouds, content just to sprinkle a few magnanimous drops of rain down onto the fields below in whimsical, haphazard gestures designed more to draw attention to the abstract ontology than to nurture a greater understanding of particular times and places.
>
> (Stones, 2005: 76)

A further difficulty with Giddens' structuration is what Margaret Archer (1995) calls the elision of structure and agency, which she contends must be viewed as a *dualism* not a duality. Unless we are able to keep structure and action analytically distinct, as indeed she argues they exist in reality, we will not be able to understand, trace or unpick, the relationship between them. For Archer structure is the ever-present precondition of action, and the outcome, but this can only be understood as a temporal process in which precondition, action, and outcome follow each other in a sequence. Archer says Giddens does not allow us to understand or even recognize this sequence. Part of the problem here comes from Giddens' contention that structures are virtual, or latent. Giddens seems to argue that structures exist in two forms: in 'memory traces' and in 'material form'. Both are latent (or virtual) and not actual until they are drawn on by the agent. They then appear as the prior conditions that made an action or interaction possible, they inform or guide, appear as the pre-existing knowledge or understandings, and are then instantiated structures. But Archer is arguing that if structure is latent then it is only ever *actual* in the actions of the agent; therefore it cannot be separated from the agent and thus cannot pre-exist before them. Archer wants to retain the sense of pre-existing structures. However, Stones (2005) does not believe Giddens ever meant structure not to have any causal or pre-existent role. He acknowledges that Giddens is unclear about the boundaries between structure and agency but does not conclude that Giddens therefore conflates the two. Agents are usually unaware of the boundary between their knowledge of circumstances that constrain their action (awareness of how much money they have at their disposal, to use his example) and their actions that take that knowledge into account. But that does not mean that a sociological researcher needs to also elide the two moments; conditions are pre-dated, outcomes are post-dated (see also Bakewell, 2010). Archer (1995: 138) suggests there are 'discontinuities in the structuring/restructuring process which can only be grasped by making analytical distinctions between the 'before' (Phase 1), the 'during' (Phase 2) and the 'after' (Phase 3), none of which is to deny the necessary continuity of human activity for the endurance of all things social'. This is a useful contribution as it enables us to put forward a practice theory that does retain some distance between external structures, internalized structures, and outcomes, and that recognizes a temporal sequence in the playing out, or the practice, of events.[4]

Finally, there remains a difficulty in defining structures that are external to the agent and yet internalized, enacted and embodied. John B. Thompson (1989) criticizes Giddens for rather loosely and simplistically reducing structure to rules and resources, and then being neither clear nor consistent about what he means by rules and saying very little that is concrete about resources. He is also somewhat vague about what is involved when structures are drawn upon by agents, and ignores the wider (institutional and organizational) frameworks within which rules and resources exist. The term 'rule' can be used in myriad ways, including moral rules, traffic rules, etiquette, and rules of the game (Thompson, 1989: 63), and can overlap with what we otherwise think of as norms and undertake uncritically as practices. The idea of rule-following is, therefore, an overly formalistic way of summarizing the complex ways in which agents act on 'internal structures of signification and legitimation' (Stones, 2005: 46). For Stones this is a failure to identify a meta-theoretical notion of structures as rules, norms, interpretive schemas, and resources, which is distinct from a more conventional notion of structures as broad patterns, larger networks, longer sequences, and employed in huge comparisons (ibid: 50). Bourdieu's work, on the other hand, has been accused of being elliptical and opaque, and thus able to be rendered as all things to all people; while his concept of objective structures remains somewhat taken for granted (Jenkins, 2000). There is a distinct emphasis in Bourdieu's work on what we might call culture, and a reluctance to define what is objective beyond what has been internalized into the habitus, even while there is an implicit assumption that structures do exist at a different ontological level than actions and actors (Jenkins, 2000). It is useful if we can draw from earlier, objectivist, sociology and employ a more traditional concept of social structure to apply when we are referring to this wider framework or different ontological level:

> The implication is that it is only by first delineating the wider, more traditional conception of social structure that one can situate and understand

the structural pressures on agents within each enterprise to draw on certain rules and resources in some ways and not others.

(Stones, 2005: 48)

The Key Concepts for a Theory of Practice

Drawing on practice theory, and taking on board the various arguments outlined above, it is now possible to outline some key concepts for a theory of practice for international migration. These include *external structures* (including those that are distant and more proximate, hard and more malleable), *internal structures* (including habitus, conjuncturally-specific internal structures), desire and projection (as the third dimension of *agency*), *communities of practice* (and external conjuncturally-specific structures), and *outcomes* (which can take form in any or all of the above).

External Structures

It is possible to preserve some notion that structures can appear to an agent (a would-be migrant, a host, a family member) as objective things, as detached and external (Stones, 2005). But these may take the shape of 'upper' and 'more proximate' structural layers (see Morawska, 2009). External structures as a whole are wider forces that confront an agent as more or less malleable (and the extent of this malleability remains a question for each study to address). They are, conceptually, the context that exists before the 'agent in focus' (from Stones, the agent to whom we are giving our attention in the given piece of research) acts. Global inequalities are a good example of external structures framing migration, as are colonial histories and their legacies. External structures are autonomous of the agent, and can have causal influence on actions, both enabling and constraining. This is not to reify social structures (as Sewell, 1992 warns us against), nor is it to imply stability. These 'traditionally conceived social structures do not work by themselves; they work on the basis of agents acting *in situ*, drawing on and being influenced by interpretative schemas, conceptions of values and norms, and power resources' (Stones, 2005: 52). They become relevant in a theory of practice as they enter the horizon of the agent: the actors themselves or the researcher is aware of them as relevant at the particular point, event or action being studied. They can, however, exist without the awareness of the agent and thus can have unintended consequences (see Bakewell, 2010). Researchers and students may thus identify structures and opportunities of which an agent was unaware, such as employment demands that lead women to seek migrant labour to help in the home. In a research project external structures are identified by asking the given agent, by observing the context itself, and/or by analysing the situation from a more distanced and abstract level (as in macro level research and broad-brush studies). For a student of migration, external structures might be identified in the existing literature that has employed those same techniques.

Upper structural layers include what Stones (2005: 6) calls 'large, historical and spatial forces', which act as 'framing devices' for action. External structures can include global forces or social transformations (in Castles' 2007 and 2010 term) identified by grand, macro theoretical frameworks and large sweeping analyses. They include wider conditions of action, general cultural shifts, technological advances, ideological frames, global power shifts, and broad policy agendas. These are especially discussed in Chapter 5.

Proximate structural layers include constraints, of what is and is not (more or less) possible, and changes that are directly or indirectly related to the wider context of action. These structures include laws, rules, organizational arrangements, and local policies. They may also include physical/material things (built/made by people), such as trains, houses, building arrangements, as well as the natural environment. As Stones notes, structures also include more small-scale and context-specific constraints and opportunities. In Ewa Morawska's (1996) work on Polish immigrants in America, for example, they include a coal strike, a flood, recession, and those who Polish immigrants rely on as customers at a more local level. It may, in practice, be very difficult to distinguish these external layers and context-specific structures from the meso level and micro level internalized structures and communities of practice we discuss more below, since they overlap to a great extent.

External structures can be separated conceptually into more or less malleable forms. In less malleable forms the external structures are *hard structures*, they have a great deal of autonomy, they are (perhaps entirely) independent of the desires and wishes and actions of the given agent; these might include health care institutions, employment structures, the housing market, war, and famine, all of which can affect migration processes. They may be what Stones (2005: 109) calls 'unacknowledged conditions of action', which in their turn might be 'the basis for unintended consequences of action'. This is because they are so hard or resistant that the agent may be unaware of them, and certainly will not conceive of them as something he or she can change. These are often best understood in the first instance by the researcher using studies and theories of broad scope: a macro perspective and general theory, and students will need to seek them in that literature. Sanctions will also be imposed by other agents – there can be no separate social structure without agents – but these may not be the agents central to a given research project.

External structures can also take more malleable forms. Some norms, pressures, vague rules, and imprecise laws may be more resistible or pliable than others. However, the extent to which they are malleable depends on how the individual understands them. Structures are, therefore, not independent of the way the agent perceives them and thus require a methodology that examines perceptions. To give an example, a Filipina domestic labour migrant in Hong Kong (see Chapter 6) may feel under pressure to extend her work contract by a further two years when her existing one ends. She could decide to go back to the Philippines, especially if she is unhappy, but she is constrained by her habitus, the norms associated with this migration, the communities around her, all of which remind her that the responsible thing to do is to carry on earning so that she can send money home to her family. These forces are therefore value-dependent. She cannot, however, change the fact that she is only offered temporary contracts, that she may not find any work at all at home (an external, fairly resistant, causal structure), or that her family lives in poverty.

Acknowledging the malleability of structures involves an analysis of how much power an agent actually has (and not forgetting some have plenty). In order to feel as if she can resist external forces, an agent must first imagine that she has the power or capability to do so. She would also need sufficient knowledge of what was possible and what the consequences might be of different actions, and would need to be capable of sufficient reflective distance (to be able to stand back and consider actions before she acts). Giddens calls these knowledge, power and critical awareness. They vary, with social elites often having more of the resources with which to resist and children and minority groups having less. In many cases, external structures influence the lives of agents to a great degree, sometimes to the extent that people do not even realize they want anything different. This is why, perhaps, for all that migration has become such a vast topic still only approximately three per cent of the world's population has ever moved internationally.

But to avoid a slide into determinism here let's remember that social life is constituted through actions. The external structures discussed above are sustained by the daily ongoing practices of agents within them – networks of people drawing on their own rules and resources, (power, opportunities, constraints, norms, habitus). They do not exist externally to all agents everywhere; they have been made by and will be transformed or reproduced by other agents. For Morawska, structures are also more or less enduring, interacting frameworks with inbuilt tensions that create gaps in their inconsistent capacity to enable and constrain. As she says, the multiplicity of structures imbues them 'at all levels with inherent tensions or even direct contradictions that create "gaps" or "loopholes" in between different social arrangements and, resulting from these imperfections, an inconsistent and mutable capacity both to enable and to constrain human agency' (Morawska, 2009: 3).

Internal Structures

In addition to external structures that confront an agent, or provide opportunities for action, structures are also internalized in the form of habitus and conjuncturally-specific internal structures. Habitus is being used here in the same way that Bourdieu employs the term, as structures embedded in corporeal schemas and memory traces. Habitus (singular and plural) are 'systems of durable, transposable dispositions, structured structures predisposed to function as structuring structures' (Bourdieu, 1990: 53). They are the multitude ways of being and thinking, of seeing and doing, that we each, in groups and as individuals, acquire through socialization, through generations of past practices, and through our own repeated practices. They are complex, and sociologists could turn to various theories to try to understand them better (theories about embodiment, the emotions, the taken-for-granted view of the world), but essentially they are people's habits, conceptual frameworks, repeated practices, internalized social structures and norms; the result of experience, habit and socialization. They are the outcomes of the interaction of actions and structures through daily practice over generations, and over and during one life-course. They include skill, knowledge, and personal resources (or human, social and cultural capital) – the extent to which agents can change things because they have the power and resources and the extent to which they will try to depending on how they understand the situation and the norms they have internalized. The concept of habitus has been elaborated by Bourdieu in many publications (1977, 1984, 1990), and by others elsewhere (e.g. Reay, 2004). It acknowledges, to a limited extent, an individual's actions might significantly vary from the usual activities of their social group, particularly when an individual encounters an unfamiliar field as in migration, or during periods of rapid social change prior to or following migration. But, for Bourdieu, the overall effect is of reproduction. Although we may be unaware of the objective constraints inscribing the possibilities open to us (Bourdieu, 1990), they mould what is considered achievable and worth aspiring to. Furthermore, even as times change and the objective probability of obtaining certain things also changes, the practical experience of one's early years remains formative. Habitus, Giddens (1979: 217) suggests, acknowledges that actions are not the same as conscious motivations; that is we cannot simply impute a motivation to an action as in push-pull forms of migration theory (see Chapter 3).

The habitus is both formed (a structural force) and continuing to be formed (an action), and is an attribute of individuals and of groups.

In empirical studies it is relevant within the wider context of action or can be studied as an outcome (Stones, 2005). We might explore, then, the forming of the group or individual migration habitus, or ethnic habitus, as a research interest. It is important to consider the habitus of both the individual and the groups within which she is located, and the interactions between these – that is, the hermeneutic frame of the agents.

Stones' (2005) 'conjuncturally-specific internal structures' are a crucial step in understanding the meso (or intermediate) level interaction of structure and agency in the practice of daily life. Conjuncturally-specific internal structures are the shape of the internal structures that become relevant at the given juncture, or given set of circumstances. They are specific at the point of action, or the way agents 'confront the immediate context of action' (Stones, 2005: 166). Conjuncturally-specific internal structures are not the same as general habits, dispositions, ways of seeing and doing (although it draws on these), but specific reactions to and knowledge of specific features, conditions, external structures and constraints – what we know about, and how we have learned to deal with or react to, this policy, at this time, that asylum seeker or this neighbour, in these circumstances. In other words it is how the given agent (perhaps a migrant, perhaps not) perceives the specific context of action, how the external circumstances (including the contexts which are described more below) are understood in this place and time. Engaging in the practice of social life relies on knowledge and awareness gained over a period of time, and put together quickly as an event unfolds. Conjuncturally-specific internal structures emerge with knowledge of how to go on in a given set of circumstances. This 'proximate' knowledge also draws on one's habitus.

Conjuncturally-specific internal structures involve some knowledge (on the part of the agent) of networks, roles, norms and power relations; they entail understanding how proximate others might behave, what power they have got, how they seem to interpret the world around them, and then acting on the basis of what is understood about all these things at a given time. Here it is worth noting, as Stones suggests, the insights from analyses of the practice of everyday life such as the phenomenology of Maurice Merleau-Ponty (1962), the ethnomethodology of Harold Garfinkel (1984), and Erving Goffman's (1990) symbolic interactionism. This is knowledge and awareness that is internal to an agent; that is part of her own understanding of the world around her at a given time, but that is specific at the point of action. It is part of internal structures because agents are always suspended within networks of power, norms and interpretations – networks of social relations. The proximate knowledge of the roles, norms, power and structures within which we are located (and the likely outcomes of action) can be viewed as constraints and/or opportunities. As Morawska (2009) notes, migration creates an unsettling of routines and a questioning of the taken-for-granted world, that tends to get overlooked when we examine either structure or agency and do not link them well. In everyday engagement, actors adjust their habits and goals as they assess practical situations, and thereby (re)create structures. 'New situations, in particular, enable actors to reinterpret schemas and redesign resources' (Morawska, 2009: 4). This is, then, a much more dynamic approach than that proposed by Bourdieu's concept of habitus.

It may be easier to understand the notion of conjuncturally-specific internal structures with reference to the theory of *situated learning* proposed by Lave and Wenger (1991). These authors' theoretical perspective on learning is based very loosely on general theories of practice in which wider structures are both preconditions and variable outcomes of action.[5] Learning, they suggest, is something we all do all the time, while co-participating in everyday situations. Here, we are not so interested in what we learn (or a traditional approach to education) as how we alter, what we think we know, how we feel, or what we do in order to co-participate within 'communities of practice' (discussed below). The concept of conjuncturally-specific internal structures recognizes the way agents achieve the 'practical consciousness' that Giddens talks about, yet is able to lend more of a sense of time to his concept. Let's take the British National Party as an example. This extreme right wing organization has an 'ideal' (general, overarching, organizational) discourse of racism and anti-immigration guiding members' actions and perceptions, which has become inscribed in their habitus. However, in practice the members and the hierarchy have come to learn that if they voice this opposition to all migration (and its inherent racism) too overtly they will not be accepted in British politics and their ideas will meet with strong public resistance. As a result they have learned to tailor both their discourse and their actions, in this case retaining the 'ideal' discourse for some purposes (Richardson, 2008).[6] Another way to think about this might be as the strategies we learn and internalize as ways to get by; strategies that will eventually become part of the habitus. For de Certeau (1984: 53) strategies, like 'taking a trick' in a game of cards, or little acts of resistance, (as in the work of Scott, 1985), involves 'an ability to maneuver (sic) within the different conditions' the hand one has been dealt or the rules of the game. Migrants may learn to disguise aspects of their culture, for example, or agents of the state may learn to overlook certain policy transgressions where there is economic demand for migrants (see Chapter 5).

Practices

Practices take place within the horizon of action and involve active agency, communities of practice and conjuncturally-specific external structures. *Active agency*, or the daily actions of agents (Stones, 2005), includes both routine and reflexive (thoughtful, purposive, strategic) action. Although they may appear constrained by habitus and conjuncturally-specific internal structures, agents' actions do not therefore become predictable based on these. Their agency comes from their habitus being as much an individual as a group one, from the fact that any individual is at any one time the bearer of any number of role positions and is subject to a diverse range of norms and expectations. Agents also hold multiple identities framed by different socio-cultural maps. An individual can therefore be a mother, wife, manager, professional, Christian, black, daughter, national subject, refugee, migrant, with specific tastes and interests not related to any of these. But more than this, a theory of practice acknowledges that all these internal structures are enacted within communities whose members each have their own internal structures and structural constraints and opportunities, power, knowledge and reflexivity. For Morawska (2009) everyday engagement (active agency) reproduces and transforms structures, and cultures. The source of the transformative capacity of agency is in the structural gaps discussed above, the individual reactions and projections, discussed below, and the enacting and interaction of structures and agency within practice. Agency, in a theory of practice, thus takes the shape of individual, reflexive reactions to specific circumstances, albeit that these reactions are always to some extent circumscribed by previous events and experiences. An important element is the ability to imagine a different way of being and doing, thinking and feeling. For Bourdieu, what agents desire is always circumscribed by the logic of a particular field, so that individuals tend for the main part not to desire what is impossible or unimaginable. In research on migration, which always presupposes a change in circumstances, a move from the familiar to (perhaps) the unfamiliar, we do need to consider that agents might make future-oriented projections. For Emirbayer and Mische (1998: 963) human agency is

> a temporally embedded process of social engagement, informed by the past (in its habitual aspect), but also oriented toward the future (as a capacity to imagine alternative possibilities) and toward the present (as a capacity to contextualize past habits and future projects within the contingencies of the moment).

Active agency thus consists of three elements: the iterational, the projective and the practical. Emirbayer and Mische's discussion around the iterational does not add anything beyond what is already provided by Bourdieu's concept of habitus (and Morawska prefers the term habitual). Their discussion of the practical element of agency contributes to the creation of conjuncturally-specific internal structures outlined above (see Stones, 2005). It involves making sense of problems based on what is known (characterizing), adjusting habits consciously in changing contexts (deliberation), more or less conscious decision-making, and execution. The projective element on the other hand recognizes that habitus can be overly deterministic and that humans do have the ability to create and to pursue goals. Social life, Emirbayer and Mische suggest, includes challenges and uncertainties to which actors respond. Actors' desires and dreams are culturally embedded, but they are not predetermined. Actors plan and project, as the Chicago School pragmatists and interactionists James Dewey (1922), Alfred Schutz (1972), and George Herbert Mead (1934) taught us; drawing on what they know they imagine alternatives to current situations, visualize proposed solutions (and how they might be achieved), test out their ideas (perhaps moving temporarily or going somewhere on holiday, or just finding out from others who have done the same), and modify them constantly as they 'move within and among...different unfolding contexts' (Emirbayer and Mische, 1998: 964).

The important bridge between macro and micro perspectives, missing in so much empirical research, is provided by analysis of the interaction, using *practice theory*, of individuals (with desires, habitus and conjuncturally-specific internal structures) and the wider structures (as enacted by people in positions or roles or statuses, in relation to each other). In other words, we must consider the horizon of action and who takes part in that in relation to who else; 'structuration theory's emphasis on *praxis* involves a 'decentering' of the subject in favour of a concern for the nature and consequences of the activities in which social actors engage during their participation in day-to-day life' (Cohen, 1989: 11). Etienne Wenger's (1998) work on communities of practice is a useful way to think about the various contexts within which agency and structures are enacted. *Communities of practice* are not communities in the taken-for-granted, common-sense (cosy and comfortable) understanding of the term. Rather they are diverse groups of individuals that engage together in the doing of social life and in the negotiation of meaning, and so may include both peers and school staff (e.g. for refugee children), transnational communities, neighbours, ethnic groups, volunteer agencies, state agencies, and so on. 'The concept of practice connotes doing, but not just doing in and of itself. It is doing in a historical and social context that gives structure and meaning to what we do' (1998: 47). Practice is the acting out of social life (not to be confused with the adjective 'practical' or the verb 'to practise', which means to try something out or to repeat it). Practice, Wenger says, includes what we might recognize (traditionally) as structures – codes, rules, regulations, procedures – but also 'implicit relations, tacit conventions, subtle cues, untold rules of thumb, recognizable intuitions, specific perceptions, well-tuned sensitivities, embodied understandings, underlying assumptions, and shared world views. Most of these may never be articulated, yet they are unmistakeable signs of membership in communities of practice...' (ibid: 47). In other words practice is about knowing (and working out) how to go on in given circumstances suspended within networks of other people and groups each with their own internal and external structures. Not only do individuals each have their own desires and habits, but also ways of knowing how to go on (conjuncturally-specific internal structures) that are continually learned and relearned within what Wenger calls communities of practice of others all doing the same, and all with their own norms, habits, desires and conjuncturally-specific internal structures, power and constraints. A community of practice is not just a group or network, it involves sustaining 'dense relations of mutual engagement organized around what they are there to do' (ibid: 74). Indeed in all social situations of everyday life, individuals need to negotiate their way forward, each bringing to the situation their own internal structures and adapting their own goals and expectations in line with the experiences, norms and practices of others. Communities of practice are not homogeneous, Wenger notes; participants have different roles, backgrounds, identities, histories, goals, statuses, power; communities of practice are interrelations that arise out of engagement in practice rather than entities we might try to objectively describe as a community.

Communities of practice (social and institutional life, if you like) thus provide the context within which an agent is constrained and enabled by the external structures. These are embodied and enacted through roles and positions of those within an agent's communities of practice. *Conjuncturally-specific external structures* are a way of bringing what sociologists have referred to as roles back into the frame, while recognizing that they entail some element of action; that while they are structural and constraining (slots for people to slot into), roles also involve them doing things in order to reproduce (or transform) them. Conjuncturally-specific external structures, like conjuncturally-specific internal structures above, are therefore useful ways of conceptualizing the intermediate level between structures and actions, within communities of practice. They direct the researcher or student to explore social webs, and direct and indirect influences on action; they involve analysis of the context of action. The evidence for these could be found in obligations, prerogatives, routine practices, – things people do because they are expected of them in their given role, office, sets of expectations, the way they perceive their relationships, their power, and so on.

Outcomes

What people do and the ways in which they interact will have an effect for subsequent perceptions, expectations, conjuncturally-specific internal structures and habitus; in turn these affect communities of practice and conjuncturally-specific external structures, and wider structures are reproduced or transformed (to varying degrees) in the process. Outcomes can be intended or unintended, and can lead to innovation or consolidation. Outcomes take the shape of all of the above: external and internal structures, practices and communities. The specific outcomes of interest to an empirical researcher could include specific events, an identified set of surface appearances, the difference (or indeed continuity) between intentions and outcomes, or social change more broadly conceived. Morawska (2009) says that studies in the US have tended to look at how structures shape immigrants' options and how they then act on these. There is thus more attention paid to how immigration has transformed immigrants than on how they transform host and home societies, or how immigrants (re)constitute the structures. Morawska examines various outcomes of migration to the US: the impacts of resettlement, assimilation trajectories, and transnational involvements at home, for example, in an attempt to 'encourage immigration researchers to undertake investigations of the transformative effects of immigration activities on the society they are embedded in' (Morawska, 2009: 6). This involves analysis of what she calls one full sequence of the structuration process. The outcomes are diverse, she says, because of the different backgrounds, and changing circumstances, but using structuration theory Morawska identifies some general patterns in migration trajectories.

Methodology

The set of concepts above can be used to inform and to frame empirical research and provide a rich understanding of international migration processes for students. But the extent to which they (and the entire framework) can be applied to substantive, empirical work depends on the level of understanding required and the richness of the evidence that can be made available. There is a place for broad-brush studies, 'most structuration studies will benefit from being placed within a broader historical and geographical framework' (Stones, 2005: 127) but the findings would always be approximate and provisional, because a complete practice story requires close attention to the interaction of:

- external structures
- internal structures
- practices, and
- outcomes.

Studies that are broad and sweeping can provide very general suggestions about wider patterns that may inform the upper structural layers and the more proximate social surroundings; but the causal process is complex, forms of power intertwine, different institutions have varying internal power dynamics. Macro historical and theoretical studies, as we shall see in Chapters 4 to 6, can thus act as a frame within which to examine the specific interaction of such wider external forces and the hermeneutic frame of actors. Broad accounts of ideological schemas (neoliberalism, for example, or those informed by colonialism) or frameworks (such as transnationalism or globalization) are useful for trying to locate how these are embodied or located in the habitus of individuals and groups, combined with other dispositions and cultural schemas. Methodologically, this involves conceptualizing and learning about these wider structures from a macro perspective; it can use both grand theorizing and learning practically about the smaller, local, relevant context. But, such abstract level arguments should always be linked overtly to the analysis of the practice of daily life.

For Giddens, structuration is an *approach* – a term that conveys its methodological implications: 'Social theory has the task of providing conceptions of the nature of human activity and of the human agent which can be placed in the service of empirical work' (1984: xvii). But rather than looking for generalizations the task of a social theory like structuration is explanation that 'is contextual, the clearing up of queries' (Giddens, 1984: xviii). This leads to a tendency for close study. It is only through the analysis of 'situated action' that we can see the outcomes of the interaction of structures and their perceptions. As Wenger (1998: 68) notes, 'In a duality, what is of interest is understanding the interplay, not classifying' the separate elements. Although we have established some basic elements in the duality of structure, it is their interaction that interests us, and this takes place in practice. Here we seek, for example, 'detailed manifestations' of discourses, the lived experiences, the micro level of daily life. This is where we can begin to understand how the forces of habitus and external structures meet the daily contingencies, the specific circumstances and how they are perceived and acted on. A theory of practice examines the daily lives of agents as they are lived (the practice of daily life) in the context of wider social structures and historical forces; the meso level provides an ontology with which to think through and examine how these two levels are interrelated. It enables us to explore daily practice at the intersection of wider forces. This is the level that is often overlooked in research on international migration.

Telling Practice Stories

Employing a theory of practice could involve paying attention to either/or external structures, internal structures, practices, or outcomes, but this inevitably leads to questions about the other parts. For example, an interest in conjuncturally-specific internal structures would lead a researcher to examine politics, power relations, and so on; whereas a focus on the habitus leads a researcher to examine an agent's phenomenological view of the world, and to look outward from that towards where these ideas and views might have come from and what their structural implications are in the longer term. Studies thus need to be brought together into practice stories that illuminate the process of social life. It would be impossible for one lone researcher to study all interrelated aspects of a phenomenon through a practice theory. An analysis of the conjuncturally-specific external structures, for example, involves engagement with the context, and with the agents within that context, in order to gain as complex an understanding as possible of the relevant norms, rules, and practices which constrain or frame an agent's choices. It involves the researcher understanding the context for herself, the various agents, their power, their roles, norms, etc. Understanding conjuncturally-specific internal structures involves trying to work out retrospectively how an agent might have perceived the world around her, by enquiring into her actions; or a researcher can engage in the world of the agent as they make meaning. Conjuncturally-specific internal structures mediate between the habitus and the external structures. Recognizing this entails knowledge of the context and how it is perceived and interpreted by the agent. Habitus needs to be understood through hermeneutics and phenomenology, but can also be posited as entities by the researcher with knowledge of the environment and history. They need a meso level of conceptualization and a micro level of analysis and data collection. In order to understand an outcome or a set of actions and behaviours, even a set of attitudes (like racism), an identity (like an ethnic one), a decision to migrate, a decision to migrate temporarily, or a decision to control migration, we need to draw on all these levels with a basic understanding behind our analyses of how the levels interact in practice. And this must be temporal. Giddens says we must 'situate action in time and space as a continuous flow of action' (1979: 3). We should avoid snapshots of society and equating time with social change; social reproduction and continuity also take place over time (and space). Students can piece together practice stories about diverse migration trends by drawing existing studies together. This will yield a complex understanding of the relevant processes, though it may of course also draw attention to gaps in existing knowledge.

Methods

In terms of method, the above need not prescribe the use of any one particular technique, but methods such as in-depth interviews and ethnography are likely to bring the researcher closer to the action. Giddens (1984: xxx), does 'not believe there is anything in either the logic or the substance of structuration theory which would somehow prohibit the use of some research technique such as survey methods, questionnaires or whatever'. However, as he also acknowledges, structuration theory views agents as at least to some extent knowledgeable and therefore demands at least some attention to what they believe and say. On the other hand, what he calls 'practical consciousness' (Giddens, 1979) often involves doing something without being aware of it, so we must also find a way of studying the practice of daily life and understanding it without relying solely on the views of agents. Making sense of a form of life, Giddens says, involves generating recognizable characterizations of life through immersion in it.

> Immersion in a form of life is the necessary and only means whereby an observer is able to generate such characterizations. 'Immersion' here ... does not, however, mean 'becoming a full member' of the community, and cannot mean this. To 'get to know' an alien form of life is to know how to find one's way about in it, to be able to participate in it as an ensemble of practices. But for the sociological observer this is a mode of generating descriptions which have to be mediated, i.e. transformed into categories of social scientific discourse.
>
> (1976: 161)

Bourdieu (1996 and 1999) reminds us that we can no longer attain the positivist's dream of findings that are not constructed; findings are produced through construction and understanding, and the best we can achieve is a '*reflex reflexivity* based on a craft, on a sociological "feel" or "eye", [that] allows one to perceive and monitor on the spot, as the interview is actually taking place, the effects of the social structure within which it is occurring' (1999: 608). It is interesting to note that the examples Stones uses of composite studies revealing structuration processes in detail include a twelve-year long, extensive ethnographic study (Morawska, 1996) and analysis of 'a very localised slice of life' as illustrated in Ibsen's play *A Doll's House* (Stones, 2005: 148). In the telling of practice stories it is likely a combination of methods will be used.

The Role of Social and Substantive Theories

Before we move on to the next chapter it will be useful to think a little about the role of other theories, concepts and perspectives within a theory of practice. Essentially practice theory attempts to develop the basic insights of Marx's maxim, that people make their own history but not in circumstances of their own choosing. As such it is a meta-level or general theory; rather than a theory of something substantive, it is a theory about the fundamental processes of social life. It is thus perfectly logical to incorporate theories, concepts and approaches from other traditions.

A researcher or student may use all sorts of useful terminology – theoretical concepts, theoretical frameworks, social science perspectives, sensitizing concepts – in order to help her identify external structures, and this need not detract from their position within the wider frame. A study may be informed, for example, by Durkheim's (1938) description of 'social facts', or Karl Marx's socio-economic forces; more contemporaneously (and especially in migration studies) she is likely to use theoretical perspectives such as globalization, cosmopolitanism, and mobility. Structures can include ideologies, for example, as overarching frames, but ideology theory reminds us that ideologies are also perceived and interpreted by agents. Discourse, similarly, can be understood as *sui generis*, as a pure discourse (therefore an external structure), but also must be considered in a theory of practice as discursive frameworks (habitus) that get adapted and adopted, or translated, in situated action. Studies of discourse and ideologies are useful framing devices linking studies to wider social forces. But in many cases, these studies of discourse are 'not wedded closely to an analysis of the process of agents' conduct in situ' (Stones, 2005: 139). But they could be. Similarly, we can use various theories to help us make sense of the learning that takes place within communities of practice; for example the pragmatism of John Dewey (1922), and the interactionism of George Herbert Mead (1934), Herbert Blumer (1969) and Erving Goffman (1990). Here ideologies, for example, take shape in the habitus of agents in context. The conjuncturally-specific external structures discussed above include things relevant to migration such as the way the police monitor residence permits, the way policies are interpreted in the practice of those in context. This is really about what happens on the ground, through practice. The traditions of ethnomethodology (from Garfinkel, 1984) and discourse analysis may inform understandings here (see Wenger, 1998: 281 for further examples). Several theories will be useful for understanding conjuncturally-specific internal structures; interpretivism, for example. Here we are drawing on the tradition from Emanuel Kant, through Max Weber, phenomenology and hermeneutics, to modern day past-modern realism or post-positivism (see O'Reilly, 2011 for an overview). With a particular interest in migration and physical movement, we might draw on Henri Lefebvre who sees space as perceived, conceived, lived, and thereby recreated, or Herbert Gans, for whom space and its use should not be divorced from its wider political and economic context (see Kidder, 2009). In order to think about habitus in more depth, we might use Peter Winch's (1960) idealism, which says people's views of the world are framed by language and concepts shared by groups. This draws our attention away from habitus as a specifically individualistic practice and towards its communal origins and outcomes.

Understanding a society and the individuals in it involves understanding its language, concepts and rules, or its world-view. But we would not take this to its relativist conclusion because we are also examining the interaction of these world-views with pragmatic decision-making and external structures.[7] A theory of practice is a general theory that will draw from other social theories as well as more substantive theories that are addressed to specific issues or problems. Rather than being irresponsible eclecticism, or an 'anything goes' approach, this involves drawing from the diverse insights that have been developed over decades of social theory in critical and informed ways within a coherent framework. As Giddens (1984: xxii) says, there is 'an undeniable comfort in working within established traditions of thought'.

Conclusion

In this chapter I have argued that migration research will gain coherence from being located within a meta-theoretical practice theory framework. The chapter outlines the key concepts and understandings on which this theory is based, and traces its roots in a range of different theorists, especially Bourdieu, Giddens and Stones. This theory of practice relies on a few basic concepts that can inform data collection and analysis as well as providing a theoretical framework within which students of international migration can begin to understand work that has already been undertaken. Practice theory views practice as the ongoing processes involved in the constitution of social life; it favours neither subjectivism nor objectivism, but instead works to understand the interrelationship at the meso level of structures and actions. Key concepts identified here are: external structures, internal structures, practices, and outcomes. External structures are constraints and opportunities that confront an agent. They can be separated conceptually into upper and more proximate structural layers, and are more or less malleable. Internal structures can be separated into habitus and conjuncturally-specific internal structures, which become relevant as one learns how to go on in a given context. The practice of daily life takes place within communities of practice, and here the agent in focus confronts the habitus and conjuncturally-specific internal structures of the other individuals within the context. Active agency is nevertheless unpredictable, based as it is on habitus, learning how to go on in specific circumstances, as well as desires and projections. The outcome of practice is the reproduction and transformation of social life into newly (re)shaped external and internal structures, dreams and desires.

Practice stories will be told by scholars or students drawing work together to reveal the structuration processes involved in any given migration trend. The demand to pay attention to all parts of the structuration process, to external and internal structures, to practice and outcomes, as well as to temporal processes, means that one researcher is unlikely to manage it all, and that people should work together in uniting empirical research using this framework. Finally, a theory of practice is a meta-theoretical framework, a theory to frame theoretical and empirical approaches; it is therefore perfectly logical to incorporate theories, concepts and approaches from other traditions. In the concluding chapter, I have summarized some of these points so readers wishing to remind themselves of the key ideas in this chapter may wish to look there.

3

Theories and Perspectives in Migration

This chapter will outline some of the more substantive theories, perspectives and concepts that are widely used in the study of international migration. The goal is not to be exhaustive in reviewing all approaches in every discipline; the field of migration studies applies an unlimited range of theories in attempts to understand all aspects including motivations, responses, and outcomes to migration. Indeed, their toolkit of theories is not restricted to what we might think of as migration theories. Migration theories are often implicitly informed by, or supplemented with, what we might call social theories. Nicole Constable (2007, see Chapter 6), for example, uses theories of power, discipline, resistance and accommodation to understand domestic labour migration to Hong Kong. Here, her interest is in how the migrants cope and adapt. Ligaya Lindio-McGovern (2004), alternatively, uses alienation theory to frame her ethnographic work with Filipina domestic workers and to illustrate the way in which migrants can become commodities for the profit of others.

While practice theory offers a more general, sociological, theory of how all of social life unfolds through the practice of daily life, substantive theories also have a role to play in illuminating specific aspects of international migration or certain parts of a structuration cycle.

The study of international migration has traditionally been the domain of demographers and human geographers, but in the past 20 to 30 years, as migration has grown in extent, spread to all corners of the globe, and diversified beyond all attempts to define types and flows, it has attracted the attention of sociologists, anthropologists, political scientists, policy analysts, historians and more besides. Disciplines differ somewhat in their focus, sometimes as a result of their methodological approach, sometimes as a result of their specific interest in culture, space, place, social or political life, but the field of migration studies has also become increasingly inter-disciplinary. Some analysts begin their work with migration itself as the problem to explain, some with the nature of settlement. The theories drawn on and elaborated in these cases tend to reflect the demand to understand specific aspects. Theories are often implicitly liberal or critical. There are linear and more circular perspectives. Theories have also tended to bring with them a macro or micro (objectivist or subjectivist) perspective and to be concerned with either structure or agency. Furthermore, behind many theories developed specifically for migration and settlement is an underly-ing theory about human behaviour or social life, as I will illustrate. This is not meant as a map or an exhaustive list of theories and perspectives for the study of migration, but I hope the following provides something of a critical toolkit for theories that may (or may not) be employed within the framework of practice theory. It is assumed that readers will already have read Chapter 2.

Micro-economic Theories of Migration

Economic theories have been extremely influential in the field of interna-tional migration, for sociologists, geographers and other social theorists besides economists. Several theories employed to explain migration over the last century, in various versions, are modifications of Ernest George Ravenstein's *Laws of Migration* (1889, 1976). Ravenstein sought laws of behaviour to explain why, based on empirical evidence collected in the nineteenth century, people tended to move from densely populated to less populated areas, from poorer to wealthier areas, and from low-wage to higher-wage areas. He concluded that migration is governed by a series of favourable and unfavourable economic conditions that serve to push and pull people or populations in certain directions. Later, generalized theories continued to reduce explanations (or perhaps descriptions) of migration to this simple dichotomy of push and pull factors. 'Push' factors are those that compel people to leave the country of origin (or the place in which they currently live) and include political oppression, poor living standards, and low economic opportunities. 'Pull' factors attract them to a different place, and include a demand for labour, the opportunity for higher living standards, and political freedom. The approach is still employed largely in economics, geography and demography, where reasons for, or causes of, migration are sought, and the actor's individual decision to migrate is the focus of enquiry.

   In neoclassical economics, the approach tends to treat economic fac-tors (poverty as a push factor, better economic opportunities as a pull factor) as paramount, and relies on a rational choice model of human behaviour, which posits the existence of rational, profit-maximizing individuals who weigh up the costs and benefits of various options then make their independent choices before finally acting. This makes the assumption that outcomes are simply the result of individual actions, and can be understood in terms of what motivated agents. It also relies on a macro perspective, linked to neoclassical economic theory more broadly, and linking migration of the universal human being to the global supply and demand for labour in universal markets, in which countries with more work, higher wages, and fewer workers will attract workers from countries with lower wages and less work. It thus supports a politically liberal view, positing the notion that if left to work naturally (relying on the actions and choices of the rational individual) then eventually everything should equal out in the open migration market: the poorer move to richer countries and the crowded move to less populated areas, and everything ends up even. The difficulty is that this does not happen, partly because it is rarely the very poorest who have the resources to migrate, but almost certainly because (as discussed in the previous chapter) social processes cannot be reduced to the motivations of individuals.

Push and pull theories of migration were especially directed towards understanding various labour migrations of the past, where they have been able to offer a seductive and apparently common-sense interpretation of events. Juss (2006) believes push and pull factors remain useful for shedding *some* light on the reasons for migration, and others continue to refer to the dichotomy at least as a starting point for explanations. Having described in rich detail the way adolescent girls are lured, persuaded or cajoled into domestic service in Nigeria (implicitly examining the communities of practice and conjuncturally-specific external structures within which they are located), and having concluded that the girls have no real choice, Okafor (2009) finally anchors the explanation for this internal migration on push factors of widespread unemployment and abject poverty and pull factors of increased labour demand (in the home) in urban centres where increasing numbers of women are working in higher status employment. However, push and pull theories are a bit weak, do not reflect reality for the majority of migrants, and disregard many wider, structural and historical factors (Castles, 2010). They overlook the fact that population growth, poverty, and unemployment are of themselves insufficient conditions to promote migration (Castles and Miller, 2003; Sassen, 1988). They neglect a host of factors that influence moves, including family and community dynamics, the role of intermediaries encouraging migration by arranging passage, and the role of states in recruiting labour, granting (or withholding) permits, establishing policies on refugees and asylum seekers, and deciding citizenship rights. Furthermore, they aim only to account for movement at the individual level, positing inertia rather than wanderlust as the natural human condition (Richmond, 1993: 7).

Everett Lee (1966, in Skeldon, 1997) modified Ravenstein's approach by introducing intervening variables into the model. Here he was beginning to acknowledge the role of other, more proximate, structures such as geographical distance between origin and destination, and political barriers, and he even started to include things we might now call the habitus, and personal attributes which affect this, such as gender, age, class, and education. Network or relational factors (or communities of practice) are also acknowledged when researchers mention (as does Okafor, 2009, for example) the role of family members, knowledge of the receiving country, and so on. We are beginning to see that there is a lot more to the decision to migrate than the focus on a male decision-maker and a simple model of societies as either poorer or wealthier can explain.

From a practice theory perspective, economic theories of migration that begin by assuming the existence of a rational individual who makes choices based on the logical balancing of options, is centred on external structures with causal influence on individuals. Though its explanatory force lies with the active agency of individuals, it takes no account of the phenomenology of the agent-in-focus, and does not permit any explanation of why some people decide not to migrate under conditions that are patently favourable. We can only understand this (as many are now acknowledging) by trying to understand men's and women's choices in the context of their families, friends and the networks within which they are located, as well as in context of the structures they have internalized and go on to shape.

New economic theories and dual/segmented labour market theories merely refine the above. Dual labour market theories see the economies of the developed world as dualistic or segmented into secure and well-paid work on the one hand and a glut of temporary, insecure work that comes and goes (a secondary labour market) on the other hand. The secondary labour market, it is argued, is avoided by the locals and attracts cheap, temporary labour from abroad. Still the argument is an economic determinist one, giving causal primacy to markets (albeit these are assumed to act through the rational choice of actors). It remains uncritical, simplistic and politically liberal. Gonzalez and Fernandez (2003: 46) say in this theory that post-industrial economies are seen to have an 'insatiable thirst for cheap labour'. This emphasizes the pull, or demand, side of the equation, but it also begins to explain some outcomes of labour migration, specifically the tendency for foreign labour to be located and to remain in low-wage, low-status, often temporary jobs. However, Arango (2004) notes that one of its flaws is that many migrants now come of their own initiative, not just in response to demand but creating jobs that would not otherwise exist. This is especially true of women migrants (Kofman, 2000), and demands something more than an objectivist approach.

New economic theories of migration (Castles and Miller, 2009) acknowledge there are also some intervening variables (networks of family and friends who help anchor people in their new communities, or of middlemen, labour brokers, contractors) but still tend to rely on push and pull theories and their determining power over active agency, in the last instance, and see the networks merely as facilitating or hindering moves. They rarely consider the internalized structures (the habitus and the daily learning how to go on) of the agent or of her communities of practice. Examining the reasons for what he calls the United States' crisis in immigration, Phillip Martin (2004: 99), for example, says push and pull factors are 'like battery poles; both are necessary to start a car or a migration stream. Once started, intervening variables such as networks influence who migrates where'. If a government wants to stay in control it must deal with all of these three aspects, he suggests. Economists continue to perceive migration in terms of supply and demand economic models and their implications for individual decision-making. Barry Chiswick (2008), for example, uses the methodology of economics (testing theoretical models against quantitative empirical data) to address the question 'who moves and who does not' by comparing motives, ability and skills; that is by looking at the *supply* side of migration. He concludes that all migrants (especially economic migrants) tend 'on average, to be more able, ambitious, aggressive, entrepreneurial, healthier ... than similar individuals who choose to remain in their place of origin' (2000: 64). That is, migrants favourably self-select. This begins to address the relationship between (some) external conditions and active agency to a small extent but it ignores the role of internal structures, communities of practice, and other proximate external structures.[1] For Arango (2004: 23), 'it is doubtful whether the disparate ingredients that make up the new economics of migration are sufficiently woven and logically integrated as to constitute a coherent theory, or whether it is no more than a critical, sophisticated version of neoclassical theory'. Clearly it needs to be underpinned by a more general theory of social processes as described in Chapter 2.

Theorists of migration continue to emphasize independent decision-making when they explain migration in terms of a search for a better way of life, for community, for work, or even for family reunification. Gonzalez and Fernandez (2003) suggest all such theories (implicitly or otherwise) assume the acting out of a conscious choice. They also suggest that these are all versions of the push and pull theory. Not all are implying that eventually an equilibrium will be reached, nor do they all ignore other factors in the decision-making. Instead we should see them as making assumptions about the phenomenology of the agent, without always asking the agent herself what influenced the decision to move; or with no analysis of how systemic changes and structural forces are understood and interpreted by agents. We thus need to evaluate the adequacy of their explanations in terms of a general theory about the *practice* of social life. As Pierre Bourdieu (1990: 46) says of rational choice theories,

> the relations between agents and objective conditions (or structures) that is implemented by economics constantly oscillates ... between an objectivist vision that subjects freedoms and will to an external, mechanical determinism ... and a subjectivist, finalist vision that substitutes the future ends of the project for individual action.

World Systems Theories

World systems theory conceptualizes the entire world as a single capitalist system, in which the undeveloped and poorer nations of the periphery provide cheap labour to support the wealthy and powerful core of the developed nations (Wallerstein, 1974). Its predecessor is dependency theory, which explains the poverty of poorer countries in terms of their political and economic dependency on wealthier nations – a theory on which many contemporary critiques of global capitalism are based. World systems theory thus takes both a global and critical perspective. In a broader sense, it relies on Marxist political economy, emphasizing the unequal global distribution of political and economic power and resources, and viewing migration as a by-product of global capitalism. For this theory migration is just another element in the domination of the Third World and works hand in hand with military and economic control.

Versions of this approach became particularly prominent in the 1960s and 70s, directed towards explaining mass labour migrations from Southern/Eastern to Northern/Western destinations that are to some extent continuations of colonial relations. They drew attention to the important role played by historical connections, colonial and other trading networks and the development of transnational corporations and international banking systems in the construction of a global economic system. Migration in this perspective takes place as a feature perpetuating a single overarching system characterized by uneven development and an international division of labour (see Portes and Walton, 1981; Sassen, 1988).

While micro-economic models ignore the role of the state and many other structural and historical factors, world systems theory focuses so much on historical and structural factors that the role of the individual (and factors that impinge on the individual's daily life) in making the decision to move is often overlooked. This perspective is much more focussed on structures than on actions, as if the structures of global capitalism have a life of their own; the actors appear as no more than pawns in a chess game (Arango, 2004); and the complexity of migration is ignored (Castles and Miller, 2009). Global systems theories tend to overlook female migration and cannot explain how labour migrations became long-term and established, nor how migrants were eventually joined by their families in what became a chain of migration (see below). They ignore the role of remittances in bringing economic advantage to sending countries. World systems theory also tends to reduce capitalism to commercial relations, rather than 'social relations, property patterns, ideologies, political institutions' (Gonzalez and Fernandez, 2003: 48).

The role of this kind of theory is, however, not to be overlooked. It has the status of a macro-theoretical explanation of broad scope; as such it can serve to highlight, in a practice story, the historical relationship between colonialism and many contemporary flows, the role of the state in migration processes, and the unequal political and economic relationship between states (see Skeldon, 1997; and Faist, 2010). The reproduction of the world system can be understood to work through processes of structuration: the nation states, which constitute variables in the system, use hegemonic power to maintain the disequilibrium, but this has to be mediated through and enacted by individuals in networks of social relations. This brings me to the concept of postcolonialism, which has informed later migration studies. Postcolonial societies are those which previously were colonized and a postcolonial relationship implies continuing exploitation, relations of inequality, economic ties based on prior appropriation, and/or cultural links informed by previously unequal relationships. I prefer the term 'traces of colonialism' as this leaves the nature of such traces for each research project to examine including its nature and constraints or the opportunity it provides, the habitus that may have become inscribed, and the social structures that have become hardened over time. Several authors discussed in the following chapters refer to colonial and postcolonial relations and their effects for, or impacts on, a given migration trend. There are numerous works that bring a postcolonial perspective or framework to the study of migration. Readers might enjoy the special issue on Examining Expatriate Continuities in the *Journal of Ethnic and Migration Studies*, Volume 36, Issue 8 (2010).

A particular concern that Gonzalez and Fernandez (2003) have with regards to world systems theory and postcolonial theory is that it 'elevates the degree of "agency" of Third-World elites', according them a higher degree of autonomy than is justified. Faist (2010) is concerned about the economic bias in world systems theory, which tends to overlook political and cultural processes. However, a theory of practice (as outlined in Chapter 2), because of its emphasis on structures as they are relevant to the given agent, will question how such power is enacted and embodied, perpetuated, strengthened, or challenged and transformed by agents. This is superbly illustrated in Rob Stones' (2005) strong structuration analysis of Ewa Morawska's (1996) *Insecure Prosperity: Small Town Jews in Industrial America 1890–1940*.

Migration Systems and Networks

The theories above tend to perceive migration as a one-off move to a new, permanent destination. They also tend to be centred on explaining (male) labour migrations. They are inadequate in their explanation of complex migration processes that take place, become consolidated, change in nature and shape, and emerge anew over time. They also favour either a structural or an action-centred approach (see the previous chapter). Migration systems theory, alternatively, understands migration as a complex process incorporating the ongoing interaction of macro, meso, and micro level elements within a wider migration system. Castles and Miller (2009) thus advocate a research agenda where interdisciplinary research examines the role of structures and actions, as well as the intermediate level of agents and intermediaries in the decision-making processes and the outcomes of migration. Rather than focus on individual migration decisions, migration systems theory acknowledges that moves tend to cluster, can be circular, and take shape within wider contexts and systems. Understanding migration processes thus involves moving out from the individual to the wider and interconnected sets of circumstances within which an individual agent is located.

A migration system connects two or more societies, each with their own economic and political systems, hierarchical structures (in other words, their own sets of external structures) that can be interrelated with other states in complex ways, through trade, culture, and politics. Thus, for example 'migration from Mexico originated in the southwestward expansion of the USA in the nineteenth century and the recruitment of Mexican workers by US employers in the twentieth century' (Portes and Rumbaut, 2006: 354–355 in Castles and Miller, 2009: 27). Interestingly, the growing retirement migration of US citizens to Mexico is now a more recent feature of this complex migration system (Kiy and McEnany, 2010). Migration systems imply durable relationships that can go back as far as colonial rule, or can be newly formed systems in the making. The approach accepts that there are prior links within the system that facilitate, inform, or describe the migration. Thus, Algerian migration to France can be understood in the context of France's prior colonization of Algeria. Pakistanis, Bangladeshis and Indians migrated in such large numbers to Britain, because Britain once colonized their part of the world and then turned to the same area to recruit when they needed workers after the war (Castles and Miller, 2003). British people moved to Spain in great numbers because it is geographically close, but also because they have usually been there first as tourists (this migration is thus a continuation of package tourism, see Chapter 4). Domestic labour migration from the Philippines to Hong Kong is better understood within the context of the wider Asian (economic) region and even benefits from some analysis of the cultures of British colonialism (see Chapter 6). But we are not simply concerned with the historical relationship between two places or states; Castles and Miller (2009) say a main focus of systems theory is on *regional* migration systems. Systems include those such as the Southern African migration system, involving cross-border labour migration to South Africa from its immediate neighbouring states; and the West African migration system, from rural to developed, capitalist urban centres. Agadjanian (2008) interestingly theorizes these systems in the context of both wider, historical developments, including colonization and apartheid, and contemporary practice. Others talk of the African or European migration systems. This was a first step towards looking beyond separate countries, to connections between them, and to the industries that arose mediating (and perhaps profiting from) migration. There is still a tendency to focus on economic systems, but culture and social ties and connections are also seen as relevant, which has the side effect of bringing women more into focus in migration stories (Kofman, 2000).

Migration networks theory involves acknowledging the role of the family and community in migration decisions, in encouraging, or funding the passage, in facilitating settlement and/or retaining ties to home. It recognizes that migration is an ongoing process; that a movement once established can become self-sustaining through the use of these networks. Migrant networks aid settlement and enable community formation. Migrant groups develop their own social and economic infrastructure, with associations, clubs, places of worship, shops, cafes, and even professionals such as doctors and lawyers. Hein de Haas (2010) has recently argued that networks theory tries to understand the internal dynamics of migration systems and is good at understanding how they become sustaining or self-perpetuating, but is less good at understanding how migration systems and networks are (differentially) initiated, their diverse trajectories, or what he calls their breakdown. Haas suggests analysis of 'feedback systems' in sending and receiving countries that serve to trigger and eventually end migration flows. This is a useful way of thinking about the role of communities of practice and conjuncturally-specific structures for migrants at home, away, and in-between.

Migration systems and networks theories are an acknowledgement of the macro, micro and meso structures (in Castles and Miller's terms) involved in migration processes. Macro structures include state policies to control migration and the role of governance, the global political economy (as in world systems theory), smaller-scale trade agreements, and broadly conceived international relations. Micro structures, they say, are the informal social networks that migrants develop to enable the migration process: family connections that help with obtaining legal residence or financial aid in setting up businesses, the role of the family and community in migration decisions. This links to the theory of migration chains, which recognizes the nature, shape, and form of migration progresses like links in a chain; and to Massey's (1998) theory of cumulative causation that suggests that each migration and its outcomes in turn alters the situation and social context within which subsequent migration decisions are made and the outcomes of these. The relationships between previous and newer migrations and the networks that are drawn on, built and developed as a result, often get researched now as social and cultural capital (as Castles and Miller, 2009 acknowledge). These newer approaches would work well located within a theory of practice. However, what Castles and Miller term 'meso structures' are not quite the same as the meso level structures outlined in Chapter 2. For these authors, the meso level includes the intermediaries, individuals, groups and organizations that 'mediate between migrants and political or economic institutions'. This includes a migration industry, smugglers, gang-masters, lawyers and agents (or what they term 'exploiters and helpers'). Castles and Miller (2009: 28) conclude their section on migration systems and networks arguing that 'Macro-, meso-, and micro-structures are intertwined in the migratory process, and there are no clear dividing lines between them ... It is essential to try to understand all aspects of the migratory process'.

Harzig (2001) demonstrates how examining the more complex picture of migration revealed by networks and systems theories reveals the part women have long played in migration, in contradiction to the linear approach with its notion of the male pioneer. She says, for example, 'Women who had moved from the Swedish countryside to work as maids or in the textile trades and then decided to move on to Chicago were as much aware of their labour market value and the higher wages they could realize abroad as their male counterparts' (2001: 18). And Watters (2008) uses network theory as a bridge between micro and macro perspectives in an attempt to understand how refugee children come to be construed as a threat to social cohesion. The approach importantly draws attention to the fact that migration takes place within sets of historical and relational constraints and opportunities, and is the outcome of the interaction of structures and actions in the context of family relationships and intermediaries. However, it does not fully theorize the interrelationship of structures and agency and spends little or no time thinking through how structures become embodied practice. If employing practice theory, researchers might examine macro structures in the context of the wider migration systems that Castles and Miller refer to, but then focus their attention on the upper and more proximate structural layers (state policies, trade agreements) of the given agent (or group of agents). This can be done by the researcher or through the perspective of the agent: as Castles and Miller recognize, the individual in question may or may not recognize that she is located within a wider system of migration. The micro analysis would then include understanding habitus (e.g. attitudes towards the host country, being a labourer, expectations of poverty) and conjuncturally-specific internal structures (the internalizing of the norms of the group at hand, the expectations of agents and intermediaries, family pressure). In a theory of practice the meso level analysis brings in the communities of practice and conjuncturally-specific external structures, which might include agents and intermediaries but also includes families and friends (the networks that Castles and Miller locate at the micro level).

Migrants in Society

Migration as a process also has outcomes for sending and receiving countries (and for the individuals and their families) and many theories are applied to trying to understand these. A great deal of literature dealing both substantively and theoretically with migration actually concerns itself not so much with migration as a process but with the impacts of migration in terms of the societies in which they settle. As with many of the perspectives above, this is often based on a unidirectional, linear approach in which it is assumed the migrant will move from one society or state to another, to settle long-term. Many migrations do not fit this model and yet it is still an assumption behind much research in the field. As Koser (2007b) notes, the issue of migrants in society remains a pressing contemporary debate, especially at the level of the mass media, political and public opinion, and is therefore reflected in academic research. Large and rising numbers of migrations across the globe are depicted as having (often negative) economic, demographic, social and cultural impacts that demand theorization. This is better understood if we consider the concept of nation.

Nations and Nationalism

Nations frame international migration as states, with policies, populations, polities, citizenships rights, and other hard upper level structural layers, but also with identities, imagined histories, and ideas and discourses about belonging (and excluding). As Day and Thompson (2004) suggest, in their useful overview of this topic, nation, nationalism and national identity are sociological phenomena that should be understood and theorized within the context of changing facts and changing ideas, including broader currents in social theory. Nations should not be reified as facts, even though they will often frame migration as hard external structures. Nations are a relatively modern phenomenon, that were intentionally created mostly during the nineteenth century, and yet the members are sometimes prepared to die for what sociologists see as a social construction. Day and Thompson distinguish classical and post-classical approaches to nation. The 'classical' approaches, that were elaborated in the latter part of the twentieth century, were concerned to explain 'what happened to transform people's sense of the world so fundamentally that they came to identify with, and be moved by, the idea of the nation' (Day and Thompson, 2004: 3). Some theorists, such as Gellner (2006), relate the development of nations to other modern developments, such as industrialization, capitalism, and major political change. Prior to the rise of the nation state, different territories each had their own local government and laws. As states unified territories into larger units there was a need to unify the people so that they felt they belonged and could be subject to the same, now centralized, laws, rules and regulations. The best way to do this was to draw on and build the sense that the people shared something in common: a blood, soil and identity (Bauman, 1992). For Ernest Gellner (2006), industrialization required a workforce with a general, basic, common education, and this was more functional where there was a shared culture. Benedict Anderson's (1991) explanation is somewhat more materialist, linking nationalism to the rise of 'print-capitalism'. Nations are communities of people – imagined communities, because there is no real connection, the members do not all know each other, some may have been migrants decades or centuries earlier, they are not genetically the same, and not all of same blood or heritage. A nation with a strong sense of community, belonging, and identity, has citizens more likely to abide by its rules, and even make sacrifices for it. Ethnicists, however, trace the roots further back, to pre-modern ethnic identities. For Anthony Smith (1979 and 2009), the origin of nations can be traced back hundreds of years via ethnic groupings, and what nations do is simply draw from and unite these identities and cultures into an homogenous grouping with allegiance to the state. Classical theorists thus show how the rise of nations needs to be located in wider historical social forces and institutional developments (Day and Thompson, 2004: 11).

Post-classical approaches critique the way in which nations are seen as a sociological reality. Feminist approaches, for example, draw attention to the 'relationship between nationalist discourses and symbolism and patriarchal practices and ideology' (Day and Thompson, 2004: 13), or demonstrate the interlinkage of nationalist and gendered discourses, especially with regards to sexuality and reproduction. Yuval-Davis (1997) criticizes the primordialism in some classical approaches (such as Gellner and Smith), that sees nations as natural phenomena rising unproblematically from kinship relations; and she draws attention to the central role of women 'and not (just?) the bureaucracy and the intelligentsia' in reproducing nations biologically, culturally and symbolically (1997: 2). She draws attention to the ubiquitous fiction of the state that purportedly encircles or controls a homogenous society and culture, and thereby 'constructs minorities into assumed deviants' (1997: 4), focussing always on a specific culture or a specific religion or language, to the exclusion of others. She also brings to our attention the role of border guards, whose role it is to defend the state from 'invasion' by non-members of the collectivity (1997: 23). Critical theory, postcolonial theory, and cultural studies approaches also challenge the foundational bias in classical approaches, and draw attention to context, the making of meaning, discourse and practice (mirroring wider developments in social theory), as opposed to grand narratives and consensus. Mick Billig's (1995) work, for example, focuses on the day to day aspects of banal nationalism. Here he is not only referring to the passionate or shocking expressions of identity such as flag-waving and ethnic cleansing, but to the 'ideological habits which enable the established nations of the West to be reproduced' (1995: 6): school children pledging daily allegiance to the flag in the US, politicians' daily reminders of who 'we' are, national newspapers that speak for the supposed nation, and calls to support the nation in sporting events. These are so banal we rarely notice they are there, yet, in the words of practice theory, they are everywhere enacted and embodied and thus inscribed into the habitus. Post-classical approaches are thus much more likely to question and challenge ideas of cultural and religious homogeneity, to highlight conflict, to look at experiences, for what nation means to members of multicultural societies, than to try to explain the rise of the nation state. However, sometimes these are not in direct contradiction to the classical approaches but build on and develop their implicit social constructionism.

Assimilation

Because migration was understood as a one-off permanent move to a new destination, migration outcomes tended to be perceived in terms of the extent to which the migrant became assimilated or incorporated into the new (supposedly homogenous) culture and country. This perception took the form of an ideological frame of reference, state policies and practices, and sets of assumptions a migrant faced (or brought with them) in the new destination (see Zadie Smith's *White Teeth* (2001), for an illustration of these assumptions and practices in what became a popular novel). As Eriksen (2002) notes, the establishment of the system of nation states we now take for granted in effect created both indigenous (majority) populations and ethnic minorities. 'Indeed the very term minority is meaningful only in the context of a state' (2002: 121). Of course minority does not necessarily mean migrant, nor vice versa. The Yanomamö, for example, claim to be both an indigenous population and minority group, as a result of being incorporated into the wider state and capitalist system (Eriksen, 2002). Nevertheless, the term minority in many cases also maps onto the

term migrant. Even in the US, which is certainly not easily seen as an ethnically homogeneous nation, there remains an assumption that migration
leads to ethnic mixing and thus to problems. Assimilationist policies and
practices assumed a permanence of migrants combined with the expectation they would blend in with the rest of society, adopting the same
mannerisms, dress, language and culture, leading to what was called a
'melting pot'. The goal was part of the national project in which national
unity and national identity are seen to depend on sameness, and difference
is seen as a threat. As Cohen (2006: 6) notes: 'A century ago the USA was
committed to an ideology and often a practice of Americanization' sym-
bolized by the opening in 1908 of 'Israel Zangwill's Broadway hit musical,
The Melting Pot'.

What this often amounted to was migrants giving up their own traditions and adopting those of the majority culture. Some did this happily
in order to avoid prejudice and discrimination, or because they had incorporated these assumptions into their own habitus. However, attempting
to hide one's 'race' is not always possible and local actors, through their
zenophobia or racism, often managed to limit assimilation through practices of discrimination. Many ethnic groups, alternatively, have strongly
resisted the eroding of their cultures and religions. What you get when people insist on keeping a tight hold on their differences in the face of policies
and attitudes expecting them to assimilate is marginalized and excluded
ethnic minority groups; some living in ghettoes physically separated from
the mainstream society, others marginalized in terms of their networks,
friends, contacts and language. Being unsuccessful in terms of the ideal
goal of assimilation usually leads to a subordinate position in the division
of labour (Eriksen, 2002). Thus these concepts, analysed critically, can be
useful tools for examining migration outcomes.

Castles and Miller (2009: 247) suggest, '*Assimilation* meant that immigrants were to be *incorporated* into society through a one-sided process
of *adaptation*' (my emphasis). The language of adaptation and assimilation make assumptions that it is the migrant who is supposed to be doing
the adapting and assimilating; they are therefore value-laden concepts that
nevertheless continue to hold strong currency. Some modern immigration
countries (France, for example, and Britain increasingly) continue to insist
on cultural assimilation at the level of the individual before they will grant
citizenship rights. And, as Bagby (2009: 474) contends, there remains a
general, lay theory, that 'immigrants and their children will inevitably
assimilate into American culture and move away from their "traditional"
culture, as they become integrated into the socio-economic life of America'.
Here, a very different group, protecting its difference and its values can be
portrayed as extremist, hostile or dangerous.

Within a theory of practice the concept of assimilation is best employed
to analyse the extent to which there is an ideology of assimilation (and

on the part of whom), and the extent to which this ideology, or set of assumptions, is inscribed in policy and practice. The outcomes of these assumptions and policies will be visible as something to explain. One could empirically analyse or try to theorize the extent to which a migrant is incorporated into a society (be it the one they left or the one they migrated to, or both) and what this might look like in practice. In this latter case it is probably safer to not use the concept of assimilation, or to use it carefully and critically.

Multiculturalism

Multiculturalism is another concept through which we can begin to understand behaviours, expectations and policies. Castles and Miller (2009: 245) rightly ask how migrants can become part of the societies they move to, and how state and civil society can facilitate this process. Assimilation could not work with clearly visible ethnic minorities, with the increase in labour migration in Europe and the US after World War II, with guest-worker policies failing to deter settlement, and with clear differences in the culture and religion of migrant groups. Now, where governments have accepted the permanence of their incomers they have usually moved from policies of assimilation to some acceptance of long-term cultural difference, to pursue what Cohen (2006: 6) refers to as the rather more nebulous goals of 'multiculturalism', 'pluralism', or 'rainbow nationhood'. Multicultural societies treat their minorities as distinct but equal; they offer the same education, the same welfare rights, equal standing before the law, but allow ethnic groupings to display their differences, for example in areas that become known as 'Little Italy' or 'Chinatown'. The multiculturalist policies in Canada, the UK, Australia and Sweden since the 1970s have thus involved granting cultural and political rights to minority groups. In the US multiculturalism is more of a cultural ideal than a state policy. However, living with difference can be difficult. Identifying oneself as different is one thing; being labelled (and therefore treated) as different is not always the same thing. Furthermore, increasing levels of immigration into Western and North European countries, combined with increasingly blatant and visual expressions of difference on the part of some groups have stretched people's tolerance for diversity.

There appears to be quite a lot of slippage in the language used when discussing incorporation, with people mixing acculturation (acquiring or mimicking the dominant culture), assimilation (becoming similar to the dominant culture and society), and adaptation (adapting to the majority culture). The term 'assimilation', in my opinion, should be seen as an ideology inscribed in practices, not as an ideal or goal pursued by social scientists. It should be used critically. Nevertheless, researchers do continue to pursue it as a goal, or ascribe its success or failure to certain groups. Eriksen (2002) for example, contends that second or third generation migrants do tend towards acculturation in terms of values and general orientation, though they may retain a mixed ethnic identity. But, he goes on to say they may be prevented from full *assimilation* (assuming this is a good) because of discrimination. Later, Eriksen takes assimilation to mean diminished ethnic identity. It would be far safer to stick with the language of incorporation, or at least to be very specific about what is being meant or implied; these words should remain questions to address not normative assumptions. People still tend to theorize/explain settlement in terms of acculturation, assimilation, multiculturalism, ethnicity, racism and discrimination, but there is more likelihood now they will ask questions about the extent and nature of incorporation rather than begin with the assumption that assimilation or multiculturalism is the best outcome. For example, one theoretical explanation for continued segregation is that migrants tend to move to poor neighbourhoods and thus a concentration effect limits opportunity (Jargowsky, 2009). A general theory about the recursive practice of social life would be useful in informing this sort of analysis (see Chapter 2).

Ethnicity

The term ethnicity refers to 'aspects of relationships between groups which consider themselves, and are regarded by others, as being culturally distinctive' (Eriksen, 2002: 4). It involves identifying (or being identified) with a group, and can be conceived as a sense of belonging that is based on ideas of, or beliefs in, a common origin, history, culture, language, experience and values. Members of a given ethnic group are not identical with regard to all these elements but they consider they are similar enough, and different enough from other groups, to be part of the same collection. Ethnicity is not the same as minority, since majority groups can also identify ethnically. In the social sciences the term was developed to draw attention to the social construction of 'racial' identities, as a means of addressing concerns about the essentializing and primordial connotations of the concept of race. Nevertheless, ethnicity has itself now come to refer, in some usage, to fixed categories and permanent groupings, and it is often used, ascriptively, to mark one group from another (often relying on physical markers like colour, but also religion, region of origin or other supposed determinate differences) in the construction of boundaries of exclusion and inclusion. This is a dangerous development: atrocities in Rwanda and the former Yugoslavia, for example, were conducted in the name of ethnicity.

Theories of ethnicity attempt to explain ethnic identification and related behaviours and practices. Barth (1969b), for example, suggests that we think of an ethnic group in terms of a relationship rather than in terms of an entity. It is not the ethnic *category* that should be theorized but the process of ethnic categorization on the part of the actors involved in that process. Using ethnicity, individuals and groups identify with and against in order to gain a sense of belonging. Specifically, these are processes of boundary construction and maintenance, thus 'the ethnic *boundary* that defines the group, not the cultural stuff that it encloses' should be the focus of studies of ethnicity (1969: 10). In opposition to Barth are those who see his emphasis as subjectivist, holding that 'ethnic distinctions, ethnic organisation or even ethnic stratification may well exist without the acquiescence or even the awareness of the agents themselves' (Eriksen, 2002: 55; see Worsley, 1984). Practice theory would not see these as opposing positions. Rather than conclude ethnicity is either/or a subjective association or a structural object, we can theorize its role in the constitution of social life as a more or less malleable structural layer and/or part of the habitus of the agent and her communities of practice.

The concept of ethnicity is used in sociological studies in some ways and in policies and practices in other ways. It can be used to understand the formation and mobilization of group identities; it could be seen as inscribed in the habitus of both the agent and the groups that form her communities of practice and as informing conjuncturally-specific internal and external structures. Ethnicity can also be seen as a structural constraint where it is a form of categorization, and is best understood in the context of other sociological concepts with a much longer history, such as stigma, labelling, categorization, stereotypes, and discrimination. Ethnicity, along with other social divisions, may come into play when networks are used to obtain jobs or finance, in the formation of associations and friendships. The concept of ethnicity is useful because it questions the relevant context, the relevant communities of practice, as opposed to imposing boundaries by pre-identifying the agent as a member of a certain tribe, race or nation. In other words it asks who people are networked with and what is the relevant hermeneutic context rather than imposing this as part of the design of the study. Studies of ethnicity also now recognize the fluidity and complexity of contemporary life, discussed more below, and examine ethnic identifications (in process), hybridity, and complex, shifting identities.

Race and Racism

Sociologists rarely talk about race these days and usually in inverted commas. This is because geneticists are having to admit that putting groups of people into categories based on a range of phenotype or biologically transmitted characteristics (genes, blood types, hair colour, facial shape) is almost impossible and always arbitrary. There is far more difference between individuals of any one supposed race than there is between the 'races' themselves. Furthermore, the historical tendency to talk of races emerged in the West during a period of extreme racism (particularly the late eighteenth and early nineteenth century) and was used to justify racist policies, actions and attitudes that supported slavery, colonization and even on into the extermination of Jews, gypsies and homosexuals in the Holocaust. Assumed problems with trying to assimilate certain groups coincided with seeing them as 'races'. Jews in Britain, for example, were initially seen as 'an introspective "alien race", which threatened the stability and harmony of the nation' (Kudenko and Phillips, 2009). Racism continues, also, in the form of prejudice towards a group or person because of his or her *perceived* ethnic or 'racial' group. Racism is a destructive and pervasive form of prejudice based on the belief that one racial category is innately superior or inferior to another.

Despite evidence and arguments to the contrary, 'race' continues to exist as a cultural construct and, like ethnicity, it can be used to categorize, essentialize, and discriminate. It is therefore a useful concept in the theorizing of these more general processes. Theorists also use the history of the idea of race to help explain how people have become categorized, labelled hierarchically, and how prejudice is justified. They also theorize how discrimination is subtly and almost imperceptibly perpetuated over time, and is not adequately resisted. It can therefore be relevant at many junctures in the practice of social life. Let's take Britain as an example. Some say that since the 1970s economic restructuring (changes in wages, employment, the nature of work) which has threatened livelihoods, social conditions, and general well-being, has been accompanied by the arrival of new ethnic minorities. Some, especially extreme right political groups, have used this conjunction of events to promote the idea that one is exacerbated by the other. In other words, people who suffer worst from changes in work and employment, blame the ethnic minorities for taking the jobs, pushing down wages, pushing up house prices, draining social services, as well as for causing political and social unrest, and rising crime rates. These changes go hand in hand with the weakening of the labour movement (and trade unions), the decline of class cultures, the erosion of community, all of which have left social spaces for racism.

Segmented Assimilation

The concept of segmented assimilation offers a significant theoretical framework for understanding the process by which the second generation, the children of immigrants, become incorporated into the system of stratification in the host society and the different outcomes of this process. The linear model of assimilation above posits that over time all ethnic groups eventually assimilate, first culturally, then structurally, then even maritally. However, this assimilation can sometimes only be into certain sectors of society, into low-paid jobs, for example, and into continued experiences of racism. Segmented assimilation argues that some groups (Mexican Americans, especially) assimilate into an alternative, third culture and structure. In an analysis reminiscent of Paul Willis' (1983) *Learning to Labour*, Portes and Zhou (1993) show how some Mexican American groups exemplify an invisible thread of social reproduction between first generation achievements and later generation expectations. Seeing their parents and grandparents confined to menial jobs, and increasingly aware of discrimination by the white mainstream, the US born children of earlier Mexican immigrants readily join a reactive subculture as a means of protecting their sense of self-worth. Participation in this subculture erects serious barriers to upward mobility because school achievement is defined as antithetical to ethnic solidarity. While the newer immigrant, and some second generation children generally do quite well in school, later generation children who make up the above subculture generally do poorly. The term segmented assimilation has informed a host of subsequent academic papers, studies, and analyses. The term has been enthusiastically embraced, extensively applied, and also widely criticized, especially for being deterministic, and not applicable to other settings. More recently it is being amended and adapted to suit diverse circumstances, see Song (2010) and Stepick and Stepick (2010) for interesting discussions.

Contemporary Approaches

Massey et al. (1998) have argued that migration scholars tend to examine either 'determinants of migration' or 'immigrant assimilation'. This is reflected in the review of theories and perspectives above. But there are other relevant divisions drawn on in the literature, such as that between internal and international migration. Studies may also be linked to development (see Skeldon, 1997), to area studies, or to poverty research, and forced migration is often treated as a separate category. Increasingly, scholars are paying attention to issues of race, ethnicity, class, and gender (Castles, 2010) and to intersectionality (Lutz, 2010). Castles (2010: 1565) proposes linking migration to broader theories of social change and 're-embedding migration research in more general understandings of contemporary society'. This is what I have provided in the previous chapter. Castles proposes a social transformations perspective for migration, which attempts to understand the connections between human mobility and wider social change. For Castles (2010) social transformations are not gradual and subtle changes but fundamental shifts: 'This implies a "step-change" in which all existing social patterns are questioned and many are reconfigured. Social transformations are closely linked to major shifts in dominant economic, political and strategic relationships' (2010: 1576). He uses Polanyi's (2001) work as a starting point, and goes on to draw from a range of ideas such as the concept of glocalization, critiques of neoliberalism, and network theories.

Changes in the world always seem to run parallel with changes in academia – we are engaged in our own processes of structuration. So, our increasingly mobile and interconnected world has led migration researchers 'to depict flux and process, ambiguity and complexity in their analyses of social worlds' instead of trying to theorize activities in the context of isolated, static, homogenous units (Eriksen, 2002: 10). Researchers are also increasingly looking beyond states, borders, and incorporation into societies to ask questions about movement, migrancy, mobility and transnationalism. Within migration research, the terms globalization and transnationalism have almost become buzz words. 'Globalization' has been used to explain many widespread changes, sometimes with the writer inadequately explaining the detail. Yet it is a central concept for understanding both widespread changes and local processes. 'Transnationalism' has dramatically altered the direction of research agendas, to focus attention on specific aspects of a migration, or to frame a study across rather than within a country. Sometimes too much is taken for granted when these terms are used, and, unfortunately they are often used to mean different things, in different ways, with different political agendas, or implicit political stances. However, they are central concepts for telling practice stories about migration, especially if some effort is made to define how they are being used and their role in the more general theory of practice. The next section briefly introduces some of the themes, scholars, and publications that draw attention to some of the vast changes that are affecting our world today.

Gender and Migration

Notwithstanding the fact that one of Ravenstein's (1889) laws of migration was that 'females are more migratory than males' (cited in Lutz, 2010: 1647), there has been a tendency to perceive migration in terms of the male pioneer blazing a trail to new destinations, followed eventually by the female partner and family. This male bias in migration research continued throughout most of the last century, despite overwhelming evidence of the migration of women (Morokvasic, 1984). Even where it was acknowledged that women made up perhaps half of some flows, they were seen as involuntarily accompanying men (like children) and it was therefore deemed unnecessary to try to understand their motivations (Lutz, 2010). This demonstrates starkly how a perspective can serve to exclude. If we begin with real lives and practices rather than with a specific, substantive, theory or concept we are less likely to exclude certain types of migrant simply because of a set of personal attributes they may or may not have (Harzig, 2001). Two things have changed: feminist and gender aware researchers have increasingly paid attention to female migrants (e.g. Sharpe, 2001; Kofman et al., 2000; Ruiz, 2008), while at the same time the migration of women alone has been on the increase. Castles and Miller suggest the *feminization of migration* is one of its key contemporary features, by which they mean women are increasingly playing a major role in migration, on the one hand, and on the other hand 'awareness of the specificity of women in contemporary migrations has grown' (2009: 12). Possible explanations for the omission of women include the fact that fewer women worked in academia, 'work' was seen as a male phenomenon, while non-productive (care and domestic) work was overlooked, and the tendency not to pay much attention to the private sphere (Lutz, 2010). Some feminist literature has sought to put women back into the picture (e.g. Hellman, 2008; Phizacklea, 2004), while others have paid attention to the contribution they made to migration and to the power struggles that inscribed the process (Lutz, 2010). Women migrate for family reunification, but also in their own right. They migrate as labour migrants, as students, as refugees, and as entrepreneurs (among others). They make an important contribution to the economic and social life of the countries they leave and arrive in, and yet their role is often overlooked because it is more likely than male migration to be undocumented, irregular, and/or casualized (Kofman, 2000).

A further version of feminist-informed migration studies has taken the notion of gender as its focus. This perspective, informed by gender studies more broadly, and with the notion of the social construction of gendered identities at its heart (Lutz, 2010), has begun to explore 'the roles migration plays in shaping social orders, geographies of inequality, spatialized subjectivities, and the meanings of difference across scale' (Silvey, 2004 in Chattopadhyay, 2010: 87). It also aims to understand how gender asymmetries are both the product of social structural constraints, and yet also produce the structures that constrain (Lutz, 2010: 1651). In other words (in the language of practice theory outlined in Chapter 2) a gendered perspective on migration examines the role of gender as informing habitus, conjuncturally-specific internal structures, and agency, and how these become hardened into less malleable external structures. Chapter 6 explores one specific female migration in depth.

Globalization

In the past two decades the world has changed to such an extent that we take globalization almost for granted, and it would now be difficult to imagine a study of migration that did not to some extent recognize the role of global networks, global interconnections, and global level phenomena in social change. But what the term means, when employed by diverse scholars, the mass media, and the general public, can vary (Castles, 2010). In social theory, globalization describes an increased awareness of the world as a single place (Robertson, 1992); a world characterized by complex mobilities and interconnections (Held, 1999); a world where boundaries and borders are increasingly porous (Inda and Rosaldo, 2001). In the globalized world the authority of the nation state is attenuated in the face of supra-national, transnational, and global institutions (Rosenau, 1997; Sassen, 1996). But to describe a situation as affected by globalization, is not always a neutral or objective statement. Globalization literature can be Marxist and critical – viewing the changes as damaging and as increasing inequality – or liberal – embracing the changes as unavoidable, natural and eventually of benefit to us all. Those who describe 'neoliberal globalization', as we shall see in some of the following chapters, are often (at least implicitly) critical of the application of neoliberal economic (and some would say political and cultural) ideas, policies, agendas, or practices to the global economy.

The globalization of migration, it is argued, has involved an increase in the numbers of people moving within and across state borders, to the extent that what was once seen as a temporary aberration, and a problem, is now considered the norm, with increasing numbers of countries being affected at any one time (Annan, 2006; Castles and Miller, 2009; Massey et al., 1998). Indeed, migration has been described as constitutive of modern life: in 'liquid' modernity we are compelled by the need to keep moving even when we are no longer clear why (Bauman, 2000; Papastergiadis, 2000: 12). But, not only has migration increased, especially in the past 30 years, it has changed its form. Where migration was traditionally a one-off move to a new life in a new place, contemporary moves are multidirectional, blurring the distinction between migration and tourism (Williams et al., 2000). As a result (it is argued), space has a new irrelevance; it may now, literally, be traversed in no time (Bauman, 2000); home and belonging are no longer place based; and the local has become less meaningful, as we experience time-space distanciation (Giddens, 1990).

Globalization theory, Faist (2010: 1667) argues, 'takes a birds-eye view'. It takes world-spanning structures as a point of departure and asks how such structures and associated processes impact and shape lower-level processes and structures. But some perspectives, especially in anthropology and migration, take a much more action-centred or bottom-up approach (see the collection by Inda and Rosaldo, 2001). Globalization has relevance in a theory of practice as a framework, enabling us to acknowledge broad developments that can be economic, political, cultural or social, and needs to be enacted and embodied, and can be negotiated and amended, through the practices of agents. In the following chapters, the term is often used when describing the external structures enabling agency. But globalization is an uneven process with very localized renderings, 'while some people may possess the political and economic resources to trot across the world, many more have little or no access to transport and means of communication' (Inda and Rosaldo, 2001: 4). Globalization is thus something that can feature in the daily lives of agents, creating constraints and opportunities on the ground, as it is interpreted, mediated and enacted via cultures and communities.

Transnationalism

During the 1990s migration literature began to criticize the methodological nationalism inherent in mainstream social science, accusing it of positing the nation/state/society as the natural social and political form of the world (Wimmer and Glick Schiller, 2002a: 302). Instead scholars proposed the concept of transnationalism as a more appropriate way to describe and explore contemporary, novel, migrant identities and communities (Faist, 2000; Glick Schiller, 1997; Urry, 2000; Vertovec, 1999). Alejandro Portes et al. (1999: 217) contend that we have witnessed the emergence of a new social field in which mobile individuals and communities increasingly live dual lives, forging social contacts and making a living across national borders, while speaking the language of both countries and retaining both as home. Nina Glick Schiller and her colleagues use the label 'transmigrants' for the individuals who maintain these affective and instrumental relationships across national borders (Basch et al., 1993; Wimmer and Glick Schiller, 2002b). The transnational elites, a term used for highly skilled professionals in global cities (Beaverstock, 2005), are the archetypal transmigrant; the nomadic worker, the embodiment of flows of knowledge, skills and intelligence who occupy segregated communities in cross-border space (Castells, 2000). Transnationalism is a concept, or a perspective (Faist, 2010), that enables us to think/see across boundaries, to observe connections between places and peoples, to consider links people have outside the nation, and to look at the impacts of these in terms of identities (or habitus) and actions and structures.[2] It is also a call to researchers not to ignore things outside of the state (not to be methodologically nationalist). It thus has a massive contribution to make to practice stories of migration.

   Migration studies has long recognized that migrants retain ties with their origins through correspondences and remittances, (starting perhaps with Thomas and Znaniecki's 1927 *The Polish Peasant in Europe and America*), but by the 1920s and 30s researchers began to concentrate more on settlement, adaptation, and social exclusion. Transnationalism therefore serves to ensure that researchers do not restrict their gaze to only trying to understand assimilation or incorporation or its lack. There can sometimes be a tendency in transnationalism literature to ignore restrictions to movement, and the continuing power of the state to contain and exclude. It also tends to overlook the power of the state to encourage mobility. It sometimes tries to contain migrants within transnational spaces, just as earlier literature tried to contain it in nation states. Beck (1992) believes transnational connections undermine sovereign national states, leading to multiple identities and citizenship; certainly developments in transnational theory have led academics to rethink rights and obligations outside state borders. Faist (2010) suggests 'transnational studies' could benefit from combining a transnational perspective with a world systems approach. Transnationalism is good for addressing 'how "old" national, international and local institutions acquire "new" meanings and functions in the process of cross-border transaction' (2010: 1666) whereas 'world systems theory is useful in outlining the asymmetric power relationships between emigration and immigration regions' (2010: 1671).

The perspective has informed a growing and important interest in the role of women, families, households, relationships, networks and emotions in migration as well as interest in institutions and organizations that connect places. It also contributes the idea of social space to migration studies, not opposed to but working in interaction with physical space and time (Faist, 2010). Using a theory of practice as a general framework for migration, transnational activities and identities may be identified as proximate structures constraining or enabling actions in the form of 'global or cross-border connections' (Vertovec, 2001: 573). They involve exchange (of goods, money, resources), communication (virtual, face to face, letters), organizations (charities, political organizations, and participation in these). They may form part of the conjuncturally-specific internal structures and the context, the communities of practice, norms, rules, and other conjuncturally-specific external structures enabling and constraining an agent's practice. But transnationalism is also relevant to the habitus (it both reflects and contributes to the ways people see themselves and their ways of being and doing). Transnational connections have outcomes both here and there, and in between. A focus on transnationalism has led to a proliferation of diverse studies and to a focus on the important role of remittances, and their impacts. There are also cultural impacts in the form of changing habitus, actual ties like marriages, and patterns of economic interdependence. Transnationalism, as a concept, encourages a focus on processes, on networks beyond physical spaces, and on how states are undermined.

Mobility

Changes in migration types and flows, increases in the complexity of migration and other wider developments, have coincided with a change in focus towards mobility rather than migration. Theories and concepts are developed in response to changes in the world but they, in their turn, change the way things are understood; they are themselves part of any practice story. Hand in hand with the above developments a multi-sited ethnography is emerging (Falzon, 2009); along with conceptions of multi-local affiliations (Rouse, 1995), researchers are analysing transnational (and translocal) spaces (McGregor, 2009), or are using the concept of migrancy to draw attention to the movement of given agents (Harney and Baldassar, 2007). For John Urry (2007: 3) 'It sometimes seems as if all the world is on the move'. He proposes that the concept of mobility be used as a perspective or paradigm for contemporary social science, in which all kinds of movement (including standing, walking, travelling by car or train, or with the aid of crutches, the movement of images and information, and even movement up or down social hierarchies) are examined as central to social life and social relations. This emphasis on movement, is an attempt to develop ideas he asserted in *Sociology Beyond Societies* (2000), that global networks and flows have undermined the power of social structures (previously identified in a sociology fixated on the notion of society) to reproduce themselves. Indeed, he even talks of a post-societal phase.

The mobilities approach is important for challenging the hegemonic notion of the male pioneer 'daring to venture into the unknown' (Harzig, 2001: 16), which sees migration as essentially unilinear and permanent and which paid far more attention to North America and Europe than other parts of the world. However, while some contemporary attempts to describe the modern world increasingly rely on such metaphors of mobility, fluidity, flux and flow (Bauman, 2000; Hannerz, 1992; Papastergiadis, 2000; Urry, 2007), others are increasingly noting the existence of counterflows to globalization and restrictions to movement. This is a new version of the agency/structure debate discussed in the previous chapter. Among others, Brubaker (2005) has argued there is no reason yet to herald the era of unprecedented porosity of borders and Faist (2000) notes that place still counts when the role of states is so crucial in determining the fates of migrant groups. Cunningham and Heyman (2004) use the concept of a mobility-enclosure continuum to acknowledge the tension between processes that enable and induce movement and the ongoing processes of border maintenance that delimit and restrict the movement of ideas, people and goods. Acknowledging that globalization has not been able to wipe out all aspects of the local, a range of studies have explored *inter alia* the roles that borders play in the contemporary world economy: struggles around state borders; identity documents and surveillance; the cultural construction of space and place; and ongoing nation-building and state-making processes (Cunningham and Heyman, 2004: 289–90). Borders are not simply territorial sites but 'ongoing, dialectical processes that generates (sic) multiple borderlands spaces, some of which are not located very close to the official international boundary itself' (Spener and Staudt, 1998: 4, cited in Cunningham and Heyman, 2004: 292). Borders are continually made and remade in the context of mobilities (of goods, people and ideas); they are 'places' where nation states play a role in shaping the lives of border people but also places where social identities are negotiated and contested. One again, there seems to be an implicit theory of practice at work here, a theory that understands social life as an ongoing process that unfolds through the embodied acting out of daily life, in communities.

Conclusion

Migration has been theorized either in terms of movement or settlement processes. Movement was understood in terms of *push and pull* theories which simply took the person's decision-making as their focus, and asked what had pushed them to leave one place and what attracted them to another. In some sense this was also a macro approach because it drew on large-scale differences between sending countries and receiving countries and between regions. Another macro approach was that which saw the entire world as a single system and then asked how people were migrating within this overarching system. This tended to be a critical approach, drawing on some version of Marxist political economy. The best known of these approaches is Wallerstein's *world systems theory*, but Saskia Sassen also wrote about migration in terms of a global system. Later, theorists are arguing that we need a more integrated approach to migration that includes intervening, or meso level, variables such as families, networks, intermediaries, and connections.

In terms of settlement people first started to ask to what extent migrants had become *assimilated* into the culture and society to which they had moved. This included academics who assumed that this was the healthiest outcome, and policy makers took it for granted that heterogeneity was a bad thing. Later, there was an attempt to theorize settlement in terms of *multiculturalism*, which wanted to explain that people could live side by side retaining their separate cultures without these meaning they inevitably clashed and without thereby denying them citizenship rights and membership of the collective. Later still, Portes and colleagues began to talk of *segmented* assimilation, of how, over time, migrants became assimilated into segments of society rather than into the mainstream. Ethnicity and race have been important concepts in these developing analyses.

Many earlier theories took linear moves and (male) labour migration as their focus, overlooking non-linear, circular, temporary, affluent, and asylum seeking migrations, and the migration of women. Now, however, there is an increasing array of concepts that encourage a focus across and between borders of nation states. Globalization, for example, acknowledges broad, sweeping global developments affecting and affected by migration. Transnationalism is a relatively new concept that is used to enable the theorizing of processes that occur across borders, between and beyond nation states. The mobilities paradigm is another approach challenging linear, national perspectives. Similarly, attention has been drawn to the role of women in migration and (as we shall see in later chapters) to forced migration and even to affluent migration. To conclude, there is now much more recognition, in migration theories and perspectives, of the existence of different types of move, much more of a focus on links between countries, less attention paid to (or assumptions about) unidirectional moves, and much more emphasis on the many macro, micro and meso level factors that impinge on an agent's experience of the whole migration process (including those who don't move but can still be affected). Several of these approaches might have a role to play in the telling (or piecing together) of practice stories about given migrations.

4

Lifestyle Migration: British Migration to Spain's Coastal Areas

This chapter will examine a small selection of case studies of lifestyle migration, bringing together theoretical and empirical work within the framework (and employing the concepts) of a theory of practice. Lifestyle migration has become a quite extensive field, so here I will focus especially on a numerically and conceptually important phase: the rapid growth of migration of Europeans to Spain during the late 1980s and through the 1990s, and specifically on British migrants. As I go along I will consider how other theories and perspectives might have helped draw attention to other, overlooked, aspects and provide more coherence to the overall picture. Finally, I will consider what gaps remain in the story that are more easily identified when we use a broad social science framework. One of the most interesting things to notice for this chapter is how the structures take the shape of opportunities rather than constraints so much more often than in the cases discussed in later chapters. This case study is therefore a useful illustration of the argument, made most forcibly by Giddens, that structures should not be seen simply as constraints to action.

The Studies

British migration to Spain is a vast phenomenon, with British who live in Spain for at least some of the year making up Spain's largest minority group (statistical analysis by author, see www.ine.es).[1] As a trend it has been growing (with some ebbs and flows) since the mid 1970s. This is quite different from the other migration trends we will look at, and is an instance of what is becoming known as lifestyle migration (Benson and O'Reilly, 2009). This is migration motivated more by quality of life than employment or escape from poverty or hardship. We might even see it as the postmodern escape from the social ills of modern life; recognized also in the phenomena known as 'downsizing', counter-urbanization, and alternative living. There has been a plethora of studies on British migration to Spain, already enough to give a quite complex picture of the process. However, many studies begin by restricting their gaze in one way or another (to older people in most cases). The field does somewhat suffer from a prior designation of the 'set of surface appearances' (Stones, 2005) as retirement migration or as residential tourism. In my own work I have tried to understand the wider phenomenon from a variety of vantage points. But I, too, have tended to restrict my gaze to a phenomenology of the agent with far less focus on independent structures. This chapter will concentrate on two monographs (King et al., 2000 and O'Reilly, 2000) and to a lesser extent two papers (Oliver and O'Reilly, 2010 and O'Reilly, 2007), the work of several other authors, such as Mantecón (2008), Rodes (2009), Casado Díaz (2006 and 2009) and the edited collection of Rodríguez, Casado Díaz and Huber (2005). The goal is to try to understand a given migration trend by piecing together a practice story about it. Practice stories understand a series of linked events in terms of a broader process, and thus lead to multi-dimensional, dynamic, and extensive explanations.

The *British on the Costa del Sol* (O'Reilly, 2000) is based on 15 months ethnographic fieldwork in Southern Spain between 1993 and 1994. The other two papers referred to here (Oliver and O'Reilly, 2010, and O'Reilly, 2007) draw on data collected then as well as during two further periods of intensive fieldwork in 2004 and 2005 and numerous shorter visits in the intervening years. I have been a peripatetic migrant and second home-owner in Malaga province for over ten years and have been both a member and an ethnographer of the British community in Spain for that time. The paper with Caroline Oliver also draws on ethnographic data collected by Oliver during two extensive field visits in the 1990s and 2000s. The book, *Sunset Lives*, by Russell King, Tony Warnes and Allan Williams (King et al., 2000) reports on a large multi-method research project examining international retirement migration (IRM) of British older people to Malta, Tuscany, the Algarve and the Costa del Sol. The research was undertaken between 1995–7 and included secondary analyses of existing statistics, reviews of published data, a questionnaire survey among British residents in the four regions, and in-depth interviews with both British migrants and other British and non-British 'key informants'. The study is therefore vast and complex but limits itself to retired older people (50 and older) living in the destinations for at least four months of the year. Of the many other studies undertaken with Europeans living in Spain, special mention should be made of the work by Vicente Rodríguez and his colleagues at CSIC, which involved a large questionnaire survey with over 300 retired North Europeans in Southern Spain (the vast majority of which were British), and the similar study by Casado Díaz in the province of Alicante, 43 per cent of whose respondents were British (see Rodríguez, Casado Díaz, and Huber, 2005). Many other studies have since been conducted on and around this topic; see Benson and O'Reilly (2009) for an overview.

The chapter will draw on the range of concepts outlined in Chapter 2 (and see Chapter 8 for a summary). These all describe interrelated phenomena that develop, change, emerge again, and reshape into something we might better describe using a different concept, but for the sake of linear organization, the discussion will be split into two sections, one looking at the decision to migrate and one looking at settlement. Later, it will become apparent that this is an entirely artificial distinction, and that it has been necessary to discuss forms of settlement and newly (re)formed structures even as I tried to concentrate on motivations and external structures framing the decision to migrate.

The Decision to Migrate

In this first section I will review what we know from these studies about the decision to migrate, beginning with what they can reveal about the broad, general changes and conditions, opportunities, cultural schemas, cultural shifts, technological, economic, material, social and cultural factors that enable and constrain this migration trend. These broad shifts are generally revealed using theories and studies of broad scope, rather than through interviews and ethnography, since some will be apparent to the agent, and some not. First, I would like to draw attention to an interesting point: that is that none of the authors I review here begins by discussing the forces that work towards people not moving. This is true, it seems, of migration research generally. Every explanation of why people move first begins with an assumption that this is something to explain. This is also as true of the British in Spain themselves as the researchers studying them. We have all (including the respondents) forgotten to mention that the broad external forces facing these agents at the time of making the decision to move include deep-seated assumptions that (especially retired) people will not move away from their home town or country, their families, their nation, or history. The family, state, familiarity, identity, commitment, ties, security, belonging, all remain so taken for granted that we have all forgotten to mention them! But they are there in the voices of all those we have interviewed when they come to explain how they made the decision to move, or how they justified it. These are all constraints to movement that need to be overcome by those making the decision to move, and they remain the taken for granted hermeneutic frame within which most migrants make and explain their decision to do otherwise. In order to resist these dominant structures a migrant must first imagine that she has the power or capability to do so. She would also need sufficient knowledge of what was possible and what the consequences might be of different actions, and she would need to be capable of sufficient reflective distance (able to stand back and consider her actions before she acts). Levels of knowledge, power and critical awareness vary, with social elites often having more of these resources with which to resist, and children and minority groups having less (Stones, 2005).

Tourism as External Structure

There have been a whole host of social transformations, some of which are very general, even global (upper structural layers), and some of which are more specific to western societies, to Europe and to Britain in relation to Spain specifically (the more proximate social surroundings) all of which help us to understand the wider forces, constraints and opportunities, facing a migrant as external structures. One of these transformations we might label 'tourism', a concept that embraces a gamut of material, economic and cultural changes. Both *Sunset Lives* (King et al., 2000) and *The British on the Costa del Sol* (O'Reilly, 2000) acknowledge the important role played by tourism in the migration of the British to Spain. Indeed most respondents in all the studies had first visited the area as tourists, before becoming migrants (see Rodríquez, Fernández-Mayoralas et al., 2005). During the twentieth century, tourism evolved from a fairly elite and often educational pastime, through a middle class pursuit of exotic otherness, to a mass phenomenon based on seasonal escape in search of sun, sea, sand and hedonism (Urry, 1990). The development and marketing of all-inclusive package tours was especially critical in the growth of mass tourism in European coastal areas, leading to the creation of entire cities or towns 'built solely for consumption' (Shaw and Williams, 2002). The Costa del Sol is often referred to as the archetypal mass tourism destination, with other regions in the Mediterranean following a similar model. New resorts such as Torremolinos and Fuengirola emerged during the 1960s and attracted British tourists in large numbers, many of whom returned year after year. The subsequent migration, of especially British and Germans, to these towns did not occur overnight but in stages with, first, a few individuals buying retirement or holiday homes, or a small tourist business in the 1970s. Increasing numbers visited these homes more frequently through the 1970s and 1980s, with more people retiring to the area, buying properties and businesses to serve the tourist and settled migrant communities from the late 1980s onwards (Hall and

Williams, 2002). This all coincided with other relevant developments for North Europeans, some discussed below, such as increases in expendable wealth, leisure time and the number of paid holidays from work, political changes in Spain after the death of Franco, a UK property boom in the 1980s, and the processes we might label 'Europeanization'. Tourism brings people to an area, but it also constructs an area, providing an infrastructure and amenities from which both local residents and prospective migrants can benefit. Almost imperceptibly places become 'reconstructed from a tourist point of view'(Lanfant, 1995: 5), with many, wide implications. Mass tourism, as King et al. (2000: 34) note, 'pays scant attention to most of the indigenous cultural features of the destinations'. Later, in this chapter, I illustrate how this frames subsequent actions of some British migrants in their pursuit of leisure and hedonism (O'Reilly, 2009a).

Without being particularly overt about what its role actually is in the migration, both monographs (King et al., 2000; O'Reilly, 2000) thus demonstrate the relevance of tourism as a wider social change and set of material/infrastructural developments, as things that have led people to have contact with an area, and (combined with other developments) have provided opportunity for this migration. To put this more overtly in the framework of a theory of practice, tourism provided a material, legal, practical and cultural infrastructure that later supported more permanent settlement. British people (and not only British) visiting the area began to see that another way of life was possible, and started to project their futures into the new setting. As we discuss in later publications (O'Reilly, 2003 and Hall and Williams, 2002), theories from tourism literature can be useful to explain the way in which early tourists and migrants blaze a trail for later ones to follow, taking back stories, making connections, triggering the imagination and facilitating practically through people they get to know, lessons learned, and changes in the host attitudes (see Franklin, 2003).

During the 1990s, when mass tourism to Spain faced something of a decline, the Spanish authorities actively sought to remedy its seasonal and polarized nature by encouraging investment in property, in the form of what has become known as 'residential tourism' (O'Reilly, 2009a). But this did not occur to them out of the blue. Individuals had already started to buy holiday and retirement homes, and property developers had caught on to this new potential market (Mantecón, 2008; Rodes, 2009). Structures thus emerge out of the consolidation over time of actions. Tourism, however, also framed what sort of life migrants to the area would seek. Mass tourism was not about other cultures but about sun, sea, sand and hedonism; it often implied leisure and escape and being able to travel abroad while remaining safely ensconced in one's own cultural milieu.

Earlier Migrations as External Structure

The longer-term history of British migration to Spain's coastal areas, as an ongoing process, also creates new structural layers that in turn frame the contemporary trend. In *The British on the Costa del Sol*, (O'Reilly, 2000) I recognize that there were other migrants, mostly backpackers and intellectuals, to Spain's coasts long before mass tourism. A general framework informed by broad social science understandings (a theory of practice), enables us to see that the actions of early individual migrants and travellers led to unintended consequences in the form of connections, links, ties, shared cultures, and more concrete, material change. However, a further effect these earlier migrations had was to plant the seed of an idea in the minds of local residents that British migrants to Spain are wealthy, elite, and very different to the members of the rural communities they lived amongst (see Waldren, 2009). This becomes relevant later, within the communities of practice of migrants and the conjuncturally-specific external structures constraining their behaviour. British migrants are aware that they are viewed as wealthy and elite and therefore do not require the advice and support that other migrants might warrant. My monograph (citing King and Rybaczuk, 1993) also describes how, between the 1950s and 70s, Spain gradually changed from being a country marked by emigration, to one characterized by immigration. More recently (see Aledo, 2005), it has become a country impacted by migrations from across the globe but especially from Africa, Latin America and Eastern Europe. These are broad historical facts, not constraints or opportunities framing British migrants' decision to move, but they become relevant in Spanish reactions to British migrants; perceiving them as different to other migrants. These upper structural layers are enacted at a more proximate level, affecting how much attention Spanish authorities feel they need to pay, and how much help they think these supposedly wealthy migrants need, in comparison with other immigrants.

However, a perhaps more relevant antecedent, that could help explain this migration is retirement to the seaside, which became something of a movement in the UK in the 1960s (see Karn, 1977). Increased car use, rail and other transport improvements, have all brought opportunities for trips to the seaside, which in turn brought experiences and desire. Increased affluence brought opportunities to turn those trips into retirement. Some government policies were introduced to encourage this development, such as the 'Greater London Council's scheme to provide bungalows by the sea for their retired tenants', but this had limited effect compared to owner-occupiers buying property in cheaper areas (Karn, 1977: 2). It is perhaps this development more than the migration of other groups to Spain that put retirement elsewhere onto the cultural agenda of British people.

Europe as External Structure

A further upper, and in many ways proximate, structural layer takes its shape in Europeanization. 'European and Spanish legislation have coincided to make it easier for Britons (and other Europeans) to purchase property, to reside, to work, and to move freely within Spain' (O'Reilly, 2000: 33). These policies thus provide opportunities and constraints for this migration. The Maastricht Treaty especially was internalized into an expectation of 'free' movement; and Ackers and Dwyer (2004) demonstrate with rich insights how the policies *in practice* are interpreted and acted on by agents migrating within Europe. Their research with older people's use of health and social care systems in Europe reveals that middle class migrants are especially resourceful in moving freely and flexibly between states, using complicated and conflicting policies to their advantage. O'Reilly (2007) shows how policies relating to free movement are interpreted by the Spanish authorities in different ways in different areas in Spain, leading to a confusing array of constantly changing rules and conditions enabling and constraining migration and residence. I argue that the consequent condition of ambiguity enables the Spanish authorities to retain control over European immigration, which seems more problematic as the years go by and especially as increasing numbers of younger, working class, and unemployed British migrants join the earlier, predominantly middle class, retirement migrants. Indeed ambiguous rules and regulations lead to social exclusion for some British migrants. The extent to which policies are enforced or ignored vary within communities of practice, in response to *in situ* conditions, and to how these are perceived and understood by the host community. The various interpretations of policy, in turn, construct new conjuncturally-specific external conditions within which British agents make decisions, such as whether to register as a permanent resident, to take out a bank account in Spain, or even to settle permanently or on a semi-permanent, flexible basis (O'Reilly, 2007).

Economics as External Structures

As noted in both *Sunset Lives* (King et al., 2000) and *The British on the Costa del Sol* (O'Reilly, 2000), other external structures enabling British migration to Spain during the 1980s and 90s include, in the UK, strong economic recovery during the 1980s, a boom in the property market, an increase in expendable wealth across the social classes, combined with the lengthening of paid holidays, sterling/peseta/euro exchange rates (which have at different times been an opportunity and a constraint), and relative low prices in Spain, especially of property (see also Casado Díaz, 2009; Gustafson, 2009). British people were able to buy a better standard of living, a better quality of retirement, or even a small business, which they could not afford in the UK. For King et al. (2000: 26) 'increasing longevity, earlier retirement, and raised incomes and assets appear most instrumental' as independent influences on retirement abroad. For them, 'having the means to move is a necessary precondition' (ibid: 14). But in my research, many British had moved with less than adequate means, driven more by desire than by practical considerations. Opportunities raise expectations, as Bourdieu (1984) notes, but the migrants interviewed by Russell King and his colleagues are imbued with much more instrumental rationality than people generally seem to deserve. It seems in order to explain British migration to Spain we need much more than just a set of economic opportunities; perhaps desire provides more of an impetus than opportunity. Both King et al. (2000) and O'Reilly (2000) note how, as a result of the rhetoric and practice of the Thatcher government, owner occupation, entrepreneurship and self-employment were on the increase in the 1980s in Britain, providing the economic basis, but also the aspiration, of property and small business ownership. These, combined with the experience of tourism and witnessing others make such a move, creates the idea that it is possible. The migration itself also creates new opportunities, including the existence of customers for new businesses, and the potential for new friendships, networks, and the provision of services for new migrants (Casado Díaz, 2009, but more of that later). The relative wealth of Britain and Spain remains a crucial structure constraining or enabling this migration. When we were working on these monographs in the late 1990s, the pound sterling was weak against the peseta and there looked to be a return migration in process. This came full circle during the early twenty-first century as the pound picked up and even after Spain joined the Euro and the pound remained strong against that. But now we are suffering from the effects of a global recession, the building boom in Spain has ground to a halt, and many British are struggling because their pensions or their invested capital is not worth what it was in relation to the Euro. One would need to never leave the field in order to keep up to date with developments. Migration to Spain is a practice, inscribed by sets of external and internalized, ever-changing structures.

The Irrelevance of Place

In the research monographs and papers brought together for this chapter, reference is often made very loosely to other technological, material and cultural changes that apply to western societies generally and that provide external structures in the form of opportunities for the British migrants to Spain. Since we wrote these papers, in the 1990s, many of the theories discussed in the latter part of Chapter 3, describing globalization, transnationalism, and mobility (and other social theories describing post-modern or second/liquid modern society) have shaped the way scholars research and understand social change. Most of the works reviewed in this chapter describe increases in road, rail and air use as an external structure shaping the migration, but now we might refer to a rise in mobility and pay more attention to the circularity or constant flow of the movement (Urry, 2000, 2007). There is some discussion of the shrinking of the globe, using the concept of globalization, and the rise in activities and identities that cross borders (but the concept of transnationalism had not at that time become fashionable). This whole sweep of theories, directed at explaining the contemporary condition (in western societies at least), draws attention to broad structural changes that help explain why people might find it easier to resist the norms and constraints of modern society and move away from their nation, their state, their family and friends, their home town, when they clearly do not have to.

In *Sunset Lives*, King and his colleagues describe 'the rise of cable and satellite communication technology and its applications to home-centred entertainment, shopping, banking and diverse domestic services, from delivered meals to counselling by phone' (2000: 10). One likely implication of the 'networked home', they suggest, is that some locational constraints are reduced. If they were writing now, and not in the 1990s, they would have been able to draw on Castells (2000), Urry (2007), Bauman (2000), and others to frame this theory, that increased connectivity brings out there in here, makes the world more easily (virtually) accessible, and increases the desire for travel and for alternative ways of living. Technological change can lead to aspirational and lifestyle shifts, to new expectations and new desires. At the abstract level, it is simple to describe these changes and make assumptions about their impacts. King and his colleagues focussed on older people, who are also somewhat freed from the constraints of work, and even family life, as they reach an age where they are the ones likely to be cared for rather than doing the caring. But my interviews and ethnography revealed a tension between the desire and opportunity for freedom from constraint, and other cultural norms inscribed in the habitus. Women I spoke to would often describe how much they miss their children and grandchildren, how bad they feel to have left the family behind in the UK, and yet how they dare not admit this to their husbands because together they had made the decision to migrate. And even children described to me the way they felt pulled in two directions, towards family and friends back home (where, perhaps they would return for their continued education of for work later in life), and Spain, where their parents pursued a life of escape and leisure (O'Reilly, 1999).

Other broad sweep changes we might have referred to in more depth include colonialism, which has led to the structural ordering of the world in which many Westerners now move as 'expatriates' (Fechter, 2007). Many of those King et al. studied had worked abroad for much of their lives, and then had not wanted to settle back in Britain on retirement. Many theorists since the early 2000s have written about the reduction in family and class ties, and the fluidity of contemporary western lifestyles. We pay scant attention to globalization and the increased awareness of the world as a single place, increased interconnections, the increased porosity of national borders. We might also have used Giddens (1990) here to show how large-scale structural change, leading to the disembedding of social relations from local contexts, and the reorganization of time and space across non-local sites, has wrought a change in orientation towards individual self-reflexive projects. These are all themes in more recent migration literature that might have encouraged us to think more about broad structural changes and historical developments that frame, enable and constrain this migration. We do not mention the material world, the sun, sea and sand that pre-exist the desire to spend time there, nor do we use performance theory to help us make sense of how actions and performances alter and shape the material thus creating new opportunities and constraints (see O'Reilly, 2009a). The world is changing in terms of what is available and what is not, and how people react to the opportunities on the ground. The general sociological framework of a theory of practice draws our attention to migration as an ongoing process and to the various theories and concepts that might be employed to understand aspects of that process. The next section will examine how the structural shifts, at a general level, have wrought cultural shifts, and how they take shape in the perceptions and understandings of the migrants themselves.

Internal Structures and Communities of Practice

King et al. call this migration a 'consumption decision and a function of disposable income and accumulated wealth' (2000: 16). They have less to say about cultural shifts, and desires, motivations, and networks. However, they do acknowledge that tastes, aspirations and preferences actually precede what appear to be economic decisions. Perhaps, they suggest, mass tourism development and the decline of empire have brought about a change in world-view, or a cultural shift, away from the British Empire as a travel destination towards areas that offer a warm climate and relaxed atmosphere. They examine the biographies of some of those who have moved and conclude that there are common aspirations, in which finances can be conserved and quality of life improved through moving abroad. They theorize that this set of aspirations is connected to wider changes because they tend to coincide. Practice theory (see Chapter 2) enables us to be more explicit about this. Individuals, through practice, enact and embody structural transformations such as tourism, globalization, flexible working lives, and longer retirement. Thus a new set of aspirations emerges out of tourism experiences, the experience of extended holidays, and as a result of longer holiday entitlements, increased expectations of a leisured retirement, and increases in expendable wealth. The structural changes outlined above thus become part of the taken for granted world view, barely expressed and mostly implicit in interviews and conversations.

Men and women are living longer and retiring earlier in the UK than they were previously. Life expectancy has improved as a result of health advances. People are aware that average life expectancy is longer and along with that has come a set of expectations about a 'third age'. Similarly, rising affluence has led to smaller family units, less cohabitation as an extended family unit, and with that reduced responsibilities for others, especially the frail and elderly. This works both ways, it means the older people have less expectation of being cared for as they age and also, for the younger ones, reduced feeling of responsibility for the care of older family members. There have been some important cultural shifts here: the 'long-term decline of large families during the twentieth century' (King et al., 2000: 11), and other things Ulrich Beck (1992) has alerted us to in his theories about second modernity. But, while such theories help us make sense of wider cultural shifts, the networks and relations of a given agent also remain important. In other words, not everyone is as free as these theories make out. As Bourdieu notes (see Oliver and O'Reilly, 2010) even though as things change the opportunities change, still old habits die hard. The practical experiences and norms acquired during the early years remain formative. The habitus changes only slowly, so that while some may imagine a new future in a changed setting, individuals, within communities of practice, might continue to perceive family, stability, home, and stasis as the most important values. Others remain tied as a result of their own needs or the needs of others, as King et al. note, and some people are less likely to move because they are still tied to their locality through work, their partner's work, local political or institutional engagements, or close local networks. The *British on the Costa del Sol* draws attention to the way in which many people describe their reasons for migration in the context of some sort of trigger event. It is as if all the pieces of the jigsaw were in place, but still the balance between staying and going had not tipped towards going until some event caused a final push. The sorts of event described by my research participants included a divorce, or redundancy, retirement, the death of one's parents, or having been the victim of crime once too often. These are stories of practice, of external constraints and opportunities meeting internal structures hardwired into the habitus or adapted in the light of ongoing contingencies within communities of practice, in which members each have their own contingencies and habitus to reconcile.

The Practice of Migration

When we ask people, especially in surveys, why they move, they tend to answer in terms of push and pull factors. They cannot explain how it is that the structures above got turned into desires; how they resisted some norms towards staying and acted on others, towards mobility. If the theories and structural forces above explained everything, then everyone would move. The British in Spain overwhelmingly, in all studies, cite climate, pace of life, lower living costs, improved quality of social life, Spanish culture, the fact that English is widely spoken, and nearness to home as pull factors. They mention antipathy towards the UK involving high crime rates, poor social values, poor climate, and high prices, as push factors. And they refer to a receptive British community, previous family links to Spain, work or business links, and having previously bought property, as network factors (see Chapter 3). But this is because when we ask people why they did something they rationalize in a way they think is expected of them, adopting a 'quasi-theoretical posture' as they reflect on their actions. The problem is that they 'leave unsaid all that goes without saying' (Bourdieu, 1990: 91). A group of studies has concluded that British migrants to Spain are more likely to be older, middle class, fairly well educated, and to have lived abroad before (Casado Díaz, 2006). But no one attempts to explore why this might be the case except that these groups have the opportunity to experience life abroad, to afford to buy a second home, to retire early. King et al. (2000) suggest that higher levels of education might lead to more of an instrumental approach to one's life trajectory and more of a feeling of being able to take some control. This is possibly true, but there are also many younger, poorer, less well educated, people who have never before lived outside of their own country who move to Spain. How do we explain this? And how do we explain that not all older, middle class people move? What we need are stories that explain how migrants made the decision to move, in practice, drawing on, and forming, habits, norms and conjuncturally-specific internal structures; stories that reveal what power and knowledge they had, and what networks they were part of that created constraints and opportunities, and the extent to which they have internalized and transformed which norms. Although our research projects each produced the relevant material our accounts fail to reveal these nuances that a theory of practice illuminates.[2]

King et al. collected life histories demonstrating how the decision to move fits into a life trajectory. My interviews and conversations led to the same reflection on life before migration as a frame for the reason to move. Although we can assert that economic factors, technological advances, and broader cultural shifts have facilitated this migration these remain implicit to a great extent in these books and articles and in the stories of the migrants. When we examine their stories about moving we can see the structural conditions outlined above, the cultural shifts and how they affect the decision to move. We also see how these are mediated by conjuncturally-specific internal structures (the way the respondents understand what will happen if they make this decision), and by individual habitus.

As the structures, superbly described by contemporary social theories, are embodied and become part of the taken for granted, it becomes taken for granted that one can choose to move abroad for quality of life reasons, rather than simply for work or escape from poverty or persecution; mobility becomes a norm rather than an aberration. Europeanization is internalized into an identity, an expectation of a right to freedom of movement, and conjuncturally-specific internal structures that learn how to go on in Europe as an individual member of a European state. The notion that a job is no longer for life, that one must be flexible, adaptable, and amenable to change, become internalized into the Western habitus, along with increased geographical movement, and staying in touch with family and friends via modern telecommunications. Those who have been corporate expatriates have moved home a lot throughout their adult lives and have become used to the idea of migration abroad. Moving is now part and parcel of their disposition. In some people, then, we witness a desire to move, a feeling that moves can be made at any time during a life but especially at times when freed from other constraints such as work or family ties (for example in retirement), an assumption that a move need not be permanent, a comfortable knowledge that if the move fails the welfare state in the UK will provide at least some sort of a safety net, the knowledge that it should be quite easy with modern communications technologies and reasonably priced travel to go back home or to receive visitors in Spain regularly. Combined with this are the experiences of having spent time in Spain, and the desire to move somewhere like that, that offers a slow pace of life, and good quality of life. However, none of this is explicit in the interviews and conversations we had with our respondents. It is made apparent through analysis of how they tell their stories and through an analysis of broader structural and cultural changes.

Some can describe their actions as more strategic, rational choices, describing how they chose Spain among a list of options after a life as expatriates. They balanced up nearness to home, with desire not to live there permanently. But, given that no individual can possibly be in possession of all the information required to take an action that will bring about predicted outcomes, we know that in reality these agents drew on their experiences and their conjuncturally-specific internal structures to make ongoing decisions through practice. One couple I interviewed exemplified this very well. They were able to tell me that they had lived abroad most of their lives, knew they did not want to retire in the UK, tried Thailand for a while, then settled on Spain because it is 'not too far from home and still beautiful and relatively cheap'. But the story they told was much more complicated, with tales of driving through France and Spain, staying with their sister in Nerja, returning to visit young grandchildren in the UK, and eventually, back in Spain:

> **Charles.** And we drove up from the coast and we came through de la Torre, came round the corner and there was this gorgeous valley, and immediately loved it, because, it was beautiful.
>
> **Mary:** Right by the Mirador, we turned that corner there you know, where it all opens up and we said 'oh my god, this is it'.

This is much more a story of practice than of rational choice. Practice is weaving the habitus with the new conditions, within communities of practice (and the habitus and expectations of those around us) in an ongoing sense of how to go on. Many people described to me how they came to Spain and were inspired. They fell in love with the place first and then events conspired to free them of constraints they felt held them back. The stories went like this: 'we had been here several times on holiday and then we decided to buy a holiday home', 'we drove around that mountain and there it was, the view, the house', 'we had made friends here', 'we saw a TV programme and we thought: why can't we do it?' The aspirations and imaginations go hand in hand with external events; something happens to help break the ties: 'my husband was made redundant', 'my mother died', 'we got divorced'. Many migrants were thus freed of constraints, enabling them to justify the move.

The freedom from ties and obligations as suggested by Bauman (2000) and others as being characteristic of contemporary lifestyles is also somewhat revealed in the stories in these papers and books. Migrants often described their new way of life in terms of new beginnings and how they had been able to shake off old ties, revealing that they are subconsciously enacting a broad cultural shift. But freedom from constraints and obligations is still tempered by internal constraints in the shape of the habitus and the norms of those around us. Some talk of being free of ties (especially in old age, or because they lost their job, or because their parents died) giving them the opportunity to move. Others, however, demonstrate that freedom might be a contemporary ideal that is not so easy to achieve in practice. King et al. spoke of older people with caring responsibilities constraining their opportunities to migrate, but how this is resolved in practice is a matter for individual and small-group negotiation: Caring responsibilities and emotional bonds 'thrive and adapt between households as well as within four walls' (King et al., 2000: 12). Some feel they need to sever ties with home after 'coming out' (announcing to family and friends that they are homosexual) or divorce and see migration to Spain as an opportunity to start a new life in new networks. Others want to be free, to start again, to be who they want, but also to retain close ties to home. Mary and Michael (O'Reilly, 2000: 81–2) were both recently divorced and said, for example: 'We both come from the same village, you see, and everyone knows both of us. It's awful, we have got all the same friends... we had to get out'. But community ties are apparently more important than we might think since many moves were not so much a clean break but a development from holiday, to second home, to more frequent and longer visits, to eventual settlement.

'Freedom' thus takes various shapes, and many respondents say they chose Spain because it is close to the UK. The following quote from a woman cited in King et al. (2000: 99) reveals the ways in which a choice is not made alone or without a whole host of opportunities and constraints, habits and norms: 'Initially we were thinking of America and we went out there for a few months and looked around. Then my husband changed his mind... we opted for a holiday home in Spain, so people could come and visit us' (ibid: 99). The woman clearly sees her 'choice' as being heavily circumscribed by her husband, who 'changed his mind'. They have also decided to choose a place that will enable them to continue their ties with home. Few of the migrants in these studies completely sever ties with home and so it is not so much about freedom from obligations as being able to embrace some sort of freedom but retain connections.

The fact that many people had previous ties to the place through tourism is revealed in many interviews and conversations. This is therefore a fairly proximate structural factor of which the agent is conscious. Most of 'those who settled in Spain had usually done so because of their prior holidays' (ibid: 99). Gary, a retired chemical engineer in King et al. (ibid: 108) said: 'We knew Mijas from holidays'. They first bought an apartment there as a holiday home but eventually settled in Spain permanently. This was a common trajectory in both studies. Interviewees do not say 'we are here because of our colonial past which has meant many of us have travelled a lot through our working lives, and our country is relatively rich compared to others', or 'we feel more free to move these days as family ties are looser and the days of the job for life are gone'. But these ideas are implicit.

Both studies begin to hint at the fact that the migration itself creates an opportunity for new migrants through networks, friendships, business opportunities, and so on (this is developed in the work of Hall and Williams, 2002). Witnessing the need for diverse services, British started to migrate in order to set up estate agencies, car rental agencies, bars, restaurants, laundries, property rental agencies. Later still, in the early twenty-first century, there are now a whole host of businesses and services provided by and for the English-speaking community, from alternative therapies to building a patio, from pool cleaning to pet hairdressing (from the sublime to the ridiculous). Spanish lawyers and doctors are learning English in order to boost their clientele, estate agencies in the UK are marketing second homes in Spain. These are the new external structures (outcomes) framing subsequent migrations and, in turn, their nature and outcomes.

To conclude this section, people move to Spain as a result of a wide range of broad structural and cultural shifts that have led to a desire to migrate, some freedom from constraints (or a feeling that one can be free), economic, technological and infrastructural developments. But these alone cannot explain individual agency. The decision to move is made when these external structures are to some extent internalized and when personal constraints and opportunities coincide with desire and with networks that mean one feels it to be a possibility. We may never be able to understand reasons for moving sufficiently to be able to predict it. But our insights using practice theory might enable us not to draw sweeping (and simplistic) conclusions that this is a middle class, retirement phenomenon that depends heavily on economic considerations.

Settling in Spain

I would like now to think a little about how British migrants settle in Spain. This is complex and there is a lot of work in this area, so I will only focus on some aspects. We know that they do not integrate well. Many do not settle permanently or full time: I have distinguished between full and returning residents and seasonal and peripatetic visitors, and there is lots of movement from one category to another (2000: 52). Many are not working or only work a little to supplement their income. Others work in small businesses working for and with other British, and many work on their own account, or are self-employed. There are numerous British clubs and societies, many of them with exclusively British or European memberships (2000: 77). Many British migrants do not register as resident in Spain, for a variety of reasons. Most only have 'some knowledge' of the Spanish language (King et al., 2000: 129, and Rodríquez, Fernández-Mayoralas et al., 2005), but few see this as a problem.

We need to think about what power people have to integrate, if that is their desire, in the context of external constraints. The Spanish tend to assume (as revealed in a number of studies including O'Reilly, 2001, and Mantecón, 2008) that British living in Spain are generally older, retired, wealthy second-home owners, or tourists, with no desire (or need) to integrate. Indeed, as Aledo (2005) reminds us, both popular and official terminology in Spain has different terms for north-European migrants (*extranjeros*, or foreigners) and non-European (*immigrantes*, or immigrants), and little time and energy are expended thinking about policies to enable the former to settle. They confuse them with tourists and offer them shared services. There could be more research into how the locals perceive the incomers, and the interaction of the two groups. These facts form part of the *habitus* of the receiving society and will thus form part of the conjuncturally-specific external structures of the British migrants. As such, over time, they will become part of the conjuncturally-specific internal structures limiting expectations towards integration. As Bourdieu (1990) notes, we may not even be aware of objective constraints but they nevertheless mould what is achievable or worth aspiring to.

But let's look at the group habitus of the British – the shared sets of dispositions, the roles, norms and practices of the group as a whole. Remember that in *practice*, the externally determined thing is in fact objectified both in bodies and in institutions (Bourdieu, 1990: 57). Institutions, laws, constraints, norms, and so on are appropriated practically, and realized through the habitus and the action of agents. British migrants thus embrace, internalize and make a practice of the idea of mobility, which has been enabled through the development of new technologies (see Rodes, 2009). These technologies also permit the retention of ties with home. In other words increased mobility is an opportunity that becomes part of the practices in which migrants assume they can (and do) move while retaining strong ties with home. Tourism also becomes part of the habitus as migrants seek the Spain that has been marketed to them, the quaint backward Spain that promises leisure and escape and a return to a more simple way of life (O'Reilly, 2000). They have a love of Spanish culture but their idea of what this is, is filtered through their experiences as tourists. British migrants express a desire to integrate, but have no real need to because of the many services available in their own communities and in their own language. They expect and enact the freedom inscribed in the right to move freely within Europe. They often resist formal residence (ibid: 47). Their move has been enabled by relative wealth and relative escape, and to integrate would damage what they achieve by constantly balancing home and away, here and there, richer and poorer society. Many are retired and not looking for work, others have very little expectation of being able to work within the Spanish economy. Here the habitus is shaped by the limits of the possible in an area of high unemployment. There is some evidence of chauvinism or national superiority, a habitus formed through long histories of empire: 'slowly we are educating the Spanish families into our way of life here' said one man who lived in a very mixed nationality neighbourhood (King et al., 2000: 146, and see Rodríguez, Fernández-Mayoralas et al., 1998). But migrants also retain the distance of the stranger, aware (and reminding each other) they are guests in a foreign land (O'Reilly, 2000).

In terms of conjuncturally-specific internal structures, their practice of settling in Spain emerges over time in interaction with their experiences and networks and how they perceive the world and the people around them. They become aware that they are perceived as relatively wealthy and not expected to settle or to integrate in Spain. Their experiences of not working, combined with their expectations not to find work within the Spanish economy, the fact that many are not expecting to stay forever or perhaps not all year round, the expectation and later the experience of being marginal, leads them to find each other socially, to help out in the initial stages of settling, to find out how to get what, to share information and advice. Some services then arise as a response; people taking the opportunity to make a living out of these needs. Also, clubs and associations are created as spaces where people can replace their sense of identity, of self-worth, of status (lost through moving and leaving work) through their position in these institutions (O'Reilly, 2000). These in turn mean that people have less need to integrate; so that newcomers learn a different way to go on in their new surroundings, supported heavily by the settled community. The interplay of expectations, habitus, and experiences *in situ*, thus lead to new external structures framing the migration experience for both existing and new migrants. Their ethnic identity emerges over time in a process of what Ewa Morawska (1996, in Stones, 2005: 54) calls ethnicization: 'in an interplay between the cultural and the practical schemas they brought with them and the ... circumstances of their new ... environment'. These circumstances – including a low chance that they would spend time with Spanish on a daily basis, building their own communities, continuing ties with home, low need to politically mobilize or to claim a distinctive identity, low need or expectation to learn the language – results in them framing their identity as 'British but different', above all not tourists. This is the 'other' that is more meaningful to them in their daily lives. Ethnicization, then, arises out of conditions in the host environment in interaction with the habitus of the group.

Conclusion

In this chapter I have reviewed a number of studies covering British 'lifestyle' migration to Spain's coastal areas. As with later chapters, this review has not been exhaustive or systematic. Instead I have selected well known studies that illustrate, to an extent, the now taken for granted knowledge about the phenomenon. Through these existing studies we have identified structures framing this migration at an upper level in the shape of technological change, the increased connectivity of the world, and the development of mass tourism, and have demonstrated the theoretical perspectives that have, or might have, been useful including globalization, transnationalism, mobility, and colonialism. We have also seen how these wider shifts are embodied and enacted by agents as they make the decision to move and in the ways they choose to live their post-migration lives. We have learned that the practice of migration to Spain has a long history, at least going back to the migration of backpackers and intellectuals to what were then remote areas of Spain. It can also be traced back to a phenomenon we might describe as 'retirement to the seaside'. These earlier migrations created new structures in the shape of concrete ties and internalized structures (expectations, goals, dreams) on the part of both migrants and hosts. Amongst other things, we have also heard how migration and settlement take place through practice, over time, and as agents negotiate a path through conjuncturally-specific external structures (perhaps norms towards staying at home), within their communities of practice (their new ethnic communities, the family and friends at home, Spanish communities), and in the context of more proximate and more distant external constraints (including policies about registration and legalization that are variously practised by local agents).

This is just the start of a practice story of British migration to Spain, relying heavily on my own work because that is what I am most familiar with. It begins to illustrate how we can work together to understand a phenomenon in much of its complexity by drawing on the concepts of a theory of practice. A theory of practice can also be used to examine some aspects of a process in depth, as long as we then link our findings to others. Alejandro Mantecón's (2008) discourse analysis of how 'residential tourism' in Spain, and the construction of entire towns for the second homes market, gets legitimized and accepted as a good, in spite of the obvious damage it is doing, can, for example, contribute to a broader analysis of the outcomes of this migration trend. We can generalize from our research to other European groups (see the edited collection by Rodríguez, Casado Díaz and Huber ,2005). Or we can generalize beyond Spain, using concepts such as lifestyle migration (supported with rigorous empirical research). A theory of practice merely provides the meta-theoretical framework within which disparate studies can be brought together. It does not attempt to do all the work that other theories and concepts contribute, nor does it aim to replace the sorts of work reviewed. However, it does demand composite studies and the recognition that international migration is a complex, ongoing process. British (and other north European) migration to Spain continues to feature in the work of Spanish academics because of the profound long-term unintended consequences with which the country is trying to come to terms.

5
Labour Migration: Mexican Labour Migration to the United States

Introduction

This chapter examines a specific type of labour migration that has received a great deal of academic (and political) attention over the decades. Labour migration is almost the archetypal migration – ask someone to picture a migrant and most will think of foreign workers engaged in low-paid, low-skilled work in poor conditions, often on a temporary basis (see Aledo, 2005: 1) – and Mexican labour migration to the United States (US) is perhaps the archetypal labour migration (Portes and Rumbaut, 2006). This chapter summarizes and reviews a selection of the vast amount of work in this field that, combined, can begin to address the huge range of questions we might have of Mexican labour migration, from its history to its current nature. In other words, I have started to compile a practice story of Mexican labour migration to the US, and I therefore attempt to learn about the external structures constraining and enabling the migration, the habitus of the agents (the migrants), the conjuncturally-specific internal structures that develop as migration proceeds and migrants learn how to go on in their new setting, the communities of practice and conjuncturally-specific external structures that are relevant to their daily practices, and the outcomes in terms of subsequent migration, habitus, and other internal and external structures. By employing some of the concepts used in a theory of practice (while accepting they are heuristic devices, not to be reified, they overlap and interact in such subtle myriad ways, especially over time), and utilizing an approach similar to detective work, I hope to reveal a little more about what is already known by framing it within a practice story. At the same time I will reveal gaps in the story, which require more searching for existing literature or further empirical research. In the process we will come to know a specific labour migration trend that shares patterns with other labour migrations (Morawska, 2009). The chapter is therefore an illustration of a type of migration of great concern to migration scholars, policy makers, and analysts.[1]

An important focus of the work reviewed here is on what we might term 'incorporation' (see Chapter 3). Alejandro Portes and his team have been especially driven to try to understand the extent to which Mexican migrants can be considered incorporated into North American society, and they have applied a variety of surveys and other research methods in order to examine the precise nature of this incorporation and what factors aid or impede it. This work has often been driven by a desire to address (or allay) concerns in US society about the extent of immigration, and the challenges it brings. Poorly educated manual labourers, who come overwhelmingly from Latin America, make up more than half of all immigrants in America.[2] Mexicans are the largest immigrant group in America and one of the fastest growing segments of the population. Their migration has continued for over a century, and according to the 2000 census, there were then 20.6 million people of Mexican origin in the United States (Portes and Rumbaut, 2006: 134). 'Not only is the Mexican immigrant population larger than all other Latin American groups combined, but it is predominantly rural in origin' (Portes et al., 2009: 117). Their migration goes back at least a hundred years, and for most of that time has been temporary and cyclical, with workers arriving in response to short-term demands for labour and with the expectation (on both sides) that they will return home. They 'tend to be concentrated in service, construction, non-union manufacturing, transportation, and agricultural industries' (Mize and Swords, 2011: 107), and geographical settlement of Mexican migrants is also highly concentrated. 'Mexicans form by far the largest contingent settling in Los Angeles' for example (Portes and Rumbaut, 2006: 47). At various times, usually related to other circumstances in the US, immigration is viewed as of more or less concern. When it is of more concern, emotive language surrounds 'floods of immigrants', describing the threat they pose to a 'traditional' national identity, caused by their supposed lack of assimilation, and their unique characteristics (see especially Huntington, 2004, in Portes et al., 2009). It seems fair to ask: 'what is the nature of Mexican migrants' incorporation in American society'?

The Studies

This chapter specifically draws on work by Canales (2003), Portes, Escobar and Arana (2009); Portes and Rumbaut (2006); Portes and

Fernández-Kelly (2008); Ruiz (2008) and Vasquez (2010). Together they begin to provide the material we need to understand the broader processes framing, and the daily practices producing, Mexican labour migration to the US. Every selection involves leaving some things out and therefore emphasizing others; here the work of Portes and his colleagues has tended to focus on incorporation, using quantitative methods, whereas the work of Vicki Ruiz is historical and qualitative, examining the lives and experiences of Mexican women. Vasquez's study is quite specific and localized. Canales' work, alternatively, is historical with a macro perspective.

Canales (2003) provides a historical overview of Mexican labour migration to the US and so provides specific background material for our story. Alejandro Portes has been undertaking research on immigration into America for many years in the context of a variety of specific research programmes, working in collaboration with a diverse range of researchers. His work is often, but not solely, about Mexican labour migrants. Portes and Ruben G. Rumbaut's book, *Immigrant America* (2006), is a very ambitious account of immigration in America, including numbers, rates of growth, the various dynamics driving migration and its forms of settlement, and the role of policies, all within the context of larger-scale (sometimes global) changes and events. The coverage is very broad and complex, but within it we can find nuggets of information specific to Mexican migration to enable us to begin to understand it better within the sociological framework of practice. The work of Portes and his colleagues draws on census data as well as some invaluable bespoke surveys.[3] The paper by Portes, Cristina Escobar and Renelinda Arana (2009) examines the political integration of Latin American immigrants from Colombia, the Dominican Republic, El Salvador and Mexico, specifically addressing the question (invoked in anti-migration, nativistic, rhetoric): does increased transnationalism lead to decreased integration or incorporation in the US? Portes and Patricia Fernández-Kelly (2008) examine outcomes of migration, especially the assimilation of second generation immigrants. They argue that while some paths of assimilation lead upwards, others lead to 'poverty, drugs and gangs'; in other words, as Portes has made clear with his celebrated phrase (discussed in Chapter 3), their assimilation is *segmented*. Vicki Ruiz (2008) is a historian and tells the story of Mexican American migration beginning 'with the first wave of Mexican women crossing the border' in the early twentieth century. Her work is enriched with personal interviews and oral accounts, and here it is possible to learn of the communities, friendships, and trials and tribulations of daily life, especially for women migrants. Finally, Vasquez's (2010) paper, which focuses on integration issues for middle class third generation Mexican Americans, provides us with some rich insights into the phenomenological perspective of specific migrants.

The History of a Trend: Early Migrations

External and internal structures, habitus and practices change shape gradually over time. So, where the migration trend has such a long history, as in this case, it is useful to examine it in terms of (not entirely discrete) time-periods, in order to get a sense of the ongoing process. To begin at some sort of beginning, the first Mexicans in states such as California, Arizona and Texas, were not engaging in international migration at all. Some had settled in what is now the US before the conclusion of the US-Mexican war in 1848, and suddenly found themselves treated as second-class citizens in a foreign country. They responded by sharing a strong sense of identity and by cherishing long-held traditions (Ruiz, 2008). *International* Mexican migration arguably began at the beginning of the twentieth century, as railroad companies and farmers actively recruited labour for construction and agriculture by sending recruiting agents into rural areas of Mexico. Such was the demand that there was even competition between recruiters at the borders as they met Mexicans on entry and tried to encourage them to join their own workforce. As Portes and Rumbaut note (2006: 14) 'By 1916, five or six weekly trains full of Mexican workers hired by the agents were being run from Laredo to Los Angeles'. Portes and Rumbaut thus explain this migration, theoretically, in the broad context of the 'hegemony exercised by the American economy and culture over nearby countries' (ibid). These were mainly men, from rural areas, migrating for temporary work, and settling (however temporarily) in specific areas to where they had been recruited. Generally, the work was not far from the border and the migration was cyclical. Mexicans were thus not expected, and did not expect, to settle. The temporary nature of their migration led to them residing close to the border, in a landscape that was familiar and close to home, (thus reducing the cost of travel home), and they were likely to be amongst their compatriots. Others moved inland to where they were recruited, for example to work on the railways. Unauthorized migration, especially, was concentrated in the west and south-west, but this changed as immigration laws changed, and Mexican migration has spread further eastwards with time.

The external structures we can identify thus include the hegemonic power exerted by the American economy and culture, and poor Mexican economic conditions. As Portes and Rumbaut (2006) note, neoclassical economic theories explain this as the balance between demand and supply: as America needs more workers and Mexicans need employment, so more migrate to fill the gap. But, at the individual level, this suggests that individuals simply respond to demands; something we have learned in Chapter 3 is problematic. We need to also include the networks within which people make their decisions, the contacts and support they have to make this sort of move. Knowing what we know about the way social life unfolds through the interaction of structures and actions, it is necessary to know more about the external conditions in Mexico at this time, and how these are enacted and made into opportunities through the practice of agents within communities. We know that, in terms of the habitus of the migrants, these were rural, poor, and poorly-educated men (Canales, 2003), driven by a desire for a better standard of living. They probably internalized (as conjuncturally-specific internal structures) the assumption that they would not stay permanently and were simply being recruited for work. They were unlikely to feel embraced by American culture and society, and were likely to retain strong ties to their home towns, their families and their country because these would remain their relevant communities of practice. Vicki Ruiz (2008) recounts stories from women who migrated as part of this early phase, and while she agrees that economic factors were important, the women also gave other reasons for migration, such as the woman who left her abusive husband to join her sister in California. Ruiz tells us a little of the more proximate structures of the early migrants, who found themselves isolated in low-status jobs and segregated barrios, with few opportunities for advancement. And she describes some of their active agency, as they formed neighbourhood and community groups, often based on their home affiliations or on religion. Portes et al. (2009) also give some insight into the habitus when they tell us that the early migrants had a strong commitment to their home town, informed by an inscribed sense of duty and tradition. Using the concepts of a theory of practice, students could actively seek even more information on the communities of practice, the habitus, and the proximate social structures affecting the early migrants. Other existing studies, such as Hellman (2008), could tell us how they were received in the US. What were their conditions of existence? Which conjuncturally-specific external structures would be meaningful in their daily lives? Life stories, oral history work, and the analyses of (formal and informal) historical records are particularly good ways to examine the practice stories of the past, especially, as in Ruiz's work, when they relocate the women, emotions, families, and communities that tend to be removed from official records and statistics.

Later Migrations

Although he acknowledges the longer history, discussed above, Canales (2003) discusses Mexican migration in terms of three somewhat more recent phases: the Bracero phase, the post-Bracero phase and what I will refer to as the contemporary, complex phase. The Bracero programme (*Programa Bracero*) was an agreement between the US and Mexico, established in 1942 when the US joined the Second World War, designed to permit Mexican workers into the US to alleviate labour shortages. It was continually renewed until 1964 and can be seen as an external structure, enabling the circular and recurrent flows of young men working especially in agriculture. If we are to understand how Mexicans themselves perceive their migration, and the proximate knowledge that informs the friendships they make and their actions in relation to settling and assimilating, it is important to note that this was a continuation of the temporary migration, the hiring to fill a temporary need, of the earlier phases.[4]

Interestingly, the Bracero phase of recruitment for short-term needs lasted so long it had unintended consequences; it consolidated 'a system of social and family networks, which made it possible for migration to continue even after the Bracero scheme was ended' (Canales, 2003: 758). As Portes and Rumbaut (2006) put it, 'a sediment' developed. Ruiz (2008) gives some more information on how this happened, on the changing habitus of the settled communities, on the communities of practice, and internal and external structures framing the lives and informing the actions of the migrants over time. She describes attempts by Americans to restrict migration and deport illegal migrants, while assimilating those that remained into the wider culture under the aspirations of the 'melting pot' metaphor (see Chapter 3). These developments took shape as laws and policies (as fairly hard structures), but Ruiz also tells stories in which we can identify more proximate structures: the playground that Mexican children dared not play in because it was in the grounds of a Methodist church; the assimilation classes provided for migrants in hygiene, cooking, and language; the setting up of hospitals, schools, and community centres for immigrants. The women she talked to both embraced and denied American identities, and in their daily practices negotiated which elements to assimilate and which to reject, which to display and which to conceal. Some of the women converted to the religion of the churches that were providing services, but Ruiz also describes the sustaining refuge from prejudice and discrimination provided by the barrios, the constant feeling of social isolation and the 'conscious decision making on the part of Mexican women who sought to claim a place for themselves and their families in American society without abandoning their Mexican cultural affinities' (2008: 44).

Post-Bracero, the flows continued in response to demand for labour (we might call this a proximate social structure) and in the context of the networks of relationships (the changing conjuncturally-specific internal structures and habitus of the agents) outlined above, but now, without the legal framework of Bracero, Mexican labour became marked by illegality, and Mexicans increasingly became labelled 'the undocumented' (Canales, 2003). This gives us some insights into the responses to the migration of the hosts. Previously, the migration served to fulfil a need and was considered legitimate (and legal); now it was perceived as self-perpetuating and illegal. It seems the host society were happy to have a controlled, temporary pool of labour to call on in times of need and discard when needs were met, but were less happy when the migrants had some power of their own to settle, to move around without being recruited, and to stay beyond their expectations. The practice story being composed here would benefit from some phenomenological and hermeneutic understanding of the hosts. Ruiz (2008) provides some of this through life stories from the migrants. She gives us, for example, rich insights into diverse attitudes towards assimilation, and the generational conflicts that arose as Mexicans' children grew up Mexican American. The women she spoke to describe being told not to speak Spanish – 'that ugly language' – in the school playground, and the damage to self-esteem from being associated with a denigrated culture (2008: 53). But there were also those who, at last partly, embraced American culture and felt grateful for the opportunities they had. Women growing up between the two world wars were torn between emulating their mothers and becoming good homemakers, and embracing the individualism of American culture. Still, the persistent backdrop of discrimination, economic disadvantage, and struggle are always in evidence in these stories, as hard external structures (and see Hellman, 2008).

Since the 1980s, Mexican migration has become differentiated and more complex, no longer simply referring to young men in agriculture but including women, from urban areas often new to emigration, and their chances of staying in the US longer is increasing (Canales, 2003). Some studies suggest more women are now migrating and while these were initially moving for family reunification purposes now they may move as migrants in search of work themselves. Also, it used to be less educated people who migrated but in recent years Mexican migration includes higher educated individuals. As noted above, initially most migrants would expect their stay to be temporary, but as time passes and many have settled permanently so more of the new migrants expect to stay longer. Furthermore, where they settle in the US has changed, with Mexicans being more dispersed and more likely than before to settle in urban areas. Portes and Rumbaut also tell us that more recently it is the settled communities themselves that attract Mexicans, maybe for a 'stint of work in the cities of the Midwest' (Portes and Rumbaut, 2006: 41). This suggests that the migrant community itself has become something of an external structure enabling the migration, as suggested in migrant networks theory (Chapter 3). We can also assume that habitus have changed as migrants have returned home regularly and told people of their experiences in the US, thus increasing the desire to go. Similarly there are probably changed expectations (conjuncturally-specific internal structures) within Mexicans' various communities of practice. Migration and settlement become more of a reality and a possibility as more people do it and tell others about it. Canales (2003) notes that Mexican migration has a long history with changing structural circumstances to which migrants have adapted. We might also add, drawing on the concepts outlined in Chapter 2, that there are changing structural circumstances to which they have contributed, and that these external structures include more proximate structures such as their own communities giving them somewhere to live, or financing the move; and that the migration has been internalized into a group habitus. We learn from Hellman (2008: 6) for example, that 'the move to the "other side" is a central theme in music and folklore, and all forms of Mexican popular culture are filled with journeys *al otro lado*' (see Hellman, 2008 for more on this).

Mexican migration remains predominantly marked by poverty, concentrated in low skill work with low wages, and is often undocumented. It also remains concentrated in certain geographical areas. The complex phase is not about better educated, urban migration so much as it is about complexity. From the perspective of the US it must also feel less controlled, and it demands analysis using theories other than neoclassical economic, push-pull, and even network theories. Judith Adler Hellman (2008), for example, illustrates how the decision to move is often as much cultural as economic. This is not to undermine the relevance of economic factors, given the 'complete lack of viable economic prospects for poor and middle-class Mexicans in their own country' (ibid: 212). Her work draws attention to the role of family, neighbourhood and village networks in facilitating migration. There is only one lone, male pioneer in her stories, others were sponsored financially and encouraged culturally. In such cases expectations that the migrant will return remittances to Mexico are very high. Hellman also demonstrates that the experiences are a mixture of good and bad; if they were only bad how would it continue to exist as a migration flow (and settlement), she asks. Practice theory provides a framework through which we can examine, in detail, these ongoing processes.

Contemporary External Structures

Canales provides useful material to inform a practice story about more recent Mexican migration, especially the external structures enabling and constraining its shape and form, by examining the economic and political transformations in Mexico and the US since the mid 1980s 'which have substantially redefined the relations between both countries' (2003: 742). In Mexico, there has been a programme of structural readjustment, involving the implementation of neoliberal ideals, that has led to more precarious working conditions for Mexicans, undermined job security and wages, and diluted union power. Between 1980 and 1998 the minimum wage fell by two thirds, and during the 1990s two thirds of the workforce suffered a decrease in wages. Though there has been some more recent improvement, 'the current value of average working incomes is still about 25 per cent less than it was at the start of the 1980s' (ibid: 743). Given that, by this time, Mexicans would likely know of compatriots living in the US (temporary or settled, wealthy or poor), these external structures with their very proximate nature, probably meet with internal structures within communities of practice that have embodied or normalized migration as a way of life. And there are likely to be other even more proximate social structures, in the shape of friends and relatives who can assist with a move financially, morally and practically.

The US economy, Canales (2003) notes, has also been experiencing structural change during the last decades; the global economy, global competition, and the rapid growth of the information age, have wrought massive changes. There has been expansion of the formal economy, an increase in information and technical industries and therefore in professional services, but also increased levels of flexibilization and casualization as firms use these strategies to compete without having to bear the costs of downturns. Manufacturing and production together, at the time he was writing, employed just 22 per cent of the workforce. Employment in the US has become polarized and segmented, with stable high-income jobs for some and a glut of informal and occasional work for others. From a Mexican perspective it looks as if their work has become more varied, with 34 per cent working in manufacturing and construction, and just 12 per cent working in agriculture (and related work). But, as a percentage of the overall workforce, Mexicans make up 14 per cent of those in agricultural type work, and only 5 per cent of those in manufacturing. Whichever way you look at it, the work is mainly marked by low skill, low pay, and low security. Mexicans continue doing traditional work in localized processes even as the wider activity is globalized and technologically advanced (Canales, 2003). Theories of the information society and of globalization are not so meaningful for understanding their experiences or conditions (or even the external structures of relevance); even as things change they stay much the same for Mexican migrants to the US. Portes and Rumbaut (2006) say the demand for Mexican workers in the US now comes from construction, labour intensive industries, urban services, as well as agriculture, and while much political and popular rhetoric surrounding Mexican migration speaks of *invasions*, but

> an invasion implies moving into other people's territory against their will. In this instance, the movement is very much welcomed, if not by everyone, at least by a very influential group – namely the small, medium and large enterprises in agriculture, services, and industry that have come to rely on and profit from this source of labour.
>
> (2006: 24)

Nevertheless, use of the word 'invasion' does give us a little insight into how Mexicans are perceived and the conjuncturally-specific external structures they might face on arriving in the US.

To summarize, Mexican migration has become something of a tradition, which has been incorporated into the communities of practice of Mexicans at home, has changed in nature to some extent, but remains predominantly low-paid, low-skilled and temporary. In the US, demands for labour combine with a rhetoric that portrays immigrants in a negative light, viewing them as a threat even as employers benefit. America needs Mexicans to come when they are needed but to leave when they are not. Policies reflect this ambivalence, sometimes enabling workers to come but usually restricting them from staying and settling, and these policies must, in turn, be internalized into at least the conjuncturally-specific internal structures, if not the habitus, of the agents (both hosts and migrants).

Contemporary Communities of Practice

This practice story for Mexican migration to the US needs some analysis of the communities of practice of Mexicans. Portes and Rumbaut describe the relevant 'contexts of reception' for immigrants as being the receiving country's policies on migration, the condition of its labour market, and the characteristics or nature of the migrants' ethnic communities (2006: 93). The first two of these can be understood as proximate and fairly hard external structures that are enacted by individuals and groups, within communities of practice. The 1965 Immigration Act, for example, permitted employers to import temporary labour where domestic provision was inadequate, but this act, even with its 1986 reform, is legally very cumbersome and actually serves to deter farmers from employing legally, whereas an illegal supply is easy to acquire (Portes and Rumbaut, 2006). The 1986 Immigration Reform and Control Act (IRCA) granted amnesty to two million formerly unauthorized migrants, thus considerably increasing the numbers of legal Mexicans in the US (2006: 135) but, as a result of these settled, and now legal, migrants bringing friends and relatives to live with them, the act effectively dramatically increased the legal population of Mexicans in the US. This same act tightened the borders, which in turn led to a significant increase in the numbers of Mexicans who were undocumented. It has not been possible so far to discover how these things happened in practice, and yet trying to understand the settlement of Mexicans in the US does demand an understanding of how they are received, whether they are permitted to be legal, permanent, and so on. This practice story would benefit from some insight into proximate structures. There have been increasingly restrictive migration policies since the early 1990s, a more tightly controlled physical border, and the promotion of a more hostile approach, including, for example, policies that restrict undocumented workers' access to social and health services (such as

California's Proposition 187 – see Portes and Rumbaut, 2006: 22). These give evidence of declining tolerance of undocumented workers. The current situation, Portes and Rumbaut report, is one in which Mexicans suffer official persecution and are not able to receive government aid. However, it is unclear which policy or time period they are referring to. And, although Portes and Rumbaut loosely describe nativist fears of immigrants who are 'in society but not of it' (2006: 119), and continuing calls for the flows of immigrants to be contained or suppressed (ibid: 120), they are not able to tell us much about unofficial persecution, or about experiences on the ground for migrants and their communities of practice. Because their work is survey based and takes a macro perspective it provides crucial broad-brush information about policies and patterns. We need to look elsewhere to obtain the perspective of the migrants and their hosts, and for details about who enacts which structural constraint or opportunity in which way. Other questions that could be pursued are: how do Mexicans find jobs, how are they hired, what sorts of contracts do they obtain, what are their conditions of employment? What is the nature of their relations with their employers and local and national government? How much knowledge and power do Mexicans have to act on the opportunities open to them?[5]

The third of Portes and Rumbaut's 'contexts of reception', the ethnic communities, form the migrants' communities of practice. The terminology of communities of practice acknowledges the transnational links migrants may have as well as the communities within the US. Portes and Rumbaut acknowledge that, as the largest ethnic group in the US with a long history of migration, Mexicans' relations with communities in the US and with their communities of origin will be very complex and varied. Pre-existing networks are crucial; friends and relatives can provide support, familiarity, and information. 'Overall the entire process of immigrant settlement is "sticky" because new arrivals tend to move to places where earlier immigrants have become established' (2006: 63). If they move elsewhere they risk losing the moral and practical support that contribute to psychological and economic well-being. Our practice story portrays Mexicans with strong ties to home, and to their ethnic communities, but it has said little about their relations with people within the US.

Transnationalism and Incorporation

As an attempt to address concerns about the lack of incorporation and the persistent difference of Mexican (and other Latin American) migrants, Portes et al. (2009: 107) ask to what extent 'their behaviours and possible resilient loyalty towards their home countries retard their citizenship acquisition, learning of American values, and involvement in the political life of their adopted country'. In other words, are transnationalism and assimilation incompatible? They distinguish loosely between transnational activism on the one hand, and occasional activities that are transnational on the other hand. I shall refer to these as *organized* and *informal* transnationalism. Organized transnationalism involves regular, engaged activity across national borders that is a feature of the daily life of those engaged in it. It usually takes place through organizations or agents in the migrant's home country, and may be political or civic rather than merely social. Informal transnationalism includes those occasional, irregular and informal activities, such as going back for a visit, receiving visitors, communicating with home or sending remittances, that migrants have always engaged in and that, they suggest, do not warrant a special term (Portes et al., 2009: 107). Perhaps surprisingly, just half of their respondents were involved in informal transnationalism, whereas the organized transnationalism, that is believed by some who oppose migration to keep 'the attention and energies of immigrants tied to events in their home countries' (Portes et al., 2009: 107, see Vertovec, 2001) is engaged in by less than one in five.

Even more surprisingly, a study of transnational organizations revealed it is not the poorest and least educated, as we might assume, but the better educated and more financially secure who engage in *organized* transnational activities. Also the longer one has been in the US, and the more 'socially stable', the more likely one is to engage in these activities.[6] These are the same people who are more likely to be incorporated politically and socially into American life, and so assimilation and transnationalism are not contradictory habits or goals (2009: 112). It was also the oldest, the better educated, and those who had been in America longest who were most likely to have the resources to commit to regular transnational activities. Furthermore, the organization leaders interviewed did not perceive the goals of successful integration and home country assimilation as contradictory, but rather as complementary; almost 90 per cent thought being involved was more likely to help integration. Portes, Escobar and Arana conclude there is thus 'a common disposition to foster integration into American society, while retaining interests and loyalties in the home country' (2009: 125). The research with organization leaders also found that those involved in transnational organizations are more likely to be involved in political activities in the US than in Mexico (Portes et al., 2009: 126). They maintain contact with public officials, implement information campaigns, organize political debates, and engage in and run civic programmes. An obvious policy implication of this is that such transnational activities should therefore be encouraged, as clear steps towards successful integration.

Portes et al. suggest that 'recent immigrants concentrate on carving a niche in the host country rather than concern themselves with collective organization' (2009: 122). Then acculturation and political incorporation (becoming settled, staying longer, acquiring papers, a job, security, perhaps marriage, getting older) all precede initiating and becoming heavily involved in transnational activities. We might expect, then, that the longer Mexicans live in the US, the more settled they become, the more likely they are to engage in transnational activities as well as political activities in the US, and arguably the more incorporated they are. However, closer inspection reveals that the overall pattern above does not seem to be true for Mexican migrants! There is some evidence that Mexicans start to use English more over the generations (Portes and Rumbaut, 2006: 224), but they rarely achieve better jobs than their parents had (Waldinger, 2007), and they suffer from low educational achievement and high numbers of school dropout (Perlmann, 2007). Portes and Fernandez-Kelly (2008: 19) analysed longitudinal data collected from second generation children, and found that, even though this is actually an improvement on the education levels of their parents, almost 40 per cent of Mexicans had 'failed to advance beyond high school'. By early adulthood 41 per cent of Mexican Americans in their study had children: 'Hence, second generation groups with the lowest education and income are those most burdened, at an early age, by the need to support children' (2008: 19). Indeed, multivariate analysis revealed that 'children from disadvantaged groups such as Mexicans, Haitians, and West Indians continue to have a significantly greater probability of downward assimilation relative to other groups' (2008: 21). Children of Mexican migrants are also the most likely to be arrested (along with West Indians), and Mexicans have a high risk of depression (Portes and Rumbaut, 2006: 185). As they note, Mexicans are different to some other immigrants because they come specifically 'to fill low-wage labour needs in agriculture, construction, personal services, and other sectors' (Portes and Fernandez-Kelly, 2008: 16).

A study, over time, framed by a general, sociologically-informed, theory of practice, might help to work out how integration, settlement, and transnationalism all interrelate for Mexican migrants. For example, according to Portes and Fernandez-Kelly, it is relevant which socio-cultural environment migrants come from. Here they are implying habitus and communities of practice, and students could employ these terms to interpret their findings. Second generation migrants in America are raised in classed, ethnic and family communities. They are likely to retain some Mexican cultural traits, and to have a habitus inscribed in other ways as a result of their socialization. Despite what we have said above about the complexity of this migration, Mexican migration is still predominantly of people of rural backgrounds, and those who stay in the US still tend to work in low-status, low-paid jobs. Mexicans tend to have 'low human capital' that 'prevents them from joining more middle class forms of organization' (Portes and Fernandez-Kelly, 2008: 117) that tend to be more philanthropic. Instead they tend to set up and to join civic organizations that are loyal to and support their home town; this appears to be a continuation of their traditional duties, or *cargos*, to their local communities back home and would certainly serve to create a sense of belonging (and a community of practice) for second and third generation migrants.

Mexico as Community of Practice

For Mexicans in the US, Mexican society, culture and the Mexican state all exist as communities of practice, each with relevant conjuncturally-specific external structures, various sets of habitus, and in which 'learning to go on' takes place for agents. Originally, Mexicans who settled in the US were subject to the derogatory term '*pochos*' and pretty much ignored in Mexico. But towards the end of the twentieth century Mexico became aware of its emigrants as a resource. By the time that almost one in ten of its population was living or working in the US, it had come to rely quite heavily on the remittances these emigrants were sending (now the second most important source of foreign exchange for Mexico), and immigrant organizations had started to have an influence on Mexican politics and economy, with even presidential candidates benefitting from their financial and political support. A Program for Mexican Communities Abroad (PCME, in its Spanish acronym), designed to strengthen ties with Mexican immigrant communities, eventually 'came to sponsor the Dos-por-Uno plan, in which every dollar raised by immigrant organizations for philanthropic works at home would be matched by two dollars from the Mexican federal and state governments' (Portes and Rumbaut, 2006: 135), and this later became the Tres-por-Uno program. Several Mexican states are now proactive in promoting transnational activities (see Goldring, 2002 in Portes et al., 2009: 117). Dual nationality legislation was brought in, and Mexicans were encouraged to naturalize in the US. This suggests that sufficient numbers were actually engaged in transnational organizations to attract the Mexican state to the benefits of their activities. Where several home town organizations, discussed above, are formed then the state establishes a federation. There are some regions in the US, where many people from a certain home town have settled (such as Houston, LA, Chicago), with their own Mexican federations; most notably the Zacatecan Federation based in Los Angeles. Furthermore, community organizations in various Mexican cities get support from their Mexican consulate. These are not just to encourage remittances but are also Mexican federal state run or provide supported community services for Mexican migrants: libraries, language courses, medical and legal services (Portes et al., 2009: 119). While Portes and his colleagues (2009) suggest we can trace back transnational activities to the context left behind (meaning we can almost predict what form they will take based on the communities they came from) our practice story demonstrates this is more of an ongoing process of structural constraints and opportunities, practised and consolidated into newly reproduced structures. In other words, Mexican children grow up learning that they have commitments to their home town (whatever that now means to them), that involve them committing time and money to those communities and associations.

Habitus and Internal Structures

Looking at the conditions people have left can give us an insight into their habitus; their expectations of a better life will be circumscribed by what is achievable and what they learn to expect. Because the topic is so vast with a very long history, the works reviewed for this chapter have not given us a precise idea of who is migrating, where and why, with what sets of expectations, what habits and norms. Nevertheless, we can start to gather information in snippets. According to Portes and Rumbaut (2006), Mexican parents have the lowest levels of schooling of any immigrant group, and 'Immigrants often lack sufficient knowledge of the new language and culture to realise what is happening and explain themselves effectively' (Portes and Rumbaut, 2006: 119). We also learn that the Mexican immigrant population is on the whole younger and has lower than average human capital than the other Latin American groups (Portes et al., 2009), and we know women are now migrating not just to join families but also to work themselves, perhaps intentionally participating in the circular moves so typical of Mexican immigration to the US.

We have established that the first generation is likely to have arrived with little expectation of staying, and so the communities that were established shared a habitus as unsettled; they came to expect low standards of living, their communities of practice remained as much Mexico focussed as US. We know many migrants started out illegally, or 'undocumented': in 2002, 96 per cent of illegal border crossings were of Mexicans (Portes and Rumbaut, 2006: 22). Undocumented migration tends to be temporary, but still large numbers do settle. Many that are now legal residents started out illegally then married US citizens or legal residents. Many enter as family or close relatives. Mexican migrants have often struggled to get in and know they are perceived, together with their compatriots, as undocumented and troublesome. Those who have arrived in recent years may well have suffered an arduous journey. Once they arrive poverty rates are high. Some Mexicans go on to entrepreneurial activity 'setting themselves up as independent mechanics, gardeners, handymen, and house cleaners' (ibid: 31). But while the wages might be better, they still live with insecurity with regards to success of the business and their legal status. They are not very political. Even for those, who are many, that settled in the south-west in territories that were formerly Mexican, their engagement in political activism is low (Portes and Rumbaut ,2006), although *not* non-existent (see Ruiz, 2008).

A migrant that is hired temporarily or who has an uncertain status has reason to retain his or her ethnic identity and to have little interest in US society or politics. It makes sense, in terms of conjuncturally-specific internal structures, to retain a strong attachment to home and, with advances in communication technologies and travel, it has become easier to return regularly and to retain (sometimes virtual) contact. Even those who settle more permanently can return home quickly and easily, and need not view the move as permanent initially: 'the fact that their hometowns are often a bus ride away reduces the finality of migration' (Portes and Rumbaut, 2006: 146). This kind of analysis would benefit from the concept of mobility, discussed in Chapter 3. While the first generation lacks a voice, Portes and Rumbaut suggest that in the face of hostility and attacks (a brief insight into their experiences in relation to the US), the second generation gain their voice (learning about the US culture and the language) and yet use it to affirm their identities in a reactive way. Their ethnicity is thus a form of resilience and resistance (ibid: 120).

Stories of Practice

Towards the latter part of their paper, Portes and Fernandez-Kelly (2008) advocate studying the experiences of second generation immigrants, and then examine a few cases in depth in order to ask why it is that 'not all children advantaged by their parents' human capital, favourable contexts of reception, and stable families manage to succeed educationally, and not all growing up under conditions of severe disadvantage end up in permanent poverty or in jail' (ibid: 22). The stories they tell illustrate a few themes they wish to highlight, revealing the importance of parental authority and family discipline for children living in poor neighbourhoods, where drugs, crime and gangs are an easy way for young people to find community and friendship. We thereby learn that the communities of practice of Mexican American children include families as well as other youth sometimes involved in less desirable pastimes. Children appear to benefit from what we might call strong role models, or what the authors call 'really significant others'. In the language of structuration this draws attention to very close, influential and perhaps powerful conjuncturally-specific external structures. These are people who motivate, take an interest, share expertise and knowledge. They also illustrate the role of community and other groups that organize to help young people, and these are especially beneficial when they are grounded in knowledge of the culture and language that the children bring with them (Portes and Fernandez-Kelly, 2008: 27). This therefore implies from a policy perspective that fully-engaged special assistance programmes and policy interventions that understand the culture and language of the migrant group and that do not attempt to force them to sever their ties with their home towns, are most likely to be successful. This is similar to Jill Rutter's findings (Chapter 7), that one's culture and history can provide reference points 'to strengthen the children's self-esteem and aspirations for the future' (ibid: 27).

Portes' and Fernandez-Kelly's stories also reveal the role of cultural capital. Middle class children do not entirely cast off their habitus but can use it to imagine a better future even under conditions where this seems unlikely or difficult to achieve (where the objective conditions suggest little chance of success, see Bourdieu, 1985). Middle class children embody aspirations, as well as 'know-how'. Cultural capital involves 'information, values, and demeanour that migrants from more modest families do not have' (Portes and Fernandez-Kelly, 2008: 29), and calls to mind the sense of one's place, and knowledge of how to achieve one's aims that Bourdieu talks about it with his concepts of habitus and practice (see Chapter 2).

This chapter has especially demonstrated the contribution that macro studies and quantitative surveys could make to a practice story; however, there are numerous rich, in-depth studies of how Mexicans experience and negotiate migration that could be included in order for us to understand the practice of daily life, such as Ruiz's work discussed above. Interestingly, a literature search for 'Mexican Labour migration' yields more in the way of macro-perspective overviews and quantitative studies; while a search for 'Mexican migrants' yields more qualitative studies. Judith Adler Hellman (2008 and 1994) has undertaken long-term fieldwork in Mexico and reveals in rich detail the strategies migrants acquire over time, and in the practice of daily life, such as learning to live without your *abuelita* (grandma) preparing your tortillas and washing your clothes (in Hellman, 2008: xvii). She reveals how precarious life can be, and how the expectations, norms and reactions of those around them (conjuncturally-specific external structures) will lead individuals to adapt and change. As a migrant, Luis' habitus slowly changed in line with his knowledge of how to go on (conjuncturally-specific internal structures) as he learned 'to stay out of trouble', and struggled to keep hold of his job. Hellman also tells the story of Javier, who through his networks was able to settle in a rural area where there were few other migrants, and we learn that where Luis spent evenings drinking with fellow Mexicans (even from their same town), Javier was a foreigner amongst locals and got into serious trouble, eventually being accused of rape when he flirted with the barmaid, whose boyfriend was unfortunately there (Hellman, 2008: xix).

The volume edited by Vicki Ruiz and Susan Tiano (1987) examines in detail the lives of Mexican American women in the context of their home lives, families and workplaces, revealing their dreams and aspirations, their struggles and successes. The book challenges stereotypes that suggest, for example, that upward mobility is caused by the fatalistic attitude of mothers (Tiano and Ruiz, 1987). Using in-depth interviews with people of Mexican origin, Rosalía Solóranzo-Torres (1987) brings the rest of the household (both in US and Mexico) into the frame, thereby allowing us to start to think about the communities of practice within which migrants are located. The new book by Ronald Mize and Alicia Swords (2011) is enriched with life stories describing the racial marginalization, abuse and mistreatment of Mexican workers, and portraying them as America's 'disposable labourers'. However, it also recognizes their active responses by documenting, for example, the rise of various immigrants' rights movements. For these authors, it is crucial to pay attention to the policies of the state, and the ways in which these shape labour migration (in this case in response to the demand for cheap labour, and the perceived benefits of remittances), but the contemporary relevance of Mexican migration can be understood only through an historical grounding that understands the interconnection of migration, identity, the development over time of second-class citizenship and racism, and the formation of transnational communities. This kind of approach implies a practice story, and would certainly benefit from applying some of the concepts in Chapter 2 more overtly.

Finally, Vasquez's (2010) work is based on in-depth interviews with middle class, third generation Mexican Americans living in California, and here we start hear about the communities of practice and conjuncturally-specific internal and external structures for Mexican migrants (although not using that terminology). As Ruiz (2008: 45) noted for her respondents, 'class must be taken into consideration... middle-class Mexicans desiring to dissociate themselves from their working class neighbours possessed the most fervent aspirations for assimilation'. Vasquez (drawing on Keefe and Padilla, 1987) says that Mexican Americans do not simply live an amalgamation of American and Mexican life, but a distinctive 'third way of life'. Though the grandchildren of Mexican migrants have grown up American, nevertheless Mexicans continue to migrate to the US. Third generation Mexican Americans are ambivalent about these new migrants; they realize that they are viewed as a homogenous group by mainstream society, and they feel unable to successfully establish a discrete identity. Mexican men in the US are stereotyped as dark, foreign and dangerous, and though they try to distance themselves from them, the third generation are subject to the same conjuncturally-specific external structures. Mexican women are seen as docile and exotic, and the third generation describe their attempts to escape these stereotypes, by thinking carefully about how they apply their make-up and dress, by disguising their Mexicanness. These are instances of individuals acquiring conjuncturally-specific internal structures; they are learning to behave and to look different. But it does not always work. Stories migrants tell of Anglo-looking people pretending not to be Mexican in order to secure jobs, and being afraid of being caught out are real insights into conjuncturally-specific structures; even those who are of mixed origin experience racialization, stereotyping, and are unable to escape their origins. Migrants' offspring internalize stereotypical images of themselves, and the fact they are not consistently applied – they are sometimes able to 'pass' as white. Vasquez says they acquire a 'flexible ethnicity' – 'the ability to navigate two different social worlds, that is, mainstream U.S. culture and a Mexican-oriented community' (2010: 58). They acquire skills and cultural toolkits (internalize the culture of both of their communities of practice), but the amount of agency still depends on the ways in which they are perceived and received. They have to find a way to live within both communities of practice at the same time (or in the same life), and this passage illustrates how difficult this can be:

> I think it's clear that I'm probably more Americanized than I think I would like to admit. I've got my Internet... My whole lifestyle is pretty American. But I do feel, at times... when I read history books or I see the horrible things that this country has done, I'm like, 'Oh Man, I'm so glad I'm not 100 percent American'. I don't feel I fit in anywhere. I'm right in between – and it's okay.
>
> (A male respondent in Vasquez, 2010: 59)

Conclusion

This chapter has examined in detail a few studies of Mexican labour migration to the US, as an example of studies of incorporation. The work by Alejandro Portes and his team was included as examples that are well known and that have gained some authority in the field; Canales' work provided a useful macro perspective, and the work of Ruiz, Vasquez and others contributed rich, in-depth material from qualitative (especially oral historical) studies. In this chapter we learn that, for Mexican migrants, external structures beyond their control include the historical (economic and power) relationship between Mexico and the US, the economic condition of each country, and changes in the global economy (perhaps best understood using theories of colonialism, globalization and neo-liberalism). More proximate structures include the way their labour is recruited, for what purposes, and the policies that enable and constrain their migration and settlement. Details on these aspects remain a bit thin given the work that has been reviewed. However, we have been able to discover something of the habitus of earlier migrants, the majority of whom were rural, poorly educated men; but as this migration has become more complex research has needed to disaggregate the group. Studies that include all Mexican migrants, sometimes even as a sub-set of a larger group of immigrants, although invaluable in their own right, lack the necessary subtlety for a story of practice. We have learned that increased transnational activities do not necessarily negate the ability to engage fully in the communities where new migrants now live (as often assumed in popular and politically motivated discourse). Indeed, those labour migrants in the US most likely to engage in transnational activities in their home countries are also those migrants who are most settled and best incorporated in the US. But close analysis reveals this is less true for Mexican migrants than for other groups. For Mexicans their duties to their home towns remain strong, and Mexican society needs to be understood as providing perhaps the most relevant communities of practice for these migrants who were never, originally at least, expected to settle. We know that Mexicans continue to be excluded or to suffer segmented assimilation (see Chapter 3), we learn a bit from the qualitative studies how migrants negotiate these various structures of constraint and opportunity, and finally, in Vasquez's work we get some interesting insights into how third generation Mexicans negotiate external structures and habitus, in communities of practice, acquiring conjuncturally-specific internal structures that inform 'a third way' of living, balancing belonging to both Mexico and America.

Together these studies illustrate that in order to understand the structuration processes involved we need *both* studies of broad scope (macro, historical studies) and close, intimate studies of daily life. But more than that, the chapter illustrates that these approaches need to work together in an attempt to understand the meso level of daily practice. Close, intimate studies of practice, preferably using ethnography and in-depth interviews, hermeneutics and phenomenology, can really reveal who and what are the communities of practice, the habitus of the agent, the emerging conjuncturally-specific external and internal structures, but must continue to analyse these in the wider context of upper structural layers using both what the agents are able to describe and what social scientists can reveal.

6

Domestic Labour Migration: Filipina Migration to Hong Kong

Introduction

Where migration was once thought to be a male phenomenon it is increasingly recognized that not only do women have as long a history of migration as men, they are now 'on the move as never before in history' (Ehrenreich and Hochschild, 2003: 2), and millions of women are especially (and increasingly) migrating from poor to rich countries to work in service as nannies, maids and sex workers, as the labour of care is commodified for the profit of others (Lindio-McGovern, 2004). This chapter will begin to tell a practice story about domestic labour migration, specifically migration from the Philippines to Hong Kong.

Women have long migrated to join their families, to find work on their own, to get away from abusive relationships, as students, as refugees, as labour migrants, and as domestic servants (Lutz, 2010). Women also travel as business executives to exotic destinations, keeping in contact with home through the media of modern telecommunications (Fechter, 2007). Women migrants are thus diverse and from various contexts, but a vast majority provide cheap and flexible labour in the service sectors and sometimes in manufacturing. Women migrants' work tends therefore to be hidden, secondary, and individualized (Anthias, 2000; Parreñas, 2003; Lutz, 2010). As is the case in much migration, but especially in hidden forms, statistics are difficult to obtain and to trust. They tend to be inconsistent and not easily comparable (collected by different agencies for different purposes, using varying sources, with different definitions and reasons for inclusion and exclusion). But overall, half of the world's migrants are now thought to be women, varying enormously by type of flow. As is the case with migration generally, the most significant flows are south to north, from poorer to richer countries. Many migrants choose to go to countries that are geographically close and not too dissimilar linguistically, but they also follow routes previously established through trade, imperialism, and colonialism. Migration from the Philippines, Sri Lanka and Latin America can be characterized as female flows (Anthias, 2000; Ehrenreich and Hochschild, 2003). Women are in the majority in movements such as 'Cape Verdians to Italy, Filipinos to the Middle East, and Thais to Japan' (Castles and Miller, 2009: 12). The impacts and social change wrought in sending countries such as the Philippines, where 'care is now the primary export' can be tremendous (Parreñas, 2003: 4). Some refugee and trafficked flows are also predominantly women. Of course we should not overlook what has become known as the 'mail order bride' phenomenon, which is a key feature of female migration too. This chapter is specifically concerned with female domestic labour migration.

Most female labour migrants work in 'women's work', or work that has been typically undertaken by women: domestic work, service work (in hotels and hospitals), and sometimes entertainment and sex work. These are low-paid jobs, often with poor conditions and low-status, in private homes and institutions such as care homes, hospitals, nursing homes, and children's nurseries (Ehrenreich and Hochschild, 2003: 6). As female migration has increased so has the percentage of women in rich countries such as the US, England, France and Germany who are foreign born and working in domestic work. Ehrenreich and Hochschild say the rise in migrant domestic workers has occurred as increasing numbers of Western women have taken up work without a matching increase in the amount of help given in the home by men. They describe the pressures and expectations of Western women to be super-women balancing home and work lives, maintaining their houses in pristine condition and their families contented. Women's employment in developed countries has increased rapidly in recent decades, and people are working longer hours, especially those in professional and managerial careers. At the same time the employment of domestic 'help' has risen to almost ten per cent of households (Lutz, 2010: 1654). But this phenomenon is not restricted to the West; the use of domestic workers in the Middle East and then East Asia has soared in recent decades.

The Studies

The studies I examine in depth for this chapter include Constable's *Maid to Order in Hong Kong* (2007); Ehrenreich's and Hochschild's *Global Woman* (2003) (especially the editors' introduction and chapters by Nicole

Constable and Rhacel Parreñas; papers by Lindio-McGovern (2004); Tam (1999); and to a lesser extent Skeldon (1997 and 2004).[1] Nicole Constable's book was 'an ethnographic and historical account of the lives of Filipina domestic workers in Hong Kong' (2007: xix) that was updated to include other groups of domestic workers in its second edition.[2] It is based on two periods of ethnographic fieldwork in Hong Kong from 1993 to 1994, accompanied by Constable's husband and two small children. The flat they rented then came with its own Filipina domestic worker, Acosta, to Constable's surprise and discomfort, but she turned this to her advantage cleaning the flat herself and using the four hours a week that Acosta was supposed to work encouraging her to help with the research. Acosta gave her lots of insights into the experiences of the domestic workers in Hong Kong, by telling her stories of her own life and those of others, and also introducing her to other workers. Constable's work is based on informal interviews and conversations, on fieldwork in the spaces where Filipinas meet, and in migrant workers' associations. She also draws from secondary sources: statistical data, archival materials, mass media and other literature, and academic works. Field research and interviews for the second edition of the book were undertaken in Hong Kong between 2005 and 2006. Barbara Ehrenreich's and Arlie Russell Hochschild's introduction, in *Global Woman*, discusses the growing trend for domestic labour migration from a macro perspective. Constable's (2003) chapter in this book is based on her fieldwork, discussed above, looking specifically at experiences of Filipina domestic labour migrants in Hong Kong. Rhacel Parreñas' (2003) chapter examines discourses in the Philippines surrounding the phenomenon of domestic labour emigration. Ligaya Lindio-McGovern (2004) draws on ethnographic fieldwork with Filipino migrant domestic workers in Hong Kong, Taiwan, Vancouver, Rome, and Chicago, especially examining their experiences of alienation. Vicky Tam (1999) examines the employment of foreign domestic helpers in Hong Kong, from the perspective of the employers. Her paper is based on a survey of 226 female Chinese employees on their views towards childcare, and interviews with 14 working mothers who employ foreign domestic helpers.[3] Ronald Skeldon (1997 and 2004) provides a more macro level economic and development perspective relevant to the region we are analysing here, especially on some impacts of 'the Asian financial crisis' of the late 1990s.

Macro Level Explanation

At the macro level, authors try to explain this growing trend with reference to broad, sometimes global changes, some of which are specifically relevant for understanding Filipina migration to Hong Kong. In fact there is already an implicit (economic) push and pull theory in what appears to be a simple description above. This is often the case with migration, where the wider context is described in terms of the changes or developments in the receiving country that leave a gap that migrants might be able to fill. This is matched by a focus on the attractions of the receiving country for would-be migrants: the pull. Then researchers tend to move on to the sending country's wider conditions and developments there that might act as a push, an incentive to look elsewhere for a better quality of life, or something compelling people to move. The introduction above describes changes in richer countries whereby more women are going to work, leaving a gap in terms of who cares for the home and the children. As Ehrenreich and Hochschild (2003) note, women cannot rely on a male breadwinner to the same extent that they used to: in the US men's wages have declined and women often work to make up the shortfall. However, there are also cultural explanations for the increase in women working). The work women were providing in the home is not being covered instead by men or by public or social services, so women either have to do it as well as their job or they hire help. There is an expectation that 'real' women can manage it all; they can work, care for the children and the home, and look good too. This is revealed in TV images and magazines and in cultural expectations where women are praised highly for successfully balancing all these demands. It would reflect badly, Ehrenreich and Hochschild suggest, to have to admit to needing help, so there is often an attempt to deny the bought-in-help rather than celebrate it as a status symbol. As well as starting to explain why there are more migrant domestic workers in some parts of the world, this cultural shift also begins to help us understand the ways domestic workers are received and treated, their employment often hidden or denied.

Why should the demand for labour, to fill the roles left when women go to work, be filled by other women from poorer countries? To some extent they are pushed by poverty, and pulled by what Ehrenreich and Hochschild call the 'care deficit'. 'In Hong Kong, for instance, the wages of a Filipina domestic are about fifteen times the amount she could make as a school teacher back in the Philippines' (2003: 8). However, Ehrenreich and Hochschild suggest that we need to understand the relationship between the sending and receiving countries in an historical context and to understand this as a postcolonial relationship. While earlier phases of imperialism were about the exploitation of natural resources, 'Today, while still relying on Third World countries for agricultural and industrial labour, the wealthy countries also seek to extract something harder to measure and quantify, something that can look very much like love' (2003: 4). Nannies, maids and sex workers do not only do manual, but also emotional labour; they care for and attend their employer's loved ones.

Domestic labour migration is not only a benefit to the economies of the receiving countries; it can also be of great economic benefit for the sending countries and is often embraced as a tool for development. This is because women have proven (and indeed are expected) to be far more likely than men to send home regular remittances; some women send home almost all that they earn to their families. The impact for Third World countries can thus be profound enough for young women to be encouraged to go, and to stay away, and governments of sending countries (as we shall see below) establish agencies and training schemes to enable and support the migration. Poor countries are actually getting poorer; where they have turned to the International Monetary Fund (IMF) or the World Bank for loans they have often been forced to undertake measures of structural adjustment, which often devalues local currencies, undermines public services and social support, and has disastrous consequences for women and children especially (Ehrenreich and Hochschild, 2003). However, as we shall see below, it is not simply the case that the poorest move to wealthier countries. Other variables than economic ones intervene and interact with internal and external structures (with habits, norms, cultural expectations, desires, institutions and rules).

Why Philippines to Hong Kong?

'The Philippines is the country of emigration par excellence, with almost seven million of its citizens overseas' (Skeldon, 2004: 70). An increasing number of these emigrants are women; making up 12 per cent of labour emigrants in 1975, 47 per cent in 1987, and over 50 per cent by 1995 (footnote in Parreñas, 2003). In Hong Kong, increasing numbers of households began hiring foreign domestic helpers from the 1970s onwards, until by 1997, over six per cent of households in Hong Kong employed at least one, and many had more than one (Tam, 1999: 260). Indeed, foreign domestic helpers now make up approximately three per cent of Hong Kong's population, and almost half of these are from the Philippines (figures from Hong Kong statistics department, 2011).[4] They have 'become part of the social landscape' (Tam, 1999). Filipina (and more recently Indonesian and other nationality) migration is a very visible phenomenon in Hong Kong, especially evidenced in photographs for academic works on the topic (see Constable, 2007, and Lindio-McGovern, 2004). This is partly because the vast majority of these workers have Sundays as their only day off and having nowhere to go on that day (as their home is their workplace, and vice versa), they gather in public places, outdoors, in large numbers. Filipinas in Central District, Indonesians at Victoria Park in Causeway Bay, sit 'in clusters chatting, singing, praying, eating, talking on cell phones' (Constable, 2007: viii); they share stories and food, braid each other's hair, set up informal stalls selling numerous goods, and tell stories and show photographs from home (Tam, 1999). This is their significant community of practice, their home from home.

Employing a general, sociological, theory of how all of social life unfolds through the practice of daily life as a framework for migration (see Chapter 2), one of the first things it would be useful to know about this migration from the Philippines to Hong Kong is what are the conditions, the upper level external structures, framing the migration. The studies reviewed afford some details. Constable (2007) reviews historically the changes in the Philippines' government and economy. These background conditions, in some ways provided as 'push factor' explanations, are best understood using the conceptual lens of colonialism and, later, globalization (see Chapter 3). The Philippines has been subject to Spanish and then US rule until 1946, and more recently a subject of neo-colonialism as 'the United States established large military and naval bases there' (Constable, 2007: 31). Between 1952 and 1969, it managed to achieve some industrial growth, but this benefitted the former colonizers rather than leading to internal development. In more recent times, the country has been marked by a series of rebellions, internal conflicts, US interference (or influence), and finally martial law in 1972. During Ferdinand Marcos' regime, there was a period of foreign investment (notably tens of millions in military aid from the US, Constable, 2007: 31), but much of the capital that was generated left the country via transnational corporations. Constable describes a decline in industry from the 1950s, and a deteriorating economic situation during 1970s and 1980s, leading to a rising cost of living and rapid increase in unemployment, (see French, 1986 in Constable, 2007: 31). 'By the early 1980s, inflation had reached an average of 32 percent, and ... about two-thirds of the Philippine population lived below the poverty line' (Constable, 2007: 31).

A further structural force (possibly internalized into the national habitus) is the long history of temporary Philippine emigration; since the beginning of the twentieth century Filipinos have migrated for work abroad, for agricultural work in the US (especially Hawaii), in the US military, as sailors, and even a 'brain drain' of skilled workers in the 1960s. Using data from the International Organization for Migration, Constable tells us that by 2003 almost nine per cent of the population were living outside the country and more than half of these were working on temporary contracts. Working abroad for a short time has become a fact of life, a taken for granted aspect of (especially relatively young) people's lives in the Philippines (Constable, 2007: 32).

Nicole Constable (2007) tells us that the Filipino economy had suffered economic crisis for over two decades at the time she was writing, and the Philippine government has come to rely on the resources of its emigrants. Each applicant for overseas work has to pay the Philippine

Overseas Employment Administration a pre-departure fee (ibid: 21 and Lindio-McGovern, 2004: 223), and they send home valuable remittances in foreign currency. Parreñas (2003) says remittances from foreign workers, in 1999, reached seven billion dollars, and is easily the country's largest source of foreign currency. By 2003, remittances from overseas workers contributed about 10 per cent of the Philippine's GDP (IOM in Constable, 2007: 34). Emigrants, including female domestic workers, also relieve the high unemployment in the Philippines. The Marcos government's labour export policy, established in the 1970s as a temporary measure to relieve high unemployment and the 'balance of payments deficit', has become 'permanently temporary' (Constable, 2007: 33), partly as a result of ongoing pressures caused by global economic factors such as oil prices, interest rates, and, later, global recession. We begin to see that not only has the Philippines been struggling economically and is historically tied to other (exploiting) countries but also, over time, emigration has become established within the internal structures of Filipinos as an acceptable way to bolster their country's economy. It could even be seen as a patriotic thing to do.

Hong Kong Macro Level

Prior to its annexation by the British, Hong Kong was a sparsely populated island. It did not immediately become the bustling global centre for trade and commerce that it is more famous as now. It was first settled by a small number of European residents involved in shipping and trade, Chinese 'boat people' (fishermen) and a few Chinese farmers. Chinese immigrants looking for work also settled in the early stages of the colonial period. Living conditions were harsh and few European women migrated; the colonial settlers and their servants at that time tended to be male. In 1898 the 'New Territories' were signed over to the British, for 99 years. These territories included already long-settled Chinese farmers and some 'large and powerful lineages, whose households included concubines, slaves, indentured menials, and servants' (Watson in Constable, 2007: 23). Gradually living conditions improved and more women and children settled in Hong Kong (both Chinese and European). The population expanded. More pertinently, for the concerns of this chapter, it seems there has been a long history of domestic workers in Hong Kong, and as more women and children settled so these preferred female helpers. As economic conditions improved, men started to move out of service work into better paid jobs, leaving the lower paid service jobs for women. Female household workers were made up of young girls sold into servitude (*muijai*) at the beginning of the century, migrating women workers from other areas as time went by (and the hiring of *muijai* was opposed), and later still refugees from China. There is then a long historical tradition of the hiring of Chinese household workers. These earlier 'servants' were later to be remembered nostalgically, as we shall see below.

Colonialism and the shape it took are relevant. Hong Kong was able to establish itself first as a centre for shipping and trade and then manufacturing and export were able to grow, leading to a demand for labour, especially post World War II. Gradually women entered the workforce in greater numbers, especially in manufacturing, in garments, textiles, plastics, electronics and wig manufacture (Constable, 2007: 25). By the 1970s the service sector started to grow, and the demand for workers there replaced some fall in demand in manufacturing. The shift towards a service economy during the 1970s and 1980s led to more women going out to work and the demand for more help in the home increased. This was difficult to satisfy by bringing in extended families from China because space is at a premium in Hong Kong, and it became difficult to find Chinese workers as these now preferred better paid manufacturing and service work outside of the home, in better conditions. It is also important to note that domestic work was seen as servitude, as low-status work, so anyone who could avoid it would do so. Even where pay was better, Constable notes, this could not compensate for the stigma of domestic work. Chinese workers started to have other options and were not such grateful workers as employers would like (Constable, 2007: 28). Domestic work in Hong Kong is, thus, ambiguously perceived both as servitude and as a necessary, taken for granted, aspect of life, especially for dual worker households.

In a predominantly economistic analysis, Constable suggests that growing numbers of working men and women, combined with a growing and developing economy, leads to a shortage of domestic labour, and the need to look to other countries for the answer. 'At first English-speaking Filipinas were hired by European and Western expatriate families. English speakers were better suited to the needs of foreigners than Chinese speakers, and they were also much cheaper. Later, the practice of hiring Filipinas became popular among Chinese who spoke some English' (Constable, 2007: 29). By the 1970s, the practice was approved by the Hong Kong government (and so became a structural outcome). But right from the outset the imported workers had low-status, and employers felt, on the one hand, that the 'poor' foreign workers should be grateful for the work, while, on the other hand, they were resentful in that they were unable to hire Chinese workers, who, as we shall see later, became nostalgically remembered as superior workers (Constable, 2007). Here, then, we begin to gain some insight into the ways in which structural factors, such as economic change, become inscribed into practices (of hiring domestic workers), but the conjuncturally-specific internal structures at the time (the learning how to go on that led to hiring workers from abroad) are not entirely separate from the habitus that has inscribed in it the attitude that domestic workers are both servants and a normal part of daily life in the home.

Tam (1999) believes Hong Kong's economic success in recent decades is at least partly due to the increasing numbers of women going out to work, and therefore, by extension, to the policy and practice of hiring foreign domestic workers. There is relatively low formal provision for childcare – the Hong Kong government seems to assume the responsibility lies with the family – but there also seems to be low demand for it. Rather than the culture of using formal care that we might see in other countries, there seems to be a habitual use of employees in the home. Tam also uses other external factors and social changes to explain the growth in numbers hiring domestic workers. With a specific focus on childcare, she describes the move towards nuclear families that have had to move geographically in order to be near workplaces, and therefore decreasing reliance on grandparents and other relatives for care. But again, these are economic explanations that are better understood combined with cultural interpretations and an explanation of how structures are embodied and enacted by agents.

Skeldon's (1997) macro analysis also provides mostly economic background. The 'new core economies' of Japan, South Korea, Hong Kong, Taiwan and Singapore increasingly incorporated women into the workforce as the result of labour shortages as they rapidly developed and industrialized. Throughout the 1990s a new affluent middle-income group emerged, with their own demand for female domestic workers, especially in Hong Kong. The Asian crisis began in 1997 and a few countries, including Hong Kong, that had experienced some of the fastest economic growth started to go into rapid decline. From a previous average growth in GNP of over five per cent for the previous two decades, it suddenly went into recession. Hong Kong actually quickly recovered, but as a result of structural changes in the economy, poverty and unemployment did not recover so quickly and even slowly rose. You might expect a solution would be to export domestic workers, as they were no longer in such demand if there were rising numbers of people in search of jobs, but this did not happen to any great extent. In Hong Kong, foreign workers are a small proportion of the labour force as a whole (despite their high visibility in some areas), and, Skeldon suggests, the contribution they make by undertaking low-paid and undesirable work remains important to the economy. But, I suspect there may be more to this story than we are able to establish here. If domestic work is so stigmatized as servitude, it makes sense that individuals would not readily turn to it, even in times of economic downturn. Instead, it appears that the status of migrants may have been affected as a result of recession, poverty and unemployment, as foreign workers come to represent 'stolen jobs' (Skeldon, 2004: 70), even while they take on the jobs others feel ashamed to do.

An economic perspective, then, cannot fully explain why domestic workers remained in demand. A structuration analysis would draw some attention to the ground conditions of reception for migrants, to their communities of practice and conjuncturally-specific external structures (the rules, norms and practices of those around them), and to the habitualized practice of hiring workers in the home. We are left with little explanation from any of the authors reviewed here why it was the Philippines that ended up providing so many domestic workers for Hong Kong.

More Proximate External Structures

> Filipina domestic workers are a valuable source of income for hundreds of recruitment and placement agencies in the Philippines and in Hong Kong, an important source of labor for Hong Kong employers, and a crucial source of foreign capital for the Philippine government. It is therefore in the shared interest of agencies, employers, and governments on both sides of the China Sea that Filipinas continue to be docile workers.
>
> (Constable, 2007: 63)

It is probably also true to say that it is in the interest of agencies, employers and governments that the workers stay temporarily and change employers regularly. The agencies thus continue to reap the rewards of placement, governments continue to gain the cost of registering, and the Hong Kong government does not have to concern itself with issues related to offering permanent settlement. It has not been possible to fully establish the relevant policies providing opportunities and constraints for the migration of Filipina domestic workers to Hong Kong, or their settlement; I would need to look for this next to tell a better practice story. But there are a few important facts I have been able to glean from the works reviewed so far. There is a requirement in Hong Kong for employers to have a household income close to the median income. The contracts they permit are temporary, short-term, and closely regulated. Tam (1999) says visas permit the domestic worker to enter on two-year contracts only, with the work they are permitted to do restricted to household duties, for a single employer. The work contract and visa are renewable, but this depends on whether the employer wishes to renew. Tam notes that domestic workers are entitled, ostensibly, to the same employment rights as local workers but there are some concerns about whether their rights are being protected, given that renewal of the contract depends on the approval of the employer. In such a situation it is unlikely that a worker will complain, as without a contract she is not permitted to remain and so cannot look for other work. Domestic workers are expected to undergo medical examination and pregnancy tests both in the Philippines and in Hong Kong. Wages are low, Tam notes, and employers are able to keep them down even further by providing food and accommodation in the home. Tam says these workers are in a weak position also because this is women's work, in private households. It is difficult to monitor, and vulnerable to all sorts of abuses, and yet 'the general public in Hong Kong has not been empathetic to the needs and rights of the helpers who have contributed so much to the territory' (Tam, 1999: 271).

Habitus and Conjuncturally-specific Internal Structures

We can make some assumptions about the habitus of Filipina domestic workers by learning a bit about who they are from the authors reviewed here, especially from Constable (2003 and 2007). Ehrenreich and Hochschild say 'Many female migrants from the Philippines and Mexico, for example, have high school or college diplomas and have held middle-class – albeit low-paid – jobs back home' (2003: 10). Skeldon (1997) says domestic labour migrants in Hong Kong are fairly well educated (at least to secondary level) and most speak English. At the time his paper was written most were from 'Metro Manila' and a few were from rural areas. In 1997, they had an average of 2.7 children (Parreñas, 2003). Constable (2007) notes that domestic workers from the Philippines are not from the poorest sections of society (those cannot afford the costs). They may well be better educated than their employers, they often emigrate for economic reasons *combined* with a desire for travel, experience and self-improvement.

> The 'typical' Filipina domestic worker is in her late twenties or early thirties and unmarried. She supports several family members in the Philippines and her primary stated reason for going to Hong Kong is economic, although a desire for pleasure, adventure, and independence may also be factors. She is most likely Roman Catholic, has at least a high school education, and speaks English, as well as her national and regional dialect. She may have been an office worker or a professional in the Philippines, or she may have been unemployed. About one in three Filipina domestic workers is married, and they typically leave two or three children behind to be cared for by relatives in the Philippines.
> (Constable, 2007: 69)

Constable is not able to go into much detail about the decisions made by women on leaving the Philippines, but she does recount the stories of two migrants as an illustration of general themes. Belle and Elsa were sisters from a semi-rural area near Manila, both in their mid to late thirties when she interviewed them in 1993. Elsa, who left the Philippines when she was twenty-three years old, had previously worked as a domestic helper and in an electronics factory. Her father encouraged her to migrate to help pay the college fees for her younger sisters. She accepted this 'opportunity' with apparent good grace and willingness, fully aware she could earn more than her father, and she remembered how hard both her parents had worked when she was young. Her migration provided something of a dream for herself and her siblings, a dream of having something more than the poverty they had lived in as children. Belle joined her sister in Hong Kong three years later, and over the years they have been able to contribute towards university education for two younger sisters, and high school for their brother. The family has since bought a small plot of land where they raise pigs, chickens and geese, and grow fruit trees (Constable, 2007: 21). However, one university-educated sister has also become a domestic labour migrant in Italy as she was able to earn far more there than she could at home. This gives us an insight into the expectations, the taken for granted nature of migration, and the culturally-embedded desires associated with migration from the Philippines. These may be individuals who are moving but you get the sense they make their decisions as part of a wider family circle that remains central in their lives.

We know from the discussion above that migration from the Philippines has become a normal practice and is, to an extent, driven by poverty. This is likely to have become inscribed into the habitus, a taken for granted response to various needs on the ground. There is likely to be a dominant ideology within which women are expected to leave to seek work elsewhere for the benefit not only of themselves and their families, but also the entire country. Implying some normalization of the practice, Parreñas (2003) recognizes the way in which the Philippines has become dependent on the remittances of migrant domestic workers, and says the practice is thus unlikely to be abandoned. Ehrenreich and Hochschild grant domestic labour migrants some agency in the migration decision when they acknowledge that women take other things into consideration than just economic factors: 'a woman may escape the expectation that she care for elderly family members, relinquish her paycheck to a husband or father, or defer to an abusive husband. Migration may be a practical response to a failed marriage and the need to provide for children without male help' (Ehrenreich and Hochschild, 2003: 11). In other words, external structural constraints and opportunities coincide with more proximate structural constraints framing the other things she may wish to do with her life, her desires and projections. This would be something of which she was made aware or conscious of within communities of practice where migration is already seen as a sensible and acceptable option.

These women are not migrating permanently (at least not ostensibly). They are workers rather than migrants, and many of the theories that try to explain types of integration become irrelevant. Many end up semi-permanent, but remain on the margins because they were never expected to be permanent migrants. Policies in Hong Kong enable their temporary stays but disable any settlement and as a result they migrate with (at least ostensibly) an intention to return. They leave behind families including partners and children, much like the early male pioneers discussed briefly in Chapter 3, but in this case there is little expectation that their family will eventually join them. Family reunification will only occur when the emigrant returns, and her income from abroad is forfeited.

Conjuncturally-specific External Structures and Communities of Practice

There is quite a lot of information in Constable's book for us to be able to tease out the conjuncturally-specific external structures for would-be domestic workers in the Philippines, as they go through the process of applying and being placed in employment. One of the first communities of practice within which domestic workers learn to go on, and adjust their habitus, is the employment agency. Through the employment process they learn to be submissive workers, and over time this becomes inscribed into the domestic worker's habitus, in turn shaping the communities of practice of domestic workers in Hong Kong. Although, in the early stages of this migration trend, domestic workers made their own arrangements through personal contacts, in 1994, the Philippine Overseas Employment Agency effectively banned private hiring. Now the majority are recruited and placed through agencies (Tam, 1999). Applicants pay fees on registering with an agency, and so do employers. Applicants who are not hired quickly (within a few months) are encouraged to withdraw and reapply, thus running up further costs. This is a lucrative business that relies on constant turnover.

Agencies, Constable (2007) tells us, work to mould their recruits into 'obedient domestic workers', the type of 'product' or 'commodity' they assume their clients seek. The notion that this is what they seek is linked to ideas about Chinese servants as superior, discussed later (see Constable, 2007 and Chapter 3). The task of an agency is to prepare their 'product' for the market; in the Philippines, agencies work hard to produce 'a hardworking, submissive, and obedient domestic helper' (Constable, 2007: 69). But a potential domestic worker also learns from her experience of trying to obtain a position, and from others she knows, and from the way the recruitment process works. Her conjuncturally-specific internal structures include knowledge that what are required are submissiveness, obedience, willingness, and an able and placid nature. In other words, women learn to become the product that is required. Women are more likely to get a position if they are well educated and speak good English, but it becomes clear in the recruitment process that they are not required to be independent thinkers. In building their file and in interviews they are asked about their educational background and work experience, but also in as much detail (or more) they are tested for their personal circumstances, tastes, interests, and attitudes. Recruitment agencies expect deference, and friends and relatives who have been through the process themselves pass on their experiences to new applicants. These often say they are just 'playing along', for example by saying they would always defer to their employers in matters of debate or discussion, but, Constable notes, they also begin to internalize the sense of inferiority they have to portray, and so conjuncturally-specific internal structures gradually become part of the habitus. They are encouraged to be tolerant of their employer's ways, to be polite at all times, and even to avoid crying as this brings bad luck to employers! (Constable, 2003: 119).

Families and friends and the wider Philippine community will also have their bearing on the women's decisions to go, and stay. It is clear that people encourage this migration when you hear, for example, that family members and friends will happily write references for (sometimes imaginary or greatly exaggerated) prior domestic work experience. Agencies like women to have had some prior experience, so women often draw on any informal experiences and make these appear to have been formal arrangements. Women also learn to lie about their age, marital status, and whether or not they have children. This will have future implications for their relationships with the families they live with; if they have been untruthful at the application stage then they cannot risk getting too close or familiar with their employer later. Constable has a very interesting section on how recruitment of Filipina workers involves 'certain forms of body discipline' (2007: 74). This could benefit from a structuration analysis of the embodiment of conjuncturally-specific internal structures. Applicants are photographed, perhaps in hired uniforms, for the files and web sites on which they will be advertised; they are encouraged to cut their hair and fingernails, to remove excessive make-up and jewellery, perhaps even to lose some weight. They are encouraged to present themselves as clean and tidy, but not flamboyant (or sexy). They are expected not to be too dark-skinned, as Hong Kong employers are thought not to like this, nor too attractive, and their conformity is ensured by the stories that circulate about women 'whose contracts were abruptly terminated at the airport' because they were too dark or too beautiful (Constable, 2007: 75). They are expected to be healthy and strong. Domestic workers thus learn to present themselves in given ways; they modify their dress, their bodies, and even their habits in order to appear to be the ideal domestic worker. Thus conjuncturally-specific internal structures become habitualized and internalized. Women also pay substantial amounts of money to agencies, sometimes pay their own travel expenses and other costs, and often go into debt in order to secure a job. They thus learn, very early on, that they are investing in themselves and should consider themselves fortunate to have this opportunity. They are often, literally, indebted to others, with all the meanings of that term.

Households hiring domestic workers tend to be quite large and can include both children and elderly family members. Employers tend to earn close to or above the average income. Most employers hire their domestic workers for a combination of duties, including cooking, cleaning and childcare, and most prefer their employees to live in the family home with them (Constable, 2007: 64). This makes them more readily available at different times of the day and night. The system that has become established encourages employers to view the worker as a commodity. Agencies are often located in smart buildings, and workers can be selected from glossy files with photographs or video clips, or their files and images can all be viewed online at the employer's leisure. There are blatant attempts to advertise their 'products' as superior to those of others, and by this they mean better trained or more obedient. Workers who are fresh from the Philippines are often considered more desirable than those who have been in Hong Kong for a while and finished one or more previous contract. This is because established migrants may have learned the ropes better, may have learned what rights they have, may have made friends and gained some independence. All these things you would think would make these better to employ as they will be happier and more settled, but agencies seem to assume that employers prefer naïve, submissive, manipulable employees.

Tam's (1999) study revealed that ideally employers would use their relatives for childcare, and that in spite of the practice of using foreign domestic workers, most did not list that as the best solution. This suggests that parents, at least, begin by being somewhat dissatisfied with the arrangement. In fact, half of the women she interviewed said they had no other choice but to hire a migrant worker. Interviews also revealed that employers felt that hiring a paid worker might enable them to have more say and control over the raising of the children. Here we have a situation where workers are hired somewhat grudgingly, where the employers want to remain in control. The respondents' reasons for not choosing a crèche or nursery are also revealing. They feel the children may not get such close and immediate attention. They clearly want their employee to build a strong, loving relationship with the children, without becoming so committed that they start to have some influence. Interviewees also felt foreign domestic workers were an advantage over a crèche as they could also contribute to the housework, and could care for the children in the home, allowing the parents to be able to see the children regularly and for longer. On the other hand, they also expressed concerns over how to trust that you have hired the right person.

Employers also learn what to expect of domestic workers, especially through the agencies and the files that are presented. The recruitment process teaches employers that the workers may be grateful to them. Constable tells a story of one employer who was discouraged from paying the (legally required) travel expenses for her employee, telling her 'You don't have to worry. You are the all time favourite type of employer for these Filipina maids' (2007: 78). This illustrates to the employer that 'a worker is expected to make economic sacrifices to get a job' (ibid: 79). Employee files discuss the appearance of the applicants, whether or not she is likely to work hard, noting where an applicant is poor and therefore needs money, and so is likely to be an acquiescent worker. These files discuss products not people. They teach employers to expect subservience, hard work, a grateful employee, and even that they are doing workers a favour. Files say things like 'she is badly in need of work because her husband is jobless' or 'she is rather dark, but quick to respond for her age' (Constable, 2007: 80).

Interestingly, Western employers are more likely to seek better educated employees, especially those who speak good English and can help educate their children. They are comfortable in the tradition of hiring a 'professional' worker. But Chinese employers have a 'cultural tradition of segregated and hierarchical servant-master relations'. There is an assumption on the part of employers' associations and agencies that it is better to hire workers who 'know their place' (Constable, 2007: 82). Both employers and employees thus learn (and critically internalize) that domestic workers should accept the superiority of the employer.

Finally, Hong Kong Chinese employers often invoke a nostalgic memory of the 'superior' Cantonese domestic servant, contrasting this golden age with the current situation and its 'inferior' foreign domestic helpers. This ideology of the ideal servant revealed itself to Constable in complaints and grumbles from employers in conversation as well as in various outlets of the mass media. It is not a faithful representation of the past, where early domestic workers included menservants, very young (exploited and abused) women, and a whole range of household workers with varied duties. But these seem all to be remembered nostalgically and to be unified into a single image of the servant that did her job well and 'knew her place' (Constable, 2007: 44). 'For Hong Kong's upper and middle classes, the Chinese amah has become the symbol of an idealized past in which power, status, and class differences were unquestioned' (ibid: 62). As Rob Stones (2005) notes, such ideologies are enacted through internal structures constraining behaviour and are conjuncturally-specific external structures for the workers, used to control and dominate them.

Domestic Labour Migrants' Daily Practice

'Despite the high demand for and important contributions of foreign domestic workers, and despite the fact that most Hong Kong employers have continued to prefer them to other foreign workers, Filipinas have long been a target of criticism' (Constable, 2007: 37). Hong Kong residents like to think people in the Philippines live in extreme poverty and are therefore being rescued by the Hong Kong economy (Constable, 2007: 32). They criticize their domestic workers for lack of servitude and respect (ibid: 28–30). They are generally grumbled about as not being as good as Chinese servants of the past (see above). Constable tells the story of what became known as the battle for Chater Road, in which there was a media backlash against the use of public spaces by Filipinas. Between the mid 1980s and early 1990s, as the numbers of Filipinas rose, and they became increasingly visible, complaints about them arose in the editorials and letters pages of the local media. Local newspapers started to grumble about areas being 'overrun' or 'taken over' by 'guest workers' who have no right to commandeer parts of the city for their own purposes. Eventually HongKong Land, a leading landlord in the Central District, which had become a popular spot for weekend gatherings of domestic workers, submitted to the District Council an 18 page report summarizing local tenants' complaints about the effect that noise, litter, nuisance, and general degradation were having on the tone of the area. They even proposed that underground car parks might be 'offered as gathering places for domestic workers' (ibid: 7), as a way of moving the phenomenon out of sight. However, these comments and suggestions were criticized via other media, especially from Western expatriates, as racist, inhuman, and degrading or insulting. It is not clear how the battle ended; it appears to have simply fizzled out. But it is instructive in revealing the mixed attitudes of the host society towards the Filipina migrants, and provides some context within which we can begin to understand the conjuncturally-specific internal structures of the domestic workers. It is certain that the workers will internalize these views of themselves.

Employers are anxious that the foreign domestic workers cannot be trusted, and as Tam (1999) notes, stories circulate among employees about untrustworthy, dishonest, deceitful workers. This leads to employers using all sorts of techniques to keep an eye on the workers. Tam describes employers calling home several times a day, or popping back home unexpectedly to check on the worker, or sending grandparents around several times a week to make sure she is not stealing or shirking, or harming the children. This is in spite, Tam says, of the fact that most reported misdemeanours were actually very trivial and included laziness or the stealing of food. Some mothers said they wanted the workers to do their job well, but not to 'overshadow them'. But also, in Tam's study, women spoke warmly of their foreign domestic workers, and most were satisfied with their work.

From the perspective of the employee, the domestic worker is aware that she is not trusted, is expected to be like a mother to the children, but not too close. She is sometimes expected to do everything in the home, but her pay and temporary contract, and the public debates, reveal that she is not highly regarded. Beyond the learning that takes place within and through the agencies, the domestic worker also learns her place in the home, as she is subjected to various rules and deprivations. It is quite common for employers to have lists of rules that might include such as things as asking permission to use the phone, having set times for personal care like showering, and what time to go to bed and get up. Constable (2003) says these firmly establish the inferiority of the worker and can infantilize someone who may well be older and better educated than her employer (which may explain why they feel the need to do it). Rules stipulate dress, and make-up, attitude, and even what to do in spare time (if there is any). Various warnings are given to workers if they break rules, including threats to reduce benefits, withhold wages, and to terminate the contract. Many threats actually contradict government policy but the domestic workers either do not realize this or are powerless to do anything about it. Contracts last for two years, and can be terminated by either side with a month's notice, but if a worker's contract is terminated she has to return to the Philippines if she does not arrange a new contract within two weeks. This leaves her likely to accept levels of abuse that she might not wish to, or terms of employment that are less than satisfactory, because a return to the Philippines is expensive and usually involves going through the whole hiring process (and expense) all over again. And having one's contract ended (even when it was because the employee objected to physical abuse) is unlikely to lead to good references for subsequent employment. When family at home are dependent on her remittances a domestic worker is unlikely to risk her situation easily.

Domestic workers in Hong Kong spend regular amounts of time in each other's company. One of their communities of practice consists of meeting with other migrant workers, usually on Sundays (as above). There are also a growing number of agencies and groups; religion and religious communities are important in the lives of many; and some are getting involved in activism to defend or fight for their rights. But a lot of the time they spend together is spent on teaching each other how to go on in the new circumstances. Recruitment and placement activities continue in Hong Kong, since contracts are so short, and amongst themselves migrant workers tell each other the correct answers to recruitment agents' and employers' questions. Migrants teach each other to be subservient, to at least pretend to not smoke, to eat anything they are given, to never argue with their employer, and so on. Furthermore, 'the Filipino and other

domestic worker communities often encourage women to tolerate diffi-
culties for the sake of their families, to change themselves rather than the
system, and to discipline themselves for the sake of national pride' (Constable, 2007: 182). Foreign domestic workers described to Lindio-McGovern
(2004) how they missed their own families and their own children. They
described the pain of leaving, and said they would prefer to have stayed
at home. But Constable's stories portray women who hide these feelings,
who are secretive about their communications with family back home (perhaps because they have not admitted to their employers the full extent
of their commitments and ties). They internalize the external structures
outlined above; they take for granted that people in the Philippines are
dependent on them securing and keeping the work that makes them so
lonely. In turn their actions consolidate the structural constraints: as time
has gone on, the Philippine government has been able to take for granted
this income from its emigrants, and Lindio-McGovern notes they have
not created the jobs there that would remove the necessity for so many
to leave.

As Time Passes

The emigration of women and mothers to Hong Kong and other destinations has now led to its own care gap in the Philippines. Mothers who
leave their children are now being vilified in the press. Parreñas (2003) says
there is a dominant gender ideology in the Philippines in which, despite
the fact that the economy benefits so much from this migration, a woman's
place remains in the home. There have been (half-hearted and rather unsuccessful) initiatives on the part of the Philippine government to try to keep
mothers at home, and vehement debates in the media about the negative
effects on the children that are left behind. Sensationalist reports describe
abandoned families, children who get involved in drugs and gangs and
crime, and even a high incidence of incest and rape where there is an absent
mother. There are no equivalent moral panics about absent fathers working abroad. Nevertheless, the Philippines has grown dependent on their
income. New potential migrants, leaving for domestic work in more recent
years, must internalize these changes, and so must the children of migrants,
who say they will not do the same.

The effects of the migration on the migrant and on their families can be
dramatic. These are often married women and mothers of children who
now have to be cared for by someone else. Migrants also leave behind the
women's work they would have done and these roles need to be filled by
someone else. There is some evidence that they are rarely filled by men. The
migrants thus retain a sense of responsibility and guilt for having left and

a need to make it a success. Lindio-McGovern (2004) describes the ways in which migrant mothers learn to cope, or develop conjuncturally-specific internal structures. She talks of the way mothers treat their employers' children as if they were their own, in an attempt to replace the emotional bond, and the extreme effort they put in to keeping in touch with their natural family in the Philippines. Visits home are quite rare because they are so expensive and because migrants get few holidays. Instead they buy mobile phones in order to make regular contact, sometimes needing to do this out of the earshot of their employers (some do not like them owning phones), they exchange letters, communicate on social network websites when they can, and send home their wages.

Finally, there are the changes in Hong Kong to consider. Constable (2007) demonstrates how domestic workers have become a little more activist over time, and are somewhat more clear about their rights, and have more institutions to turn to in times of difficulty. But, Constable also tells tragic stories of exploitation, abuse, depredation, poverty, and intimidation of domestic workers in Hong Kong. The structural position of these workers is such that they have very little power to change things, and, worse, they come to embody, enact and reproduce their low-status position. Despite small changes, still the daily conditions seem not to have changed very much. Constable analyses the situation of Filipinas in Hong Kong using the concepts of power, discipline, resistance and accommodation. This involves analysing, in critical depth, the historically changing structures of power. For her, domestic workers learn to embody their position and they pass on what they have learned to others; they thus both choose and are coerced. Her analyses work very well with a theory of practice, and as a result she has provided us with some highly relevant empirical data.

Conclusion

In this chapter we have heard that, although migrations in the past have included women (some of whom migrated independently), migration has typically been characterized as a male phenomenon. However, female migration has been on the increase in recent decades. Specific migration flows are especially marked by feminization, flows from southern to northern, poorer to richer countries (often following prior colonial routes) for work in low-paid, low-skilled jobs formerly undertaken by women: domestic, service, entertainment, and sex work. This chapter has specifically begun to frame Filipina domestic labour migration to Hong Kong in the context of a theory of practice. The studies reviewed have been able to describe changing economic conditions in both the Philippines and in Hong Kong that have led to a series of conditions we might see as providing the pull and the push of this migration. However, the history of the migration trend (and the description of wider economic structures) has also enabled us to begin to understand the role of cultural change, and of the embodiment and internalization of practices. As increasing numbers of Filipinos have emigrated so the country has learnt to enjoy and benefit from the remittances they send. We can assume (but need to examine further) that emigration has also become something of an expectation and a normal way of life for Filipinos. Labour migration, for the benefit of wider society, has perhaps become part of the habitus. Meanwhile, the history of the settlement and developing economy of Hong Kong reveals a long-established tradition of hiring domestic workers, and of these being viewed as low-status while granting status to the hirer. This is not the hidden domestic labour described by Ehrenreich and Hochschild. In Hong Kong, the hiring of domestic labour has become a cultural norm, inscribed in the habitus.

In terms of proximate external structures constraining and providing opportunities for migration and settlement, it becomes clear that the Hong Kong government views the migration as temporary and perhaps cyclical. Workers have limited contracts and limited rights, thus their ongoing situation depends very much on the nature of the relationship with their employer. Before they leave the Philippines, however, women have learned within the employment agencies, as part of the recruitment process, that some aspects of their background are more relevant than others. They have learned to present themselves as docile workers. To some extent, these conjuncturally-specific internal structures become embodied and internalized into the habitus, combined with an expectation to be a successful migrant for the good of the family. Prior education, independence, strength of character cannot be extracted from the habitus of an educated young woman, but she can learn these are not relevant in the new circumstances and inevitably, over time, she will alter how she sees herself; her practices, expectations, habits, dress, and tastes will be modified to suit her new circumstances. Later, she will bring this modified habitus to her communities of practice, to her meetings and socialization with other domestic workers, in turn teaching them how to go on.

We have also seen how the employment agency plays a crucial role as a community of practice within which employers learn to expect employees to be grateful, submissive and naive. The attitudes, norms, practices, and rules of the agents are conjuncturally-specific external structures for the employer. Now, with the employer as the agent in focus, we can also begin to see that they too bring expectations, hopes and desires to the situation, hoping the domestic worker with childcare responsibilities can provide nurturing and care without being too independent. Employers seek ways of coping with the fact that their employee could well be an educated and strong-willed young woman with a family of her own. They have to negotiate their demands for a committed and caring worker and the structural constraints of short-term contracts.

Foreign domestic workers, on the other hand, suppress their habitus and learn how to go on, teaching others in their own communities of practice how to be the right kind of employee, in order to secure a contract, send home money to the family, and thus be good Filipinas. As time passes, the Philippines (culture and government, economy and society) has come to take domestic labour migration as a fact of life, even as mothers who leave their children are vilified by an ideological perspective that argues a woman's place is in the home. The solution to high unemployment and low industry has been found. Meanwhile, in Hong Kong, the search for the perfect subservient domestic worker continues and migrants from Indonesia and Sri Lanka are increasingly recruited.

7

Refugees and Forced Migration: Refugee Children in the United Kingdom

What is Forced Migration?

Forced migration includes refugees, asylum seekers, internal displacement, trafficking, development-induced displacement, and exile (Castles, 2003b). Individuals and groups can be forced to move, among other reasons, 'due to persecution, to flee war, to escape famine, or because of a major development project' (www.iasfm.org); they can be displaced by natural, environmental, chemical, or nuclear disaster (Rutter, 2006: 24). Forced migration includes exiles, slaves, and mass expulsions (Richmond, 1993). But forced migration is not a migration flow separate from all other types of migration; the types overlap. Forced migrants may be mobile (moving back and forth), they may be transnational, they may or may not settle (or assimilate to varying degrees), they may also be labour migrants, and there may well have been an element of choice and lifestyle aspiration in their move. According to Rutter, it wasn't until the 1970s that researchers began to distinguish between voluntary and forced migration, and it is not always a useful distinction because to some extent it denies agency to forced migrants. However, to avoid using the term perhaps gives too much space for agency where there is little. The choice of language and labels is often, at least implicitly, a political one. Initially, the main focus of migration research was turned towards labour migration, but there is now much more academic and policy attention given to understanding refugees, asylum seekers, and forced migration more broadly conceived.

Forced migration is not a central topic in migration studies, but a literature search will uncover a range of studies in diverse disciplines, scattered across a range of journals that address issues such as identities, ethnicity, policies, citizenship, nation, and gender. *The Journal of Refugee Studies* and *Forced Migration Review* are excellent resources. The International Association of Forced Migration (IASFM, www.iasfm.org), an independent, self-governing community of scholars and practitioners who are concerned about understanding forced migration was established in 1998 and has a broad membership of academics, practitioners and decision-makers. Their work is sponsored by numerous research institutes and organizations, including the Institute for the Study of International Migration (Georgetown University, Washington DC, USA), The Centre for Refugee Studies (York University, Canada), and the Refugees Studies Centre (Oxford University, UK). For this group, forced migration is about displacement of peoples within and across borders. There are now many academic journals, conferences, associations and organizations dedicated to the study and understanding of forced migration, especially in the context of policy responses.[1]

From the sixteenth century onwards migration has grown to become a mass phenomenon, with some invited, some in search of new wealth, but also some persecuted and expelled (Marfleet, 2006). Many early transatlantic migrations, for example, that were ostensibly in search of new wealth or escape, were actually the result of compulsion. Who is a refugee and who is displaced gets lost in the way that stories are told, and by whom. Marfleet gives the example of French settlers in colonial Nigeria, where migrants were mobilized to populate the new colony, many of whom were poor and lacked much in the way of choice. But the issue of forced migration has become increasingly pertinent since the end of the Cold War, and it is increasingly being viewed as a global phenomenon. However, many responses are necessarily local, with forced migration becoming a major theme of political debate in recent decades (Castles, 2003a). Figures from UNHCR describe a rapid increase with a peak of 27 million in the 1990s, and subsequent decline to around 10 million in 2003 (Marfleet, 2006: 14). However, as Castles (2003b) notes, this includes only those refugees defined as such under the 1951 UN Refugee Convention (discussed below). Other estimates can be four times this figure, with internal displacement especially on the rise (O'Neill, 2010). For Marfleet, increasing numbers of refugees worldwide has led to increasing levels of hostility; from the late 1980s onwards 'deserving refugees' became labelled 'illegal aliens' then a 'menace to society'.

The Studies

As with previous chapters, in this chapter I summarize and review a selection of the work in the field that, combined, can begin to tell a practice story about refugees in Britain, with a special focus on refugee children.

I therefore seek to understand the external structures that constrain and enable the migration, to learn something about the habitus of the migrants, to gain some insight into the conjuncturally-specific internal structures that develop as migrants learn how to go on in their new setting, to come to know the communities of practice and conjuncturally-specific external structures that are relevant to their daily practices, and consider the external and internal structural outcomes of these processes. As with other chapters, substantive migration theories also have a role to play in illuminating specific processes. Four studies have been selected for this chapter: Marfleet (2006) and Rutter (2006), and to a lesser extent Castles (2003b) and Bloch (2002). Philip Marfleet's book, *Refugees in a Global Era*, provides a critical analysis of global, historical and contemporary patterns of forced migration.[2] This is a study of very broad scope, examining general changes and conditions that give rise to forced migration, and the opportunities, policies, ideologies and cultural schemas that frame the reception of refugees in a variety of contexts. Stephen Castles' (2003b) seminal paper in a special issue of *Sociology* dedicated to global refugees, proposes a sociology of forced migration. This is a mainly theoretical piece arguing for an approach that treats forced migration as a specific field that should be examined in the context of global social transformations. Castles contends that refugees have been studied narrowly, in specific contexts, usually within the framework of a methodological nationalism. For Castles, refugees and asylum seekers are forms of forced migration, along with exile and trafficking. Alice Bloch's (2002) book, *The Migration and Settlement of Refugees in Britain*, examines the social and economic settlement of refugees in Britain based on survey research conducted in the London Borough of Newham, with a sample of 180 refugees from Somalia, Sri Lanka and the Democratic Republic of Congo (DRC). Bloch also examines the history of migration to Britain and relevant UK and EU policies, as well as theories of migration and settlement. Jill Rutter's book, *Refugee Children in the UK*, alternatively, is even more focussed and specific: motivated by concerns about negative experiences and a 'failure to make progress', she examines the experiences of refugee children in British secondary schools.

Broad-brush Approaches

It seems it is impossible not to separate the migration and settlement parts of the story, at least to some extent; and migration or movement tend to be examined much more broadly or generally, in terms of an event, whereas settlement is a more local and particular process (see Chapter 3). Both Castles (2003) and Marfleet (2006) examine the causes of forced migration using studies of broad scope. Their analyses demonstrate the world systems theory, the social transformations perspective and the transnationalism and globalization perspectives outlined in Chapter 3. Castles' argument fits well with a structuration perspective, or a theory of practice (see Chapter 2). He says forced migration, like all other types, demands a perspective that looks at the role of human agency and social networks, family, friends, intermediaries, and agents. However, here he especially wishes to draw attention to the fact that forced migration is linked to wider processes of global social change, and especially to globalization: 'First, globalization is not a system of equitable participation in a fairly-structured global economy, society and polity, but rather a system of selective inclusion and exclusion of specific areas and groups, which maintains and exacerbates inequality' (2003: 16). Increasing inequalities, especially between the global North and South, lead to exclusion, conflict and flight, the latter of which is not easy to distinguish from economic migration. But, he insists, it is crucial for bureaucracies to understand the human rights as well as the economic motivations for migrations if they are to design effective and fair policies and responses. Castles thus argues the concept of forced migration draws attention to the structural dynamics involved in this kind of migration, whereas exile and displacement seem to put too much emphasis on subjective and cultural aspects (2003: 21). His contribution to the wider context is a necessarily brief discussion of some wider social transformations. Social transformations in the South that led to forced migration – decolonization, internal wars, violence, ethnic conflict, the development of new states, and so on – cannot be understood without recognition of the prior and continuing links to Northern economic interests, to global political and economic networks, and seem to involve the imposition of Northern value systems (ibid: 19). Changes in the North, including economic deindustrialization, privatization and deregulation, have impacts for who might choose to migrate where. Forced migration, in turn, leads to social transformations in the form of transnational networks, diversity, multiculturalism and the reception of incomers. Meanwhile, intermediate countries (to use Castles' term), such as South Korea, Taiwan, Singapore, Hong Kong, Malaysia, Thailand, and some parts of Latin America are fast growing, modernizing and expanding, but are also involved in trafficking and ethnic conflict.

Individual studies of discrete groups, Castles contends, should always be informed by broader studies, by locating empirical research in the wider context of 'global social, political and economic structures and relationships – and vice versa' (2003: 22, and see Castles, 2010). He sees this in terms of a division of labour rather than every study being able to achieve all things. Studies of localized migration processes should understand the wider context, while broad-brush studies should be based in local research. Forced migration, then, should be studied as part of a wider, inter-disciplinary project with a global and transnational focus. Castles is not simply saying we need close, micro studies, and analyses of the broader context to be brought together to inform each other. He goes further arguing: 'The micro- and macro-levels have to be linked through an analysis of the complex processes that mediate between them' (ibid: 22). But he does not elaborate how this should be achieved. Castles himself locates forced migration in a wider structural and historical perspective, arguing that without understanding the various big events and changes or development we cannot understand what is happening on the ground today at the smaller scale, but he fails to discuss how the micro and macro fit together through the meso level. This is exactly what the present book is aiming to provide with a theory of practice.

Marfleet's book is also very general. We can learn from this about the wider structures framing forced migration today. This is a world systems approach and is more overtly critical of globalization. It actually complements the work of Castles, contributing a more sophisticated and critical perspective. Marfleet also uses the concept of globalization but is keen to emphasize how globalization is seen uncritically as a good thing, when in fact, dominated now by neoliberal policies and neoliberal international relations, he says, it leads to widespread inequalities. Globalization is actually a structural condition: a condition of uneven development, powerful relationships of inequality, and the intensification of global differences (2006: 36). With regards to contemporary discussions about increasingly open borders (see Chapter 3), he agrees things have changed to an extent, but contends that states remain strong. 'The global pattern is one in which states and supra-national movements of capital are accommodated by the world system' (2006: 39).

Marfleet (2006) critically examines the long history of colonial rule and its legacies, sweeping developments in world politics and economy, and the role of the International Monetary Fund (IMF) and the World Bank, while drawing on concepts of trade liberalization and privatization as ideologies driving policies and practices. For Marfleet, the role of super powers is paramount; refugee movements are often legacies of colonialism, the Cold War merely having 'an impact on many conflicts' rather than to 'precipitate them' (2006: 40). The end of the Cold War led to struggles for power, but changes in the world economy led to new pressures on weak states. Many causes of displacement, even what he terms 'new wars' have their 'roots in movements for independence from the colonial powers' (ibid: 41). New conflicts are therefore not new. Colonialism often took the shape of divide and rule, so when left to their own devices old antagonisms broke out (ibid: 41–2). For Marfleet, while we may wish to examine specific migration flows, or individual refugee's motivations, each crisis of displacement has its own distinctive features. Many recent crises, however, share certain characteristics, of which the most important is the imposition and re-imposition of neo-liberal reforms ... unrelenting pressure from the IMF, the World Bank, and creditor states and institutions has been a key factor in the mass production of refugees.

(Marfleet, 2006: 48)

Marfleet (2006) offers some analysis of developments in Somalia as an example. This will become more relevant to this chapter later. The collapse of the Somali state in the early 1990s, he argues, has been explained away with reference to local politics and culture. In fact, this is a story of colonialism and unequal location in the global nexus. Somalia has been subject to Italian, French and British rule with intense competition, the imposition of new power structures (that cut across or undermined traditional ones), and little attention to its economic health. Independence brought tensions and violence between traditional clan groups and political elites, war with Ethiopia, and interference from superpowers with their own agendas in the form of arms and aid. The IMF and World Bank introduced conditions on loans, and austerity programmes, that led to rapid decline, exacerbated by rapidly changing dependences of export and trade. Somalia had been able to benefit, under the Barre regime, from its strategic location during the Cold war but this came to an end, leaving the weaknesses of the regime exposed, and leading to conflict with rival groups, and rapid economic decline. Eventually the state collapsed amidst fighting, famine, political vacuum, and massive flight of refugees and internal displacement.

In 1995 the UNHCR (1995: 251) estimated that there were at least 535,000 Somali refugees; in 1997 the UN estimated that there were still some 1.2 million people internally displaced.

(Global IDP Survey, 1998: 84; see Marfleet, 2006: 50)

Policies and Ideological Responses

All of the above gives us a very broad-brush description of upper structural layers framing forced migration broadly conceived, and some of the more proximate layers relevant to Somalian refugees. Practice theory wants to understand what are the structural layers for a given agent or group of agents in the context of a given explanandum. This is not to say the above is not useful; it is indeed useful given that no one academic could possible achieve all this analysis plus undertake a close local study over time. But the practice story I wish to tell needs to tease out from the above, and other such broad studies, what might be relevant in terms of upper structural layers and more proximate social surroundings for the given problem at hand, as will be discussed more below.

Marfleet is also very useful for an analysis of the perspectives of the host societies and how they reached certain ideological and policy responses. These can be seen as more proximate social structures, embodied and enacted by agents within the conjuncturally-specific external structures and networks of refugees in Britain today. Over time there have been changing forms of refugees, different displacements, different regions, and changing and developing policies. I offer here a very quick summary of policies and changes in relation to Europe, as an almost arbitrary example but the one likely to be most relevant to this chapter as we proceed. We begin with a period, pre-capitalism, in which immigration is generally viewed as an asset. Then the nineteenth century witnessed massive migrations *out of* Europe and all around the globe, and, as noted before, some of these could be viewed as forced migrants since many were poor and desperate. Later, war in Europe led to recruitment, first of fighters, and then of labour, often drawing from prior colonial connections, whereas the end of the war brought enforced borders, a fear of 'aliens', and repatriation of those recruited. But, Marfleet says, it is not war itself that explains this but the changing world economy; the expansion of international capitalism, reduced demands for labour (mass production and increased productivity, that meant labour migrants were no longer in such high demand, although some had nowhere else to go and were effectively refugees) and at some periods the declining world economy (backed up by a post-war nationalism and state-centred economic policies). Borders were tightened, movements scrutinized, the 'escape hatch' was shut, and 'refugees' emerged as a defined group (2006: 73). Post WWII things changed again. During the mid 1940s mass migrations resumed, especially in the form of labour recruitment but also peoples displaced by war and ideological conflict. A long economic boom demanded labour recruitment to all Western countries, and chain migration was encouraged in order to secure an ongoing supply. Many 1940s and 50s refugees were 'escapees' of Stalinist rule. 'Their flight was depicted as a rejection of Communism and their presence in the West as testimony to the virtues of liberal democracy' (Marfleet, 2006: 147). By the 1970s there were renewed economic pressures but by now it was not so easy to stem flows that, through their networks and ties (what we might call transnational activities), had become to some extent self-perpetuating (Marfleet, 2006: 88). Recruited as labour, migrants had established roots, and their home countries had become dependent on their remittances. If the richer economies were experiencing recession then the poorer ones were really struggling. Even though some states offered incentives for migrants to leave, some simply had nowhere to go; and while opportunity in the West had motivated earlier migrants to arrive, it was the by now atrocious conditions in the South that compelled them to leave. The 1980s and

90s witnessed new wars with many casualties – religious displacements, local conflicts, large-scale 'ethnic cleansing', the collapse of communism – resulting in the creation of camps and holding stations. Emphasis came to be on containment in origin, as these new refugees raised 'uncomfortable questions about the legacy of colonialism and the instability of the world system' (ibid: 151). As they grew in number, became more long-term and long-distance, refugees in the west were increasingly perceived as a menace, and borders were tightened. There is a close inter-relationship between economic circumstances, and ideological and practical responses (see Joly, 2004).

The blurred distinction between voluntary and forced migration is a useful one in terms of understanding their migration and settlement, but it causes problems for policy. How groups are labelled and defined has implications for how they are subsequently treated. In order for finite resources to be allocated numbers need to be ascertained and definitions clarified. Policies and acts of legislation are hugely important for the ways in which refugees are labelled, treated, and perceived. Even the passport was 'a bureaucratic assertion of the power of the state vis-a-vis "its" citizens' (Marfleet, 2006: 124), while the Aliens Restriction Act of 1914 in Britain led to the reclassification of up to 75,000 citizens as enemy aliens, and the internment or deportation of around 50,000 (Kushner and Knox, 1999, in Marfleet, 2006: 124). The 1945 *Charter of the United Nations* was a general statement about human rights, but human rights, Marfleet says, are often more about citizen rights than universal rights, and serve to exclude groups (ibid: 144). The 1948 *Universal Declaration of Human Rights* was a bit more specific in affirming the 'right to seek and enjoy asylum' (Marfleet, 2006: 145–6), among other things. But it was the 1951 *Convention Relating to the Status of Refugees* (The Geneva Convention) that really specified protection for refugees. It is 'seen as a model statement of asylum rights' (ibid: 146), and is the basis of international law on refugees. The Convention has 46 articles, with the first establishing the definition of a refugee. Under the Convention, refugees have the right to certain freedoms (religious and citizen) and the right not to be returned to a country where they fear persecution. But in Britain, as in many countries, there is a process through which arrivals need to go before being defined as refugees and during this time they can be subject to different statuses, with varying rights and levels of security (Bloch, 2002). These in turn have impacts on settlement, as we shall see below. This broad range of policies informs localized responses. They are important knowledge and background, revealing upper and more proximate structural layers. But this practice story needs to focus on those that are relevant, to examine how malleable these structures are, and how they are enacted and embodied by agents in the given context. The information above illustrates that the material required to understand migration in terms of the ongoing practice of social life is not always readily available; students have to use what they can obtain to piece stories together. Researchers, alternatively, can aim to collect material to fill in the gaps or to enhance the ongoing story.

Policies and practices are often supported (and perhaps informed) by ideologies, so looking at them we begin to see how structures are interpreted and sustained in practice. For Rob Stones (2005, see Chapter 2) ideologies are one window onto the interaction of structure and agency in everyday practice. The relatively modern nation state (as discussed in Chapter 3) seeks an ethnic homogeneity that may not actually exist (or ever have existed) in reality. It achieves this homogeneity through processes of otherness (defining insiders and outsiders), labelling, persecution, and exclusions. A homogenous state is seen as a secure state and others are portrayed as dangerous and threatening. However, in many cases it has been the construction of the nation state that led to the exclusions and to the flight of asylum seekers to other parts of the world (or corners of states). States also need to appear to be controlling their borders. But, Marfleet says, they often need workers from outside as well, especially for different industries at different times (in response to fluctuating demand). States achieve this balance between permitting workers in and keeping (dangerous) outsiders out through a series of amnesties, turning a blind eye, loopholes, and changing policies. The US-Mexico border is a perfect example (see Chapter 5). Overall, Marfleet contends, it is the attempts at control that lead to undocumented migration, clandestine behaviour, seeking refuge instead of labour, trafficking, and smuggling. Marfleet and Castles, therefore, present some of the broad structural changes and conditions that may constrain or enable a given forced migration event. I will now closely examine the work of Jill Rutter, as she provides rich material about refugee children in Britain that can be framed within a theory of practice.

The Children of Refugees in Britain

Jill Rutter has a very clear explanandum (thing to explain) that I will re-word into the following research question: how can we explain the progress (or lack of progress) of refugee children in British secondary schools? She also has another, less explicit, goal, and that is to understand integration more broadly. She therefore helps her reader begin to understand how refugee children get on and get by in the new school setting. Rutter's work is extensive and provides a lot of information to help us compile a practice story. She teaches us a lot about how to understand refugee children. We learn about the various policies, their conditions at home, their experiences in school and their home lives. But, of course, there is information missing that would be useful if this phenomenon is to be more systematically informed by practice theory.

Rutter's doctoral research involved a study of the educational progress of 32 refugee children in secondary schools; subsequent research work explored the experiences of Congolese children in primary and secondary schools. Research was also undertaken through case studies in four secondary schools (this research was conducted in order to prepare a teaching resource for young people, Rutter, 2004). Each of these studies involved the analysis of quantitative data and policy documents, interviews with teachers, classroom observations and semi-structured interviews with children. Rutter also worked for the Refugee Council for several years and draws on field notes collected as part of that work. The strength of the book used for this chapter is in the way it brings together research from a range of primary and secondary sources including systematic reviews of other studies. There is a chapter on how UK children view refugees, for example, based on both a review of existing studies and the research conducted in the four case study schools. The chapter on the school experiences of refugee children uses research from five schools. In many ways this book already starts to tell a practice story: outcomes (educational progress) can be identified as she discusses refugees' experiences; communities of practice can be teased out of the discussion of policy responses and UK children's views. Here the framework outlined in Chapter 2 provides concepts through which to identify more clearly the ongoing, structuration processes.

Background

Rutter (2006) begins by outlining the history of forced migration to the UK and policy responses; much of this is discussed in Marfleet (2006) but here it has a UK focus, bringing external structures down a level to the more proximate social surroundings. She informs the reader that the UK has acceded to the Geneva Convention (discussed above) as well as to its later 1967 Protocol. She tells us that the United Nations High Commissioner for Refugees (UNHCR) is responsible for ensuring that states who have signed up to these conventions and protocol actually observe their humanitarian principles, especially the overriding one, that a refugee is someone who has fled a country of origin or is unable to return to it 'owing to a well-founded fear of being persecuted for reasons of race, religion, nationality, membership of a particular group or political opinion' (from the 1951 UN Convention Relating to the Status of Refugees). But these are broad regulations and procedures. To bring this down a level to the more proximate social surroundings, Rutter asks (2006: 17), how does one define a 'well-founded fear of persecution'? There is no real international definition to help governments decide definitively. They therefore deal with refugees differently. In the UK, asylum can be sought at the port of entry or when having entered. The latter group can include both legal and illegal entries and stays. In the case of children, it is normally the parent that has applied.

Outlining the policy context in the UK provides interesting background and this frames the later analyses, but the link between this context and the migrant children's educational outcomes is not made explicit. However, this background can be made to have a role using practice theory, if we understand it in terms of the conjuncturally-specific external structures within communities of practice. These external structures serve to constrain and enable, inscribed in the practices of agencies, organizations and individuals with whom refugees come into contact. Policy structures do not have a role via the agent's habitus (as does the background in the sending country) but they have a role in the conjuncturally-specific external structures and later the conjuncturally-specific internal structures (learning how to go on), and later become incorporated into the agent's habitus, limiting expectations and projections. Bloch (2002) notes for example that as refugee numbers have increased, legislation has become more restrictive in the UK. Asylum seekers can no longer claim social security, housing benefits or social housing.[3] This affects how they live and how they understand their opportunities. Asylum seekers, Bloch contends, are therefore marginalized and isolated. Rutter's work examines the experience of Congolese, Somali, and Sudanese refugee children.

Congolese

For the Congolese refugee children the research is based on the analysis of statistical data, classroom observation, interviews with 14 children, and interviews with teachers, parents, carers and key informants (Rutter, 2006: 165).[4] What we can begin to understand about the structuration processes for these children also draws on the other research mentioned above and other studies reviewed in Rutter's book. Rutter is (implicitly) trying to understand why Congolese and Somali children (among others) are under-achieving in relation to other minority groups and to white UK and Irish children (Rutter, 2006: 137). This was the situation in all the case study schools and using a number of different indicators. Approximately 25 per cent of Congolese and Somali children failed to become fluent in English, even after more than five years. GCSE and reading test results yield consistently lower rates of success than for other groups. And crucially, 'Congolese children who had been in the UK for all or most of their lives underachieved in relation to pupils as a whole' (ibid: 167). However, some Congolese, especially girls whose home language is French, have a positive experience of school and are 'achieving at levels comparable with or better than children of their age' (ibid: 167). We could frame this in the context of under-achievement more generally, and ask: how is it that some children are able to overcome external and internalized structural constraints, experiences in the UK of insecurity and risk, marginal close-knit communities, and high unemployment, and still succeed?

The chapter on the Congolese begins by outlining the conditions, historical experiences and activities that explain sets of dispositions (although not using this terminology). The majority of Congolese in the UK are from the Democratic Republic of Congo (DRC), although there are also those from Congo-Brazzaville. The analysis of the experiences of Congolese refugee children begins with a discussion of political upheavals in the DRC, from independence from Belgium, through President Mobutu's regime, student uprisings and repression, through later rebellions, and continuing bloody conflict and flight. In Congo-Brazzaville the story is also one of conflict and flight. Many of these refugees in the UK, then, have left as a result of intense conflict, human rights violations, and political upheavals. Some of the children in the case studies arrived with very low levels of education and had such traumatic experiences that they had to be helped to learn basic skills such as picking up a pair of scissors (Rutter, 2006: 165). Rutter presents this history as explaining the reasons to migrate but of course they also could be conceived as internal structural constraints to educational progress, or integration. The history and prior experiences enable us to understand refugees' habits, expectations, tastes, aspirations, the dreams they bring with them in their habitus and will have adjusted recently in the light of changing conditions. Rutter demonstrates that the Congolese in the UK are constituted of political activists and journalists and, later, people of 'lower socio-economic classes', whose migration was mediated by existing networks. The social and educational profile of the children is therefore very variable. Class, gender, ethnicity, and language all vary within the group and have implications for the general dispositions in relation to education. Bloch (2002) complements this information by noting that many Congolese did not choose to come to the UK, and 44 per cent of her respondents would have chosen a different destination. With these bits of background we can start to piece together some idea of the habitus of the various Congolese families. These will impact on how they learn to go on in their new surroundings (their conjuncturally-specific internal structures).

Rutter usefully draws attention to a number of policies, acts, and other external structures that indirectly constrain, limit, or enable the experience of refugee children. And when we look closely we can see there is also some evidence of the ways in which these external structures are enacted within groups. The 1988 Education Reform Act increased competition between schools and has led (inadvertently) to the concentration of refugee children in 'underachieving' or 'unpopular' schools (Rutter, 2006: 32). This is compounded by the fact of housing segregation: 'caused by the availability of particular forms of accommodation, restricted employment opportunities, cultural pulls, primary chain migration and secondary migration within the UK' (ibid: 32). 'The 2001 Census showed that 81 per cent of the UK's Congolese lived in Greater London' (ibid: 162) and then in a small number of London boroughs. The asylum application process in the UK is a powerful causal influence, leading as it does to changing statuses, temporary stays, and insecurity (and conjuncturally-specific internal structures). At a given time some refugees may be clandestine, others awaiting decisions. This is particularly pertinent for Congolese asylum seekers, since the majority are refused asylum but are left in limbo through the ongoing granting of extensions to their stay. This indeterminate state gives rise to a great deal of anxiety for parents and children. Other structural constraints that are hinted at include: the English language, the school structure, and the laws, language and culture of the UK. These are all independent, existing outside the control of the refugee child. Contemporary policies aiming to achieve integration and social cohesion, Rutter contends, contain 'assimilative associations' whereby 'they' are supposed to become like 'us' (Rutter, 2006: 12).

Rutter is also quite good at giving us some idea of how habitus meet other expectations (conjuncturally-specific external structures) in the new surroundings and how these lead to conjuncturally-specific internal structures (learning and adapting). Research in the London boroughs of Haringey and Islington, which have a significant percentage of the UK's Congolese refugees, found the population to be divided into those who are well educated and those with little or no education, so we can expect different outcomes. But to examine a few details, in the UK there is an expectation that parents will help with their children's education, but Congolese women are less likely than the men to have been educated and they therefore may not feel able to fill this new role. Children are likely to speak a combination of languages, especially Lingala in the home ('the most widely spoken language among Congolese living in the UK', Rutter, 2006: 160) but a vast majority are unable to read and write in the language. French also permeates their everyday speech but many cannot read and write in French. This is functional in the society they left but dysfunctional when attempts are made to translate their ideas in spoken and written English. We also hear that there are traditional expectations that women will not go to university (ibid: 167), and in order to tell a good practice story it would be useful to try to learn more about how some girls overcome this in practice. Unemployment is high amongst Congolese refugees and those in employment are often in low-skill, paid work. We can assume from this that refugee children will not aspire to be educated in order to obtain work. Also, parents may be unhappy, poor and uneducated themselves. But these latter comments from me are things I have surmised from the information available, and what is really needed is for them to be framed as working hypotheses to inform further research (either of existing or new data).

To summarize, this is a diverse group of refugees (some more educated than others), many of whom experienced trauma before leaving. In the UK, they are concentrated in a few areas, likely to be spending a lot of time together, many are insecure in terms of their asylum status, and many are attending 'unpopular' schools. Language problems are vast, and in terms of some of their communities of practice (the people with whom they come into contact outside of their own communities) there are assumptions towards assimilation rather than multiculturalism (see Chapter 3).

Rutter has some very rich data on the practice of everyday life for refugee children in the UK. It is not systematically addressed in terms of its outcomes, but there are scattered details that can be pulled together within a theory of practice. We learn from Rutter that when the Congolese arrive in the UK there are several means of support for them, but many of these are within, or involve mixing with members of, their own ethnic or religious communities. There is a strong music scene, the church is important in the lives of many (especially less well educated) Congolese, there are Congolese shops and newspapers. Rutter concludes that this demonstrates the need for support, but we instead could frame these as both outcomes of migration and existing conditions for new migrants, conditions that may impede communication with the wider community. Many community groups work with children in various ways, running youth clubs and parent-child mediation, but it would be valuable to have more information about these communities of practice for refugee children. This practice story needs to find out who organizes and funds these activities; what is their role in the educational progress of children? They form part of the networks within which children are located, and therefore are the communities within which children learn to get by.

Rutter describes some children becoming disaffected, and excluded, especially feeling discriminated against because of their ethnic origins, experiences we can expect would eventually become internalized into conjuncturally-specific internal structures and then the habitus. Many Congolese children (50 per cent in the study reported here) are identified as having special educational needs. Half of the children in the study do not do their homework. Teachers spoke of parents being secretive and not involved in the children's education. But the parents are often unemployed or working in low-paid jobs, working anti-social hours, they may be at work, then, or they may not be interested in the child doing well at school if they do not know how long they will be able to stay in the UK. Parents of girls may not expect them to need to do well at school, Rutter suggests. Parents themselves spoke of lack of confidence in dealing with the school, because of fear of authority and language problems. Many of the children are not even living with their parents but with other carers (aunts and uncles perhaps). We then wonder to what extent they have an interest in the child's future progress. Are they temporary or permanent carers? To what extent do they even have a long-term view? Piecing together a practice story would mean seeking more information on all of these aspects.

Rutter provides some quotes from community workers about how Congolese leave their children at home while they go to work, either not realizing that is not accepted in the UK or, perhaps, having no choice because they lack the wider support they would normally rely on. Children are late for school because parents or carers left for work early. Although there is a high prevalence of HIV/AIDS among the Congolese, the take-up of testing, drug treatments and social support is low. Implying that these are conjuncturally-specific internal structures, Rutter suggests this is because of the way Congolese think the authorities will react to them admitting their illness (perhaps refusing them asylum or leave to remain). In terms of habitus, there is stigma attached to HIV, as there is to illiteracy. Stigma prevents individuals confronting their problems, instead causing them to hide them from each other and from outsiders.

There is some information from the children themselves enabling us to begin to work out how they act and react – their own conjuncturally-specific internal structures and communities of practice. Rutter mentions the trauma they might suffer in the UK from losing parents to AIDS and from family violence. She talks of parents being too strict and not letting them out to play with friends and of parents not understanding the UK culture. On the other hand the children and parents complain that in Africa they would have been able to simply play in the street, but in the UK they cannot. Parents complain that children do not respect adults in the UK, and perhaps (I suggest) they are more strict than they might be as a way of getting back some control. Interestingly the children Rutter spoke to were often clear about their future career aspirations, many seeing themselves in professions that could be relevant either in the UK or the home country. This is a reflection of their ambivalence or confusion about where the future home might be. There is also some evidence of their conjuncturally-specific internal structures when Rutter tells us some are aware that job prospects in the UK for Congolese are pretty low. Rutter admits that 'children had developed their own strategies for coping with the often opposing cultural expectations of home and peers and most seemed able to straddle the worlds of home and school with ease' (ibid: 170). This is fascinating and much more exploration of this, of how the children learn to go on, with more focus on their conjuncturally-specific internal structures might start to reveal how some progress at school and some do not.

This is a fantastic study of Congolese children but as it stands it leaves the reader feeling refugee children are fettered by structures (including internalized ones) and there is too little focus on their agency. This is not a criticism of Rutter's work, but is simply meant to draw attention to the way a practice story needs to obtain information from various sources over time, and will never be complete. Even in this one book, when we apply the concepts of practice theory from Chapter 2, we can begin to see that the receiving conditions conflict terribly with the habitus of the agent. Parents and carers appear unable to learn, or understand, the culture of the society they now live in because they suffer from poverty, unemployment or low-paid work, and insecurity about the future. Children, who have often had awful experiences, live in insecure conditions, with communication diffi-culties, find it difficult to acquire the rules, norms, habits, and practices of other children in the school with whole different sets of dispositions. Those within some of their communities of practice (teachers, social work-ers) then develop conjuncturally-specific external structures (ways to go on) and label them as having special needs, whether these are 'behavioural' or 'learning' difficulties.

Somalis

For Somali children, Rutter's (2006) research is based on an analysis of previous research (of which there seems to be a substantial amount), partic-ipant observation in five schools, interviews with eight Somali children, and some interviews with parents and teachers. The problem to be explained is again scattered throughout this and other chapters: although there has been some improvement in recent years, the picture for Somali children is of low educational progress compared with other children. Some children do well, but Rutter believes too much attention given to these successes belies the wider picture. 'Policy makers must not be seduced by the achievements of a small elite', she suggests (ibid: 194).

Somali migration to the UK has a long history, and includes Northern Somalis who had a right to British citizenship, through to more recent refugees of the 1988 civil war, and the arrival of more elderly, disabled, single mothers and children (Bloch, 2002). This is a story of long-term settlement, established communities, as well as recent arrivals of people fleeing war and persecution. Their habitus, or general dispositions, will have been formed as a result of their backgrounds, their group history and culture, their ethnic differences within the wider group, and their (sometimes traumatic but certainly disruptive) experiences before coming to the UK. Somalis are a mixed group ethnically and linguistically, with sometimes competing ethnic clan groups each with their own language or dialects, and a strong oral tradition. There are also very different rea-sons for their leaving Somalia and many have spent time in other countries (often in camps) before settling in the UK. Rutter is, again, very good on detail with regards to the backgrounds of refugees – the cultural baggage, the linguistic skills, and the experiences that frame their experiences in the UK. The recent historical background from Marfleet (2006), above, also describes some external structures that would in turn affect the habitus and conjuncturally-specific internal structures of refugees. For the children we can weed out the following ideas. Many will have had little or no schooling, or interruptions to their schooling. Those who have been in the UK longer are likely to be settled whereas for more recent arrivals there is a very high rate of rejection of asylum applications. Some may be very insecure. The earlier arrivals were of people from middle class backgrounds whereas recent arrivals include more people from lower socio-economic groups.

Somalis in the UK have strong networks and high levels of social capital, but contrary to much literature on the topic of social capital (see Halpern, 2005), high quantities of this type of capital do not necessarily lead to high levels of employment. Unemployment is very high for this refugee group as a whole, and so, as with the Congolese, these children are living with high unemployment and poverty. For Somalis, large family sizes are the norm, and children are often also living in cramped conditions. Many households have no adult male, for various reasons.

One community of practice within which these children must learn to go on is the school. Here, Rutter is able to give us a few fleeting details of experiences and attitudes, with the occasional very detailed insight from her own work. There seems to be some tension between what parents expect and what teachers and schools expect. For example, there are expectations that parents will help with homework, while parents themselves are struggling to get by with high unemployment and large families. Teachers reveal low expectations of Somali refugees, describe difficult behaviour but also explain how they suffer from bullying and stereotyping (Rutter, 2006: 191). Children and adults commonly experience racial harassment, according to much of the literature: 'many young Somalis feel a sense of rejection by mainstream British society' (ibid: 182). We can assume that children's attempts to mix with white children will be limited. They will learn to expect rejection. Most Somalis are Muslim but there is huge variation in the extent to which refugees observe the religious practices. Some research says Somali youth happily inhabit 'two different worlds', learning 'to switch between the cultural norms of the home and school' (Kahin, 1997 in Rutter, 1986: 183). But Rutter instead tells some sad stories of children struggling to get by in school, with one avoiding physical education classes because she was embarrassed about her clothes, and others being teased and tormented. Female genital mutilation is common in Somalia and continues to an extent in the UK. As with the Congolese above, children are caught between two cultures. They are not in a position to reject this custom and Rutter tells stories of them avoiding physical education classes for fear of embarrassment, and finding passing urine difficult and painful leading to long periods in the toilet and subsequent questions and teasing.

Overall, one gets the impression that in terms of conjuncturally-specific internal structures (learning how to go on in certain circumstances) Somali children do not learn to reconcile their habitus with the expectations and norms of those around them in UK. Possibly, neither are their parents learning enough about the new setting to understand what changes need to be made to enable the children to adapt. High unemployment or low-paid jobs mean they are not learning an educational culture, or do not perceive the value of education. Poverty and social exclusion mean they are learning how to get by, not how to get on. How can they pass aspiration to their children if they have none? In order to frame this within practice theory, I would next need to try to find out some more about other communities of practice than the school – the family, their ethnic groups, transnational ties and so on. Apparently, for example, they retain strong transnational links to Somalis in other places, and even those with very little to spare are sending home remittances.

The interventions that are successful, Rutter (2006) says, are those that help both parents and adults, such as projects helping with language learning, helping parents to get together to help with children's homework, local authorities taking the time to explain the school system and the GCSE coursework to parents. If these are the most successful interventions this suggests that the difficulties lie in the contradictions between home and school, in children needing to learn to live between two worlds. This would benefit from being examined in more depth in terms of structuration processes. Rutter suggests that we might usefully use Portes' theories about segmented assimilation to understand Somali youth (see Chapter 3). 'Greater integration may be achieved through a period of greater separation', she argues (ibid: 182). There is some evidence, she says, that Somalis have a strong sense of self-help, a strong social spirit, and entrepreneurial natures (2006: 194). They work together to provide social support. But they are unable to do anything to change the wider conditions, the lack of support staff in schools, the limited extent to which local authorities work together with Somali community groups, the low numbers of Somali teachers, and the refusal to establish a GCSE in Somali (which would enable children to learn the structure of their language and would give their language status). Structurally, it seems the authorities are choosing to turn a blind eye to under-achievement in this group, and perhaps their strong sense of self-help sometimes works against them (ibid: 184).

Rutter's refugees remain victims, perhaps as a guard against the tendency in popular and mass media attitudes to refugees to blame the victim. Her refugees tend to be portrayed as pushed and continually constrained. One gets the sense that they have brought their traditions with them and that it's them that needs to change in new circumstances. There is not very much emphasis on the actions of the migrants here, on how they interpret and enact the structures that are more malleable. Practice theory begins with the agent in focus, even where that emphasis results in demonstrating how structures get reproduced. A practice story needs to ask: What precisely are the circumstances these refugees face in the UK and how do they perceive and react to them. What are they doing to change the future? Do they have any power at all? That is to say, we need to remember the duality of structure and agency at the core of structuration theory and other theories of practice (see Chapter 2).

Sudanese

I will very briefly summarize some of the material on Sudanese refugee children because they provide such a contrast to the processes and outcomes above. Here information from Rutter (2006) is based on life history and educational data from a very small sample of just six southern Sudanese children aged between 11 and 16. Sudan is ethnically diverse and this is also true of the UK population. Earlier migrants to the UK from Sudan included business people and students; it is only more recently that Sudanese migration has become associated with refugees. However, it is not easy to distinguish the groups in practice: some of the students were also forced migrants and refugees can, of course, hail from elite groups. An increase in applications for asylum in the UK has come as political opposition has been increasingly suppressed in Sudan, and so many refugees are political refugees.

Sudanese have the same problems of poverty, downward mobility, unemployment, cultural differences, and insecurity as the groups above but Rutter says they seem to learn how to get by and get on. They retain a strong and proud sense of identity, and a strong desire to achieve. Children seem to be torn between the conflicting demands of their various communities of practice, like those above. But the Sudanese have inscribed in their habitus a cultural norm that values education (Rutter, 2006: 203). 'They . . . remained committed to school work even in secondary schools where the dominant culture did not favour academic success' (ibid: 203). Some even resisted being drawn into a 'laddish' culture. This does suggest the strength of the home over the host culture, but also fewer tensions between the two sets of expectations. The communities of practice of schools and teachers are not so contradictory to their own habitus, and to the communities of practice of family and ethnic community, peers, and social life. Southern Sudanese (who Rutter's work focuses on) all enter school with some English language skills and teachers' expectations for this group are higher. Nevertheless, in the long-term it seems that relatively good progress at school does not translate into good jobs for this group. This is a fascinating outcome that a theory of practice could be fruitfully employed to explain. Rutter's work focuses on wider structures and habitus but less on a close 'analysis of the process of agent's conduct in situ' (Stones, 2005: 139). It provides a complex frame but could be more dynamic if informed by the duality of structure and employing the meso level concepts outlined in Chapter 2. It could also use migration theories and concepts to help illuminate discrete aspects of the structuration process (always bearing in mind the wider, sociological framework). With the Sudanese one gets the sense they have learned how to go on through their own networks but it would be interesting and insightful to hear more about this. Rutter's book really does give us some rich material to begin to tell a practice story. But, as she acknowledges herself, more depth is required for rich under-standings of processes and outcomes. Currently, a range of possible causes and constraints are thrown into the pot that would certainly make more sense if framed within a meta-theory explaining their role in the practice of daily life.

Conclusion

In this chapter we have learnt that forced migration overlaps with other types, but is marked by a lack of choice, persecution, and fear. The label 'forced', however, may well be a political one since the person using it thereby recognizes or imputes lack of agency. This chapter has used 'refugees' to refer to the migrants of forced migration. We have seen that one way to look at forced migration is to use concepts such as globaliza-tion, neoliberalism, and colonialism, perceiving the resultant inequalities in structural and historical terms as a continuation and consolidation of global relationships. At a more proximate level, we have also seen that forced migration overlaps with other types of migration. Where a forced migrant 'chooses' to escape to will often be affected by prior links estab-lished through other types of movement. Policies and legislation are hugely important for the ways refugees are labelled, treated and perceived. The authors reviewed here tend to summarize policies and ideologies with-out explaining how these are practised and experienced by given agents, whereas using the concept of duality of structure would enable them to understand social life as the outcomes of the interaction of structure and agency.

This chapter has demonstrated that it is easier to tell a practice story if we begin with a very clear explanandum. The chapter closely examined Jill Rutter's work on Congolese, Somali and Sudanese children of refugees in the UK, which especially tries to address their underachievement at school and, more broadly, their integration. There is a wealth of information in

Rutter's book, quite sufficient to begin analysing within a structuration framework, but of course the analysis in relation to this theory is not explicit. For a better practice story, the work could be restructured, with some supplementary information added, or one could concentrate on one aspect of structuration, or one part of the cycle. Assimilation theories (and ideologies) enable us to understand, to an extent, how refugees are received in the UK, with expectations they will adapt to the host culture. A description of the refugees' background enables us to begin to understand their habitus. Interviews with parents and teachers give us some insight into their communities of practice from where we can begin to make assumptions about how their conjuncturally-specific internal structures might develop. We thus begin to understand their underachievement as the outcome of the interaction of a whole gamut of external and internal structures and actions.

8

Conclusion and Summary of Key Points

Practice Theory for Migration Studies

This book presents a general, sociological, theory of how all of social life unfolds through the practice of daily life as a way of framing, understanding and evaluating the extensive range of empirical and theoretical work in the field of international migration. Practice theory is not an integrated migration theory, nor does it replace substantive migration theories, but it is a meta-theoretical approach that understands the broad social processes that are continually involved in the constitution of social life. It therefore underpins substantive theories and empirical research, providing a fundamental perspective. Crucially, practice theory favours neither subjectivism nor objectivism, but instead works to understand the interrelationship at the meso level of structures and actions. Practice theory understands social processes to take place through an ongoing cycle constituted by the interaction of external structures, internalized structures in agents, practices (or actions), and outcomes (with intended and unintended consequences). The cycle of structuration is illustrated overleaf. It should not be perceived as a sequence of discrete moments: both structures and agency are at all times involved in social processes.

Key concepts (or tools) involved in understanding the cycle of structuration are external structures, internal structures, practices, and outcomes. I will spend some time elaborating these in a little more detail here, as a way of summarizing what was discussed at length in Chapter 2. Other concepts that a theory of practice relies on are the *agent in focus* (the agent or group of agents with whom we are currently interested in a given piece of empirical research), and the *agent in context* (those agents within the communities of practice, the daily practice of the relevant others).

148

The Cycle of Structuration

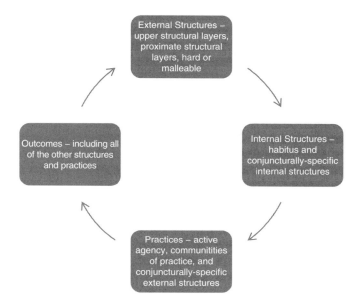

Figure 8.1   The Cycle of Structuration
(adapted from Stones, 2005: 189)

External Structures

External structures include both constraints to and opportunities for action, and can be separated conceptually into *upper structural layers* and *more proximate structural layers*.

Upper structural layers are social structures, as fairly traditionally conceived by sociologists, that appear to the agent as objective and detached. They are the wider context – the (often unacknowledged) conditions of action – and they have causal influence. They may or may not be recognized by the agent in focus (be that the migrant or the member of the host community, the would-be emigrant or the second generation settler) and therefore should be researched from a distance (not only via the agent's phenomenological perspective), using a macro perspective. However, it is important to ensure we examine those that are relevant to the given agent and the given research topic (the explanandum). Upper structural layers include large (even global) historical and spatial forces, wider conditions of action, broad patterns, global social change and social transformations. In more concrete terms this may involve such things as health care institutions, employment structures, the housing market, war, or famine. To understand them we might use theories or perspectives such as globalization, neoliberalism, colonialism or feminism. But we must always remember that the structures are drawn on, interpreted, and conceived by agents.

More proximate structural layers include wide, but not necessarily global, structures. These are the more small-scale and context-specific constraints and opportunities, and changes and developments. They include structures that are more pertinent to the given explanandum, such as laws, rules, policies, organizational arrangements, physical and material things like trains, houses and building arrangements. More precisely they may include such things as an industrial strike, a flood, an earthquake, recession, or a specific set of (perhaps migration or integration) policies. The point of conceptually distinguishing these from the above upper structural layers is not so that we can spend ages deliberating over whether something is an upper or a proximate social structure, but in order to draw attention to the fact that a structuration theory of practice demands constant attention to the interaction of structures and actions in daily practice. They can be usefully examined from the perspective of the agent and from the perspective of the researcher, because some will be unacknowledged or unrecognized by the agent. On the other hand, only the agent in focus can draw attention to those that are *felt* to be relevant.

External structures can be more or less *hard* or *malleable*, and this will depend on how the agent perceives them and the power she has to resist or act. The extent of power and resistance always remains a question for every empirical study. *Structural gaps* occur where structures (institutions, organizations, ideologies) overlap, contradict each other or have weaknesses. This leaves them with an inconsistent ability to constrain or provide opportunities for given agents. This is where their mutability comes from to an extent. Mutability also comes from the fact that at all times structures are enacted.

Internal Structures

Internal structures include both *habitus* and *conjuncturally-specific internal structures*. Habitus is used here in pretty much the same way that Bourdieu uses the term in his own theory of practice (and refers to what Stones calls dispositions), to mean structures embedded in corporeal schemas and memory traces. Habitus are the multitude of ways of being and thinking, of seeing and doing, that we each, in groups and as individuals, acquire through socialization, through generations of past practices, and through our own repeated practices. Habitus is best conceived as both a structure (formed) and an action (being formed), and it includes the skills, cultural schemas, world views, knowledge, capitals, and personal resources (including those that are embodied) of a given agent or group of agents. Habitus is/are fairly fixed but transposable (or somewhat mutable).

Conjuncturally-specific internal structures could be conceived as situated learning, or what is involved and internalized in the process of knowing or learning how to go on in given circumstances. They are the relevant internal structures (ways of thinking and doing) at a given time, specific reactions to and knowledge of features, conditions, structures, opportunities and constraints; the habitus drawn on and manipulated in the specific context of action. They involve proximate knowledge of the given context, drawn on quickly or learnt over time. Habitus and conjuncturally-specific internal structures can be learned about from the agent directly but are also likely to require some understanding of the context and the practices of agents within their communities. They can draw on a whole tradition of sociological theories in pragmatism, interactionism and interpretivism, but using a theory of practice one must also have one eye focussed on the wider structures, on power and knowledge.

Practices

Practices are the daily actions of agents in communities of practice. *Active agency* in a theory of practice, takes the shape of individual, reflexive reactions to specific circumstances, albeit that these reactions are always to some extent circumscribed by previous events and experiences. Agency consists of three elements: the habitus, practical considerations given the wider and immediate context, and projection. The projective element recognizes that humans have the ability to create and to pursue goals. Their desires and dreams are culturally embedded, but they are not predetermined. Drawing on their knowledge and experiences, actors imagine alternatives to current situations, visualize proposed solutions (and how they might be achieved), test out their ideas (perhaps, for migrants, by moving temporarily or going somewhere on holiday), and modify them constantly as contexts unfold.

Practice is the acting out of social life, it takes place within communities, and it involves aspects we might recognize as structures – codes, rules, regulations, procedures – but also implicit understandings, rules of thumb, established sensitivities, shared world views, underlying assumptions (Wenger, 1998: 47). In other words, practice is about knowing (and working out) how to go on in given circumstances suspended within networks of other people and groups each with their own internal and external structures. A community of practice may be a family, a school, one's peer group, the workplace, or any group within which members learn to act together. They are best understood by taking part. Members have, and acquire, different roles, backgrounds, identities, histories, goals, statuses and differing amounts of power. Communities of practice thus provide the context within which an agent is constrained and enabled by *conjuncturally-specific external structures*. These are the external structures as embodied and enacted through roles and positions of those within an agent's communities of practice. They include the habitus and conjuncturally-specific internal structures of the agents in context. They are best understood from a hermeneutic understanding of the context gained over time.

Outcomes

The outcome of practice is the reproduction and transformation of social life into newly (re)shaped external and internal structures, dreams and desires. Any of the above, at any time, can be viewed as outcomes (and thus as structures). This is because a structuration theory of practice is always temporal.

The Role of Theory for a Structuration Theory of Practice

In Chapter 3, I summarized some of the theories, perspectives and concepts that are widely used in the study of international migration. The goal was not to be exhaustive or comprehensive since the range of approaches employable is practically infinite, and is certainly not limited to what we might think of as migration theories. However, I did demonstrate that theories have, in the past, tended to focus on either migration as an act or an event, or on settlement as a process that takes place within a given space. Migration has traditionally been viewed as problematic, and as a linear, unidirectional, and one-off event. In more recent decades, however, migration research has increasingly acknowledged that migration has always been diverse, has always included return, circular, temporary and uncertain moves, and has always had implications within and beyond national boundaries. Perhaps it is also true that migration is *increasingly* diverse, multi-directional and transnational. Theories employed more vigorously in recent years thus reflect these interests and developments, and thus draw attention to changes wrought by globalization, mobility, and transnationalism, instead of (only) nationalism, ethnic relations, reasons for migration, and integration.

Migration researchers have also begun to acknowledge that they need to look at the interaction of wider structural changes and on the ground actions. Migration systems theory, for example, understands migration as a complex process incorporating the ongoing interaction of macro, meso, and micro level elements within a wider migration system (Castles and Miller, 2009). Rather than focus on individual migration decisions, migration systems theory acknowledges that moves tend to cluster, can be circular, and take shape within wider contexts and systems. Understanding migration processes thus involves moving out from the individual to the wider and interconnected sets of circumstances within which an individual agent is located. Ewa Morawska (1996, 2009) has applied structuration theory more or less overtly in her own work on international migration. Oliver Bakewell (2010) has proposed critical theory as a means of addressing the interaction of structure and agency. But migration theory has yet to elucidate a meta-theoretical framework that draws on existing social theory to explain the recursive manner in which all social life proceeds.

The purpose in Chapter 3 was two-fold. I felt a book on international migration and social theory should present the key theories and approaches, but I also wanted to demonstrate how these and other theories might be employed within a meta-theoretical framework of practice theory. Within the approach presented here (and in accordance with the work of both Giddens and Stones) it is perfectly logical to incorporate theories, concepts and approaches from other traditions; a researcher or student may use all sorts of useful terminology – theoretical concepts, theoretical frameworks, social science perspectives, sensitizing concepts – in order to help her identify external and internal structures, and understand practice as it takes place within communities. But above all else, practice theory demands that both structures and agency and their interaction through practice are examined, or as Stones (2005) puts it, structuration is committed to a structural-hermeneutic diagnostic. Practice theory can thus draw on, evaluate, develop, or discard other theories by considering their location in, and contribution to, the general social theory.

Economic theories have been very influential in the field of migration studies (even for sociologists). These begin by assuming the existence of a rational individual who makes choices based on the conscious balancing of available options, and is thus centred on external structures with causal influence on individuals. Though its explanatory force lies with the active agency of individuals, it takes no account of the phenomenology of the agent-in-focus, and does not permit any explanation of why some people decide not to migrate under conditions that are patently favourable. We can therefore consider them objectivist. Macro-theoretical explanations of broad scope can provide a framework for a structuration account, serving to highlight the historical relationship between, for example, colonialism and many contemporary flows, the role of the state in migration processes, and the unequal political and economic relationship between states. But they can also accord wider structures a higher degree of autonomy than they deserve. Again, there is a danger of too much emphasis on the autonomous role of structures. Newer approaches, such as migration network theory, lend themselves well to a theory of practice, if the tools outlined in Chapter 2 (and above) were to be applied more consciously. However, what Castles and Miller (2009) term 'meso structures' are quite different to the meso level structures above (the internalized and enacted structures). For these authors, the meso level includes the intermediaries, individuals, groups and organizations that mediate between migrants and institutions. This is an important contribution that does acknowledge the interaction of macro and micro processes, but it is not the same as conceiving of a meso level where structures and agents interact through practice. Practice theory goes further by theorizing the interaction of structure and agency in the practice of daily life. It therefore enables us to think through *how* the meso level structures of intermediaries, families and networks play a role. It also recognizes the important meso level of internalized structures.

To move on to theories of settlement, researchers and students can employ the concept of assimilation within a theory of practice to analyse the extent to which there is an ideology of assimilation (and on the part of whom), and the extent to which this ideology, or set of assumptions, is inscribed in policy and practice. The outcomes of these assumptions and policies will be visible as a set of surface appearances to explain. They can also empirically analyse and/or try to theorize the extent to which a migrant is incorporated into a society (be it the one they left or the one they migrated to, or both). However, in this latter case it is probably safer to not use the concept of assimilation or to use it carefully and critically. Rather than conclude ethnicity is either/or a subjective association or a structural object, we can theorize its role in the cycle of structuration as a more or less malleable structural layer and/or part of the habitus of the agent and her communities of practice. The extent to which an agent is free to identify with and claim resources for an ethnic category remains a question in every case; and each choice has its own implications. Similarly, the concepts of race and racism may be relevant at many points in the structuration cycle especially as ideas that individuals act upon in relations with others. In the structuration cycle transnational activities and identities may be identified as proximate structures constraining or enabling actions in the form of cross-border connections. In other words, a theory of practice is a meta-theory, a theory for how theories might be employed. As Giddens (1984) notes, this involves taking ideas from diverse sources and working with them, sharpening them (or refining them), and ultimately making them work together.

Telling Practice Stories

In Chapters 4 to 7 I have begun to tell practice stories about four types of migration: lifestyle migration, labour migration, domestic labour migration, and forced migration. These were not selected as illustrative of all the various types or forms of migration in existence, though they do serve to illustrate some key themes and approaches. Telling practice stories about a given phenomenon involves searching for existing material that can begin to reveal the structuration processes involved, and thereby starting to understand a set of surface appearances (or a migration trend) within the framework of a structuration theory of practice. It will always be a work in progress, but it is something both students and researchers can attempt. The wonderful breadth of work already undertaken in many fields of international migration can thus be drawn into a coherent framework in the telling of practice stories of given trends or processes.

Chapter 4 explores British migration to Spain's coastal areas as an example of lifestyle (or leisured) migration. Here I used a range of my own works, the work of Russell King and his colleagues (2000) and a selection of other studies in the field. Together these studies have been able to identify upper structural layers constraining and (especially here) enabling the migration. Macro level theoretical perspectives, such as globalization, tourism theories, European integration, the network society, and mobility, have in this case drawn attention to various changes in the world that have increased the likelihood of and the opportunities for this kind of leisured and tourism-related migration. In the chapter I drew attention to the ways in which these broad changes were enacted in practice and how they have wrought their own cultural changes and impacted on the habitus and the nature of settlement of the British in Spain. Employing a theory of practice has enabled me to illustrate this in detail where the studies reviewed often only hinted at the relationship between structures and practices. The same is true of more proximate structural layers such as policies, tourism practices, retirement and unemployment. These much closer structural constraints often revealed themselves through the life histories and practices of the agents in our studies. But I also noted how agents themselves often describe their own migration in terms of push and pull factors (though not only economic ones). It is only when we examine stories about moving that we can see the structural conditions outlined above, the cultural shifts and how they affect the decision to move. We also see how these are mediated by conjuncturally-specific internal structures (the way the respondents understand what will happen if they make this decision), and by individual habitus. Applying practice theory to the ethnographic work that has been undertaken, we are able to see the ways British migrants embrace, internalize and make a practice of the idea of mobility, which has been enabled through the development of new technologies, and the ways in which tourism practice has become inscribed in the habitus. We can interpret their settlement by remembering that their move has been enabled by relative wealth and relative escape, and realizing (from a critical perspective) that to integrate would damage what they achieve by constantly balancing home and away, here and there, richer and poorer society. Because it is based on a wide range of rich data, this chapter begins to illustrate how scholars can work together, (and students can combine existing studies), to understand a phenomenon in much of its complexity by drawing on the concepts of a theory of practice. Of course, structuration can also be used to examine some specific aspects of a migration process in depth, as long as we then link our findings to others by referring to the theoretical framework.

   Chapter 5 examined Mexican labour migration to the US as an illustration of labour migration more widely. The studies by Alejandro Portes and his team were selected as examples that are well known and that have gained some authority in the field; the studies of Ruiz, Canales and Vasquez were also selected because they provide important material that was missing in these other studies. The upper structural layers providing the context for Mexican migration to the US include the historical (economic and power) relationship between Mexico and the US, the changing economic situation in each country, and changes in the global economy. More proximate structures include the way their labour is recruited, for what purposes, and the policies that enable and constrain their migration and settlement. Details on these more proximate structures were quite difficult to locate in the chosen studies. It was even more difficult to learn about the habitus and conjuncturally-specific internal structures, and the desires and goals of the migrants themselves. There was very little in the way of phenomenological understandings of the agent in focus. I made some assumptions about the habitus of the earlier migrants, the majority of whom were rural, poorly educated men; but the migration is now much more complex. The more in-depth studies of Hellman, Ruiz and Vasquez gave more information about different types of Mexican migrants as agents in the migration process. We learned that they seem to retain strong ties to their home communities, especially their home towns, and began to gain a hermeneutic understanding of their communities of practice. This would be enriched if we were to locate some ethnographic details of daily life before, during or after migration (these do exist, see for example Dreby, 2010). We know that Mexicans continue to be excluded, or to suffer segmented assimilation, and, in Vasquez's work, we begin to get some interesting insights into how third generation Mexican Americans negotiate external structures and habitus, in communities of practice, acquiring conjuncturally-specific internal structures that lead to a third way of living, balancing belonging to both Mexico and America. Together these studies illustrate that in order to understand the structuration processes involved we need *both* studies of broad scope (macro, historical studies) and close, intimate studies of daily life. But more than that, the chapter illustrates that these approaches work well together when framed within a general social theory about the recursive nature of social life. Studies of broad scope do not enable the understanding of precise processes on the ground without the analysis of the role of structures in practice. Close, intimate studies of practice, preferably using ethnography and in-depth interviews, hermeneutics and phenomenology, reveal who and what are the communities of practice, the habitus of the agent, the emerging conjuncturally-specific external and internal structures, but need to place these in a wider context using both what the agents tell us and what we perceive for ourselves (perhaps drawing on macro studies).

Chapter 6 examined domestic labour migration from the Philippines to Hong Kong, as an illustration of domestic labour migration. The studies used were selected in order to provide something of a composite study of the field, combining macro, micro and broad-brush approaches with very close in-depth studies. These studies explained the migration using economic push and pull theories, albeit implicitly. Economic conditions in both countries have been utilized to explain why women might leave the Philippines to work in conditions that those less well educated than them in Hong Kong would not wish to suffer, and why women in Hong Kong feel they need to hire women from abroad to do the work in the home that is taken for granted as 'women's work'. Economic push and pull theories are inadequate and simplistic, but analysis of the macro elements nevertheless revealed some cultural schemas and cultural shifts that were of relevance, such as how Hong Kong women have learned to accept domestic help in the home and to see it as status enhancing, and how Filipina women have learned that to go abroad for work (and send home your earnings) is not only acceptable but a familial and national duty. New structures are revealed as we see that the Philippines has come to rely on the remittances of its emigrants, and has thus not attempted to find other ways to deal with high unemployment. The studies, reviewed within a practice theory framework, were also able to identify more proximate external structures constraining and providing opportunities for migration and settlement, such as Hong Kong's assumption (inscribed in policies and practices) that the migration will be cyclical and temporary. Of course, the studies reviewed do not use the language of upper and proximate structural layers, but these are revealed through their analyses. The material is not structured in the way I presented it, but the details are available for students and scholars to identify. There is also information in these studies to inform analysis of the habitus, conjuncturally-specific internal structures and even desires and projections. There is some very rich material on the ways in which women, through the agencies and their own communities, learn to become the docile and submissive product that is required for the domestic labour market. Communities of practice can also be examined, in the shape of the women's own ethnic communities, their home communities, and the households they move to. Migration scholars could usefully apply a theory of practice more consciously and overtly to this field, and then collect supplementary data on specific aspects (habitus, conjuncturally-specific internal structures, communities of practice, proximate structures) or a specific explanandum (for example, why is it that Filipina women in Hong Kong remain so subservient and accept being kept apart from their children and families? How does this situation reproduce itself?).

Chapter 7 looked at refugees in the UK as a window onto a type of forced migration. I selected a few studies that could begin to tell a practice story about a specific type of forced migration, with Marfleet and Castles offering more broad-brush analyses whereas (at least ostensibly) Rutter and Bloch provided closer, phenomenological case studies. In this case upper structural layers were revealed using the concepts of globalization, neoliberalism, and colonialism. Thus global inequalities that have resulted from the continuation and consolidation of historical economic and political relationships, are used to explain contemporary economic inequalities that lead to migration. Again, this is implicitly an economic push and pull explanation. The more proximate structural layers that affect where a forced migrant 'chooses' to escape to include previous migrations and the ties, networks, and other meso level institutions and organizations that result from these. Policies and legislation are hugely important for the ways refugees are labelled, treated and perceived. The authors reviewed here tend to summarize policies (and ideologies) without explaining how these are practised and experienced by agents in practice, so this is a gap our practice story needs to fill. This chapter has demonstrated that a theory of practice can especially illuminate concrete social processes when directed towards an explicit explanandum. Jill Rutter's work very clearly and expressly examined reasons for refugee children's apparent lack of success in school in the UK. She provided a lot of rich information, gathered from interviews and observation, but given that this was not originally framed within a practice theory, there are lots of gaps in the empirical data we need to fill in order to really understand the recursive processes involved. The work tantalizingly offers just enough information for us to be able to understand structuration processes using the concepts of habitus, conjuncturally-specific internal and external structures, communities of practice, proximate structures, and knowledge, power and awareness.

Methodology for a Structuration Theory of Practice

A theory of practice provides a coherent framework for scholars and students to combine existing work, identify gaps, and begin to tell practice stories about given explananda. As such it does not dictate the use of any particular data collection method. However, the ability to understand the various structuration processes will entail a combination of ethnographic research with some broad-brush studies, especially analysing external structures and wide historical or macro developments in the context of the given agent in focus and explanandum. Students therefore might usefully begin by exploring studies on a given trend that employ a variety of methods. Chapter 5, on Mexican labour migration, remained frustrating until quite near the end, because despite lots of information, it was difficult to understand the interaction of wider processes and daily practices using material that relied so heavily on quantitative methods. However, these quantitative data did reveal some crucial insights, especially in terms of patterns we might wish to explain. They also served to challenge some basic assumptions about migrant behaviours. A theory of practice then directs us to seek more answers from the qualitative data. Chapters 4, 6 and 7 contain much more rich detail, complemented by the broad-brush studies of macro perspectives. In these cases the concepts and tools in Chapter 2 are useful in drawing attention to more proximate structural layers and how they are enacted, the communities of practice and their conjuncturally-specific external structures. In the material we have available, the interaction of the wider structures and the individual (and group) agents is not clarified; the recursive nature of social life is not made apparent until the work is located within the general social theory.

Practice theory views agents as knowledgeable, which calls for empirical research to pay some attention to agents' own perspectives, thoughts and opinions. However, practice often involves doing things without being aware of it, in the context of constraints and opportunities of which agents may not be conscious. It is important, therefore, to find ways of studying the practice of daily life and understanding it without relying solely on the views of agents. As I already noted in Chapter 2, it is interesting to observe that the examples Stones uses (of composite studies revealing structuration processes in detail) include both a very long-term extensive ethnographic study and a microscopic analysis of a small-scale set of events.

Ethnography that pays attention to both wider structures and the thoughts and feelings of agents, within the context of action, would seem the best approach. Ethnography is a methodology, not a method; it is informed by a theory about how research should be conducted and therefore does not provide a recipe for techniques that can be employed (O'Reilly, 2011, 2009b). Ethnography draws on a family of methods, usually including participant observation, in-depth interviews, and conversations, and gains its understanding of the social world through involvement in the daily practice of human agents. It therefore involves immersion in the context, the building of trust and rapport with agents, both phenomenological and hermeneutic interpretations, and recognition of the complexity of the social world. It does not attempt to reduce this complexity to a few statistical or typological representations. It is reflexive about the role of the researcher and the messiness of the research process. And, if it is faithful to practice theory, then it will ensure that it employs a macro approach to gain knowledge of the wider context of action, as well as maintaining a close eye on the various ways that structures are taking effect within and through agents in practice. Rob Stones (2005) says that his strong version of structuration theory has a normative commitment to studying the complexity of people's daily lives (to hermeneutics and phenomenology), a desire to understand cultural differences, to challenge stereotypes and typification, and not to reduce such complexity. But it should not do this alone. Structures are both internal and external, so agents' perceptions can never be divorced from structural contexts, furthermore, a researcher might understand aspects of the context not perceived by the agent. Remember that a theory of practice draws attention to the duality of structure and agency, viewing practice as:

> synonymous with the *constitution of social life*, i.e. the manner in which all aspects, elements and dimensions of social life, from instances of conduct in themselves to the most complicated and extensive types of collectivities, are generated in and through the performance of social conduct, the consequences which ensue, and the social relations which are thereby established and maintained.
>
> (Cohen, 1989: 12)

Final Thoughts

Practice theory should not be applied too rigorously. In Chapter 2 there are a set of concepts for thinking through the various processes, but these should not be reified, nor applied uncritically. Broad sweeps of history and macro developments (be they economic, cultural, or political) can only be discussed at the abstract level if they are to be kept distinct from the other parts of the structuration cycle, such as communities of practice. As soon as one looks for distant and hard external structures in the context of practice, one starts to trip over conjuncturally-specific external structures within communities of practice, such as roles and norms, because this is where and how these structures are enacted. Almost immediately one needs an analysis of power, of the agent in focus and the agent in context. And as soon as one begins to address the power of a given agent, questions are raised about other agents in the community of practice, and other communities of practice. An analysis of habitus, as an element in the theory, cannot be examined without acknowledging that a habitus is constantly changing and adapting, and is all tangled up in daily practice with conjuncturally-specific internal structures, that in turn depend on the given community of practice being currently focussed on. A theory of practice entails attention to time, space and historicity: the durée of human action (Giddens, 1984). It is difficult to know where to start and finish. Structuration processes, or practice, unfolds like a spiral. But each spiral is embedded within and linked to other spirals. It is very challenging for one person to begin to draw on the entire set of concepts and insights outlined in Chapter 2, just as no researcher could use all the theories outlined in Chapter 3. However, this is no reason to abandon the attempt to loosely delineate processes, underpinned by a coherent meta-theory. I hope readers are able to see some added value in telling practice stories, beyond what would have been achieved if the various pieces of research had merely been critically reviewed in the usual way of a literature review.

The substantive Chapters (4–7) have demonstrated the role of practice theory as a meta-theoretical framework for migration by locating a few examples of work on a given topic and beginning to tell practice stories about it – stories that draw on the concepts outlined in Chapter 2 to provide coherence to the processes revealed. Students and researchers of migration can discover the existing work for themselves, as I have done, and try to identify the structuration processes involved. This will draw attention to gaps in the story that researchers can then attempt to fill with reference to further existing studies, or where necessary, by undertaking their own empirical research. This can, in turn, draw on other theoretical perspectives and approaches where relevant and where they illuminate relevant aspects of the migration process.

Anyone can apply a theory of practice to his or her research on migration by collecting survey research, undertaking interviews, doing ethnography, summarizing vast swathes of information, or employing whatever methods they see fit, while retaining one eye on the wider structuration picture, and acknowledging that whatever they achieve can only tell part of the story because social life is constituted and reconstituted through practice. What has been demonstrated is that studies informed by a theory of practice can best be achieved by bringing together studies undertaken at the smaller scale, using data collection techniques that gather rich data on daily practice, that include an element of time (they should not be snapshots), with other approaches that analyse the broader, historical changes, (social change broadly conceived), and the more proximate structural layers (including studies of policy). More than anything else I want to emphasize that researchers and students should not go out and study anything empirically without first examining very closely what else has been done in the given field. There is such a vast amount of empirical work currently being undertaken, by such a huge and diverse range of migration scholars, that it seems to me the way to advance knowledge is for us to get together to share and compare, seek a coherent story, and identify gaps before collecting yet more data. A theory of practice – a general, sociological, theory of how all of social life unfolds through the practice of daily life – might provide a sensible meta-theoretical framework to guide this programme of work.

Notes

1 Introduction: International Migration and Social Theory

1. This remains the most comprehensive review of migration theories available (Bakewell, 2010).

2 Practice Theory: A Framework for International Migration Research

1. For Emirbayer and Mische (1998) and Morawska (2009) the work of both Bourdieu and Giddens constitute theories of practice.
2. Note that Giddens does, however, build on theories of other sociologists; he simply wants to point out that they tend to overlook the interrelationship of structure and agency. In *New Rules* (1976) he both celebrates and demonstrates the one-sidedness of interpretive approaches, in *Central Problems* (1979) he does the same with structuralist approaches. *Studies in Social and Political Theory* (1977) is where he really develops structuration theory.
3. For Emirbayer and Mische (1998: 963) both Bourdieu and Giddens 'give selective attention to the role of habitus and routinized practices' viewing agency as 'habitual, repetitive and taken for granted'. However, not all scholars use structuration to emphasize agency by any means. Structuration proves really useful at trying to understand why structural or institutional change does not yield practical (or even structural) change. For example, active attempts to be more democratic or inclusive do not always lead to more inclusion (see Kruythoff, 2008, on housing tenant associations), and gender ideologies can continue to be influential despite active provision of opportunity for girls (see Cooky, 2009, on encouraging girls to take part in sports).
4. Bakewell (2010) would call this methodological dualism. See Bhaskar (1989) for some discussion of critical realism's insistence on the separation of agency and structure and the 'real' nature of social structures, and Bakewell (2010) for the implications of this position for migration research.
5. Lave and Wenger (1991) elaborate the wider, sociologically-informed theoretical framework behind their theory of situated learning in more detail in their footnotes, and it is covered in much more detail in Wenger (1998).

163

6. See Stones (2005: 141) for a further, related, example.
7. Please note that for this section, above, rather than list all the relevant publications for each author I have offered indicative reading for the student reader to pursue.

3   Theories and Perspectives in Migration

1. Quantitative studies, like official statistics, also often exclude undocumented migrants and women, especially when they use the head of the household as their reference person.
2. When I wrote my PhD thesis in 1996, very few people had mentioned the word transnationalism, but by the time I wrote the book in 2000 it was becoming a buzz word in migration studies. A search for 'transnationalism' in the *Journal of Ethnic and Migration Studies* in July 2010 yielded 130 papers! A search for 'transnational' in *Ethnic and Racial Studies*, at the same time, yielded 64 papers. A search for 'transnationalism' in *Sociological Abstracts* yielded 376 results since 2000!

4   Lifestyle Migration: British Migration to Spain's Coastal Areas

1. Other important European groups in Spain include Germans, French, Italians and Swiss. These form large visible minorities in many coastal areas.
2. The way the class habitus affects how migrants choose their destination and their social lives after moving is discussed more in Oliver and O'Reilly (2010).

5   Labour Migration: Mexican Labour Migration to the United States

1. Labour migration is a vast topic. Useful overviews of labour migration include Sharpe, P. (2001) *Women, Gender and Labour Migration, Historical and Global Perspectives*, London: Routledge and Guild, E. and Mantu, S. (2011) *Constructing and Imagining Labour Migration*, Farnham: Ashgate.
2. Some authors reviewed in this chapter use the term 'immigrant' to refer to those who have migrated to the US. I have used this term when they do to indicate the work is theirs, or to reflect the fact they are talking from the perspective of the US. But I prefer to use the term 'migrant' when I am referring to people who move, to indicate that they may be both emigrants and

immigrants (depending on whose perspective we are taking), and to acknowledge that their migration may be temporary or fluid, a process rather than an event.

3. **A note on Portes' and his team's bespoke surveys.** *The Comparative Immigrant Entrepreneurship Project* is a quantitative survey of 1,200 heads of immigrant families living in New York, Washington DC, and Providence, Rhode Island, exploring the extent and determinants of transnational activities. Since it was discovered that transnationalism was being channelled mainly via organizations as a collective and political activity, *The Comparative Immigrant Organization Project, phase 1* (CIOP -1) examined organizations involved in transnational activities and the impacts on communities of origin, particularly on development. Thirty organizations were selected for each nationality (Colombian, Dominican and Mexican) and the leaders were interviewed. *The Comparative Immigrant Organization Project, phase 2* (CIOP- 2) 'was designed to address directly the questions of immigrants' loyalties, integration and US citizenship acquisition' (Portes, Escobar and Arana, 2009: 109). Here 20 immigrant organizations with either a transnational or a domestic focus were selected for each national group and leaders were interviewed face to face about the characteristics of their members and the nature of the activities of the organization. They were also asked questions about their attitudes to 'naturalization, incorporation into American civic and political life' (ibid: 110) and whether they felt transnational activities or allegiances with the countries of origin were incompatible with successful incorporation in American life. Additionally, a telephone and internet survey was conducted with a number of small and medium size immigrant organizations, asking these last set of attitude questions of members. Overall, the sample for CIOP – 2 is 247. In 1996–97 a representative sample of more than 2,500 immigrant parents in South California and South Florida were interviewed, covering nine nationalities of immigrants (representing, they suggest, 80 per cent of the immigrant population of the US, ibid: 18). The *Children of Immigration Longitudinal Survey* (CILS) survey then followed a sample of 5,200 children from early adolescence to adulthood with three interviews at different points of their lives (Portes and Fernández-Kelly, 2008: 18). See http://dss.princeton.edu/cgi-bin/dataresources/guides.cgi for more information on these studies.

4. For more on the Bracero program and what was called Operation Wetback (a 1954 forced repatriation program) see Ronald Mize and Alicia Swords (2011).

5. It is also worth noting that Mexican migration often follows a sequence, from Southern to Northern Mexican states and then on to the US, or from Mexican villages to towns, then abroad, or to border cities, then across the border. However, patterns are very varied and many also migrate directly from rural areas of Mexico to US cities (see Castles, 2010 for some discussion of this). Also note that practice stories are never complete; I recently started to find answers to many of these questions in Hellman's (2008) work.

6. It was not actually very clear what these authors meant by the term socially stable, but they did refer to marriage, having children, and a legal status as indicators.

6 Domestic Labour Migration: Fillipina Migration to Hong Kong

1. Parreñas' (2003) chapter builds on her other work (2001), on Filipino Domestic workers based in Rome and LA. This book is able to contribute some invaluable insights into the transnational lives of domestic workers that I have not been able to cover here. I also recommend Parreñas (2008 and 2005) which would add some very rich material to the work begun in this chapter.
2. In the early 1990s there were well over 100,000 Filipina Domestic Workers in Hong Kong and just a small number of other groups. By 2006, there were almost 100,000 Indonesian workers as well as an additional 25,000 Filipinas and countless more from other areas.
3. Note that I am using the terminology of the authors here; some use the term 'domestic helpers' while others prefer 'workers'.
4. I would like to draw the reader's attention to the fact that a great deal of applied social science work has been undertaken on this topic at the City University of Hong Kong.

7 Refugees and Forced Migration: Refugee Children in the United Kingdom

1. If the reader is interested, The Refugee Council in the UK and the US Committee for Refugees and Immigrants are good places to start learning about this topic. The United Nations Refugee Agency (UNHCR) www.unhcr.org has lots of resources for teaching and learning about refugees. Donellan (2004) reviews news stories and statistics to analyse the refugee situation around the world. Rutter (2004) is a teaching resources for 11–18 year olds and includes guidance for teachers, lesson plans, refugee testimonies, and other information.
2. Marfleet (2006) uses 'refugees' and 'forced migration' almost interchangeably, which reflects his contention that refugees have little agency.
3. Note that this was at the time of writing; policies on the ground and how they are interpreted need updating for every new study.
4. Rutter 2004 has more information on the research methods.

Bibliography

Ackers, L. and Dwyer, P. (2004) 'Fixed Laws, Fluid Lives: The Citizenship Status of Post-retirement Migrants in the European Union', *Ageing and Society,* 24(3), 451–75.

Adkins, L. (2004) 'Reflexivity: Freedom or Habit of Gender', in L. Adkins and B. Skeggs (eds) *Feminism After Bourdieu* (Oxford: Blackwell) pp. 191–210.

Agadjanian, V. (2008) 'Research on International Migration within Sub-Saharan Africa: Foci, Approaches, and Challenges', *The Sociological Quarterly,* 49(3), 407–421.

Alba, R.D. and Nee, V. (2003) *Remaking the American Mainstream: Assimilation and Contemporary Immigration* (Cambridge, MA: Harvard University Press).

Aledo, A. (2005) 'Los Otros Immigrantes: Residents Europeos en el Sudeste Español', in J. Fernández-Rufete and M.G. Jiménez (eds) *Movimientos Migratorios Contemporáneos* (Murcia: Quaderna Editorial) pp. 161–180.

Anderson, B. (1991) *Imagined Communities: Reflections on the Origin and Spread of Nationalism* (London: Verso).

Annan, K. (2006) 'Address of Mr. Kofi Annan, Secretary-General, to the High-Level Dialogue of the United Nations General Assembly on International Migration and Development, New York, September 14, 2006', *International Migration Review,* 40(4), 963–965.

Anthias, F. (2000) 'Metaphors of Home: Gendering New Migrations in Southern Europe', in F. Anthias and G. Lazardis (eds) *Gender and Migration in Southern Europe* (Oxford: Berg) pp. 15–48.

Arango, J. (2004) 'Theories of International Migration', in D. Joly (ed.) *International Migration in the New Millennium: Global Movement and Settlement* (Aldershot/Burlington, VT: Ashgate) pp. 15–35.

Archer, M.S. (1995) *Realist Social Theory: The Morphogenetic Approach* (Cambridge: Cambridge University Press).

Asian Migrants Centre (AMC) (1991) Foreign Domestic Workers in Hong Kong: A Baseline Study (Hong Kong: Asian Migrant Workers Centre).

Bagby, I. (2009) 'The American Mosque in Transition: Assimilation, Acculturation and Isolation', *Journal of Ethnic and Migration Studies,* 35(3), 473–490.

Bakewell, O. (2010) 'Some Reflections on Structure and Agency in Migration Theory', *Journal of Ethnic and Migration Studies,* 36(10), 1689–1708.

Barth, F. (1969a) *Ethnic Groups and Boundaries: The Social Organization of Culture Difference* (Boston: Little, Brown).

Barth, F. (1969b) 'Introduction', in F. Barth (ed.) *Ethnic Groups and Boundaries: The Social Organization of Culture Difference* (Boston: Little, Brown) pp. 9–38.

Basch, L.G. (1993) *Nations Unbound: Transnational Projects, Postcolonial Predicaments, and Deterritorialized Nation-states* (Basel: Gordon and Breach).

Bauman, Z. (1992) 'Soil, Blood and Identity', *The Sociological Review*, 40(4), 675–701.

Bauman, Z. (2000) *Liquid Modernity* (Cambridge: Polity Press).

Beaverstock, J.V. (2005) 'Transnational Elites in the City: British Highly-Skilled Inter-Company Transferees in New York City's Financial District', *Journal of Ethnic and Migration Studies*, 31(2), 245–268.

Beck, U. (1992) *Risk Society: Towards a New Modernity* (London: Sage).

Benson, M. and O'Reilly, K. (eds) (2009) *Lifestyle Migration: Expectations, Aspirations and Experiences* (Farnham: Ashgate).

Berger, P. and Luckmann, T. (1975) *The Social Construction of Reality. A Treatise in the Sociology of Knowledge* (Harmondsworth: Penguin).

Bhaskar, R. (1989) *The Possibility of Naturalism: A Philosophical Critique of the Contemporary Human Sciences*, 2nd edn (New York/ London: Harvester Wheatsheaf).

Billig, M. (1995) *Banal Nationalism* (London: Sage).

Bloch, A. (2002) *The Migration and Settlement of Refugees in Britain* (Basingstoke: Palgrave Macmillan).

Blumer, H. (1969) *Symbolic Interactionism: Perspective and Method* (Englewood Cliffs, NJ: Prentice-Hall).

Bommes, M. and Morawska, E.T. (eds) (2005) *International Migration Research: Constructions, Omissions and the Promises of Interdisciplinarity* (Aldershot: Ashgate).

Bourdieu, P. and Passeron, J. (1977) *Reproduction in Education, Society and Culture* (London: Sage Publications).

Bourdieu, P. (1977) *Outline of a Theory of Practice* (Cambridge: Cambridge University Press).

Bourdieu, P. (1984) *Distinction: A Social Critique of the Judgement of Taste* (London: Routledge & Kegan Paul).

Bourdieu, P. (1985) 'The Social Space and the Genesis of Groups', *Theory and Society*, 14(6), 723–744.

Bourdieu, P. (1990) *The Logic of Practice* (Cambridge: Polity).

Bourdieu, P. (1996) 'Understanding', *Theory, Culture & Society*, 13(2), 17–37.

Bourdieu, P. (1999) *The Weight of the World: Social Suffering in Contemporary Society* (Oxford: Polity).

Brettell, C. and Hollifield, J.F. (eds) (2008) Migration *Theory: Talking Across Disciplines*, 2nd edn (London: Routledge).

Brubaker, R. (2005) 'The "Diaspora" Diaspora', *Ethnic and Racial Studies*, 28(1), 1–19.

Bryant, C.G.A. and Jary, D. (eds) (1991) *Giddens' Theory of Structuration: A Critical Appreciation* (London: Routledge).

Bryant, C.G.A. and Jary, D. (2001) *The Contemporary Giddens: Social Theory in a Globalizing Age* (London: Palgrave Macmillan).

Bryant, C.G.A. and Jary, D. (2003) 'Anthony Giddens' in G. Ritzer, *The Blackwell Companion to Major Contemporary Social Theorists* (London: Blackwell) pp. 247–273.

Canales, A.I. (2003) 'Mexican Labour Migration to the United States in the Age of Globalisation', *Journal of Ethnic and Migration Studies*, 29(4), 741–761.

Casado Díaz, M. (2006) 'Retiring to Spain: An Analysis of Differences Among North European Nationals', *Journal of Ethnic and Migration Studies*, 32(8), 1321–1339.

Casado Díaz, M. (2009) 'Social Capital in the Sun: Bonding and Bridging Social Capital Among British Retirees', in M. Benson and K. O'Reilly (eds) *Lifestyle Migration: Expectations, Aspirations and Experiences* (Farnham: Ashgate) pp. 87–102.

Castells, M. (2000) *The Rise of the Network Society*, 2nd edn (Oxford: Blackwell).

Castles, S. and Miller, M.J. (2003) *The Age of Migration*, 3rd edn (Basingstoke: Palgrave Macmillan).

Castles, S. and Miller, M.J. (2009) *The Age of Migration: International Population Movements in the Modern World*, 4th edn (Basingstoke: Palgrave Macmillan).

Castles, S. (2003a) 'The International Politics of Forced Migration', *Development*, 46(3), 11–20.

Castles, S. (2003b) 'Towards a Sociology of Forced Migration and Social Transformation', *Sociology*, 37(1), 13–34.

Castles, S. (2007) 'Twenty-First-Century Migration as a Challenge to Sociology', *Journal of Ethnic and Migration Studies*, 33(3), 351–371.

Castles, S. (2010) 'Understanding Global Migration: A Social Transformation Perspective', *Journal of Ethnic and Migration Studies*, 36(10), pp. 1565–1586.

Chattopadhyay, S. (2010) 'Narrating Everyday Spaces of the Resettled Adivasis in Sardar Sarovar', 16(2), 85–101.

Chiswick, B. (2008) 'Are Immigrants Favourably Self-Selected?' in C. Brettell and J.F. Hollifield (eds) *Migration Theory: Talking Across Disciplines*, 2nd edn (London: Routledge) pp. 61–76.

Cohen, I.J. (1989) *Structuration Theory: Anthony Giddens and the Constitution of Social Life* (Basingstoke: Macmillan).

Cohen, R. (2006) *Migration and its Enemies: Global Capital, Migrant Labour and the Nation-state* (Aldershot: Ashgate).

Constable, N. (2003) 'Filipina Workers in Hong Kong Homes: Household Rules', in B. Ehrenreich and A.R. Hochschild (eds) *Global Woman: Nannies, Maids and Sex Workers in the New Economy* (London: Granta Books) pp. 115–141.

Constable, N. (2007) *Maid to Order in Hong Kong: Stories of Migrant Workers*, 2nd edn (Ithaca, NT/Bristol: Cornell University Press).

Cooky, C. (2009) ' "Girls Just Aren't Interested": The Social Construction of Interest in Girls' Sport', *Sociological Perspectives*, 52(2), 259–284.

Cunningham, H. and Heyman, J.M. (2004) 'Introduction: Mobilities and Enclosures at Borders', *Identities: Global Studies in Culture and Power*, 11(3), 289–302.

Day, G. and Thompson, A. (2004) *Theorizing Nationalism* (Basingstoke: Palgrave Macmillan).

De Certeau, M. (1984) *The Practice of Everyday Life* (Berkeley, CA/London: University of California Press).

De Haas, H. (2010) 'The Internal Dynamics of Migration Processes: A Theoretical Inquiry', *Journal of Ethnic and Migration Studies*, 36(10), 1587–1617.

Dewey, J. (1922) *Human Nature and Conduct* (London: Allen & Unwin).

Donellan, C. (ed.) (2004) *Refugees* (London: Independence Educational Publishers).

Dreby, J. (2010) *Divided by Borders: Mexican Migrants and their Children* (California. University of California Press).

Durkheim, E. (1938) *The Rules of Sociological Method*, 8th edn (Chicago Illinois: University of Chicago Press).

Ehrenreich, B. and Hochschild, A.R. (eds) (2003) *Global Woman: Nannies, Maids and Sex Workers in the New Economy* (London: Granta Books).

Emirbayer, M. and Mische, A. (1998) 'What Is Agency?' *American Journal of Sociology*, 103(4), 962–1023.

Erel, U. (2010) 'Migrating Cultural Capital: Bourdieu in Migration Studies', *Sociology*, 44(4), 642–660.

Eriksen, T.H. (2002) *Ethnicity and Nationalism*, 2nd edn (London: Pluto).

Faist, T. (2000) *The Volume and Dynamics of International Migration and Transnational Social Spaces* (Oxford: Clarendon).

Faist, T. (2010) 'Towards Transnational Studies: World Theories, Transnationalisation and Changing Institutions', *Journal of Ethnic and Migration Studies*, 36(10), 1665–1687.

Falzon, M. (ed.) (2009) *Multi-sited Ethnography: Theory, Praxis and Locality in Contemporary Research* (Farnham: Ashgate).

Fechter, A. (2007) *Transnational Lives: Expatriates in Indonesia* (Aldershot: Ashgate).

Franklin, A. (2003) *Tourism: An Introduction* (London: SAGE).

French, C. (1986) *Filipina Domestic Workers in Hong Kong: A Preliminary Survey*, Centre for Hong Kong Studies, Occasional Papers, University of Hong Kong, 11.

Gadamer, H.G. (1989) *Truth and Method* (London: Sheed and Ward).

Gans, H.J. (1992) 'Second-Generation Decline: Scenarios for the Economic and Ethnic Futures of the Post-1965 American Immigrants', *Ethnic and Racial Studies*, 15(2), 173–192.

Garfinkel, H. (1984) *Studies in Ethnomethodology* (Cambridge: Polity).

Gellner, E. (2006) *Nations and Nationalism*, 2nd edn (Malden, MA/Oxford: Blackwell).

Giddens, A. (1971) *Capitalism and Modern Social Theory: An Analysis of the Writings of Marx, Durkheim and Max Weber* (London: Cambridge University Press).

Giddens, A. (1976) *New Rules of Sociological Method: A Positive Critique of Interpretative Sociologies* (London: Hutchinson).

Giddens, A. (1977) *Studies in Social and Political Theory* (London: Hutchinson).

Giddens, A. (1979) *Central Problems in Social Theory: Action, Structure and Contradiction in Social Analysis* (London: Macmillan).

Giddens, A. (1981) *A Contemporary Critique of Historical Materialism* (London: Macmillan).

Giddens, A. (1984) *The Constitution of Society: Outline of the Theory of Structuration* (Cambridge: Polity).

Giddens, A. (1989) 'A Reply to My Critics', in D. Held and J.B. Thompson (eds) *Social Theory of Modern Societies: Anthony Giddens and His Critics* (Cambridge: Cambridge University Press) pp. 249–301.

Giddens, A. (1990) *The Consequences of Modernity* (Stanford, CA: Stanford University Press).

Giddens, A. (1991a) *Modernity and Self-identity* (Cambridge: Polity).

Giddens, A. (1991b) 'Structuration Theory: Past, Present and Future', in C.G.A. Bryant and D. Jary (eds) *Giddens' Theory of Structuration: A Critical Appreciation* (London: Routledge) pp. 201–221.

Giddens, A. (1992) *The Transformation of Intimacy: Sexuality, Love and Eroticism in Modern Societies* (Cambridge: Polity).

Glick Schiller, N. (1997) *The Situation of Transnational Studies. Identities: Global Studies in Culture and Power*, 4(2), 155–166.

Goffman, E. (1990) *The Presentation of Self in Everyday Life* (London: Penguin).

Goldring, L. (2002) 'The Mexican State and Transmigrant Organizations: Negotiating the Boundaries of Membership and Participation', *Latin American Research Review*, 37(3), 55–99.

Gonzalez, G.G. and Fernandez, R.A. (2003) *A Century of Chicano History: Empire, Nations, and Migration* (New York/London: Routledge).

Gregson, N. (1989) 'On the (Ir)relevance of Structuration Theory', in D. Held and J.B. Thompson (eds) *Social Theory of Modern Societies: Anthony Giddens and His Critics* (Cambridge: Cambridge University Press) pp. 235–248.

Guild, E. and Mantu, S. (2011) *Constructing and Imagining Labour Migration* (Farnham: Ashgate).

Gustafson, P. (2009) 'Your Home in Spain: Residential Strategies in International Retirement Migration', in M. Benson and K. O'Reilly (eds) *Lifestyle Migration: Expectations, Aspirations and Experiences* (Farnham: Ashgate) pp. 69–86.

Hall, C.M. and Williams, A. (2002) 'Tourism, Migration, Circulation and Mobility: The Contingencies of Time and Place', in C.M. Hall and A. Williams (eds) *Tourism and Migration: New Relationships Between Production and Consumption* (Dordrecht/London: Kluwer Academic) pp. 1–60.

Halpern, D. (2005) *Social Capital* (Cambridge: Polity).

Hannerz, U. (1992) *Cultural Complexity: Studies in the Social Organization of Meaning* (New /Oxford: Columbia University Press).

Harney, N.D. and Baldassar, L. (2007) 'Tracking Transnationalism: Migrancy and Its Futures', *Journal of Ethnic and Migration Studies*, 33(2), 189–198.

Harzig, C. (2001) 'Women Migrants and Global and Local Agents', in P. Sharpe (ed.) *Women, Gender, and Labour Migration: Historical and Global Perspectives* (London: Routledge) pp. 15–28.

Held, D. and Thompson, J.B. (eds) (1989) *Social Theory of Modern Societies: Anthony Giddens and His Critics* (Cambridge: Cambridge University Press).

Held, D. (1999) *Global Transformations: Politics, Economics and Culture* (Cambridge: Polity Press).

Hellman, J.A. (1994) *Mexican Lives* (New York: New Press).

Hellman, J.A. (2008) *The World of Mexican Migrants: The Rock and the Hard Place* (New York: The New Press).

Huber, A. and O'Reilly, K. (2004) 'The Construction of Heimat under Conditions of Individualised Modernity: Swiss and British Elderly Migrants in Spain', *Ageing & Society*, 24(3), 327–351.

Huntington, S.T. (2004) 'The Hispanic Challenge', _Foreign Policy_, March 1, see http://www.foreignpolicy.com/articles/2004/03/01/the_hispanic_challenge.

Inda, J.X. and Rosaldo, R. (2001) 'Introduction. A World in Motion', in J.X. Inda and R. Rosaldo (eds) _The Anthropology of Globalization. A Reader_ (London: Blackwell) pp. 1–34.

Jargowsky, P.A. (2009) 'Immigrants and Neighbourhoods of Concentrated Poverty: Assimilation or Stagnation?', _Journal of Ethnic and Migration Studies_, 35(7), 1129–1151.

Jary, D. and Bryant, C.G.A. (eds) (2001) _The Contemporary Giddens: Social Theory in a Globalizing Age_ (Basingstoke: Palgrave).

Jenkins, R. (2000) 'Pierre Bourdieu and the Reproduction of Determinism', in D. Robbins (ed.) _Pierre Bourdieu_ (London: SAGE) pp. 148–163.

Jenkins, R. (2002) _Pierre Bourdieu_, Rev. edn (London: Routledge).

Joly, D. (ed.) (2004) _International Migration in the New Millennium: Global Movement and Settlement_ (Aldershot/Burlington, VT: Ashgate).

Juss, S.S. (2006) _International Migration and Global Justice_ (Aldershot: Ashgate).

Karn, V.A. (1977) _Retiring to the Seaside_ (London: Routledge and Kegan Paul).

Keefe, S.E. and Padilla, A.M. (1987) _Chicano Ethnicity_ (Albuquerque: University of New Mexico Press).

Kidder, J.L. (2009) 'Appropriating the City: Space, Theory, and Bike Messengers', _Theory and Society_, 38(3), 307–328.

King, N. and Calasanti, T. (2009) 'Aging Agents: Social Gerontologists' Imputations to Old People', _International Journal of Sociology and Social Policy_, 29(1–2), 38–48.

King, R. and Rybaczuk, K. (1993) 'Southern Europe and the International Division of Labour: From Emmigration to Immigration', in R. King (ed.) _The New Geography of European Migrations_ (London/New York: Belhaven Press); Co-published in the Americas with Halsted Press, pp. 175–206.

King, R. and Skeldon, R. (2010) ' "Mind the Gap!" Integrating Approaches to Internal and International Migration', _Journal of Ethnic and Migration Studies_, 36(10), pp. 1619–1646.

King, R., Warnes, T. and Williams, A. (2000) _Sunset Lives: British Retirement Migration to the Mediterranean_ (Oxford: Berg).

Kivisto, P. (2001) 'Theorizing Transnational Immigration: A Critical Review of Current Efforts', _Ethnic and Racial Studies_, 24(4), 549–577.

Kiy, R. and McEnany, A. (2010) _Civic Engagement, Volunteerism, and Charitable Giving: Americans Retired in Mexican Coastal Communities_ (National City, CA: International Community Foundation).

Kofman, E., Phizacklea, A., Raghuram, P. and Sales, R. (2000) _Gender and International Migration in Europe: Employment, Welfare, and Politics_ (London: Routledge).

Koser, K. (2007a) _International Migration: A Very Short Introduction_ (Oxford: Oxford University Press).

Koser, K. (2007b) 'Refugees, Transnationalism and the State', _Journal of Ethnic and Migration Studies_, 33(2), 233–254.

Kruythoff, H. (2008) 'Tenant Participation in the Netherlands: The Role of Laws, Covenants and (Power) Positions', _Housing Studies_, 23(4), 637–659.

Kudenko, I. and Phillips, D. (2009) 'The Model of Integration? Social and Spatial Transformations in the Leeds Jewish Community', *Journal of Ethnic and Migration Studies*, 35(9), 1533–1549.

Lane, J.F. (2000) *Pierre Bourdieu: A Critical Introduction* (London: Pluto).

Lanfant, M. (1995) 'Introduction', in M. Lanfant, J.B. Allcock and E.M. Bruner (eds) *International Tourism: Identity and Change* (London: SAGE) pp. 1–16.

Lave, J. and Wenger, E. (1991) *Situated Learning: Legitimate Peripheral Participation* (Cambridge: Cambridge University Press).

Layder, D. (1994) *Understanding Social Theory* (London: Sage).

Lee, E. (1966) 'A Theory of Migration', *Demography*, 3(1), 47–57.

Lindio-McGovern, L. (2004) 'Alienation and Labor Export in the Context of Globalization. Filipino Migrant Domestic Workers in Taiwan and Hong Kong', *Critical Asian Studies*, 36(2), 217–238.

Loyal, S. (2009) 'The French in Algeria, Algerians in France: Bourdieu, Colonialism, and Migration', *The Sociological Review*, 57(3), 406–427.

Lutz, H. (2010) 'Gender in the Migratory Process', *Journal of Ethnic and Migration Studies*, 36(10), 1647–1663.

Mantecón, A. (2008) *The Experience of Tourism: A Sociological Study of the Process of Residential Tourism* (Barcelona: Icaria).

Marfleet, P. (2006) *Refugees in a Global Era* (Basingstoke: Palgrave Macmillan).

Martin, P.L. (2004) 'The United States: Benign Neglect Toward Immigration', in W.A. Cornelius, P.L. Martin and J.F. Hollifield (eds) *Controlling Immigration. A Global Perspective* (Stanford, CA: Stanford University Press) pp. 83–99.

Massey, D.S., Arango, J., Hugo, G., Kouaouci, A., Pellegrino, A. and Edward Taylor, J. (1998) *Worlds in Motion: Understanding International Migration at the End of the Millennium* (Oxford: Clarendon Press).

McGregor, J. (2009) 'Associational Links with Home Among Zimbabweans in the UK: Reflections on Long-distance Nationalisms', *Global Networks*, 9(2), 185–208.

Mead, G.H. (1934) *Mind, Self and Society from the Standpoint of a Social Behaviorist* (Chicago, IL: The University of Chicago Press).

Merleau-Ponty, M. (1962) *Phenomenology of Perception* (London: Routledge and Kegan Paul).

Mize, R. and Swords, A. (2011) *Consuming Mexican Labor: From the Bracero Program to NAFTA* (Toronto, Canada: University of Toronto Press).

Mora, G.C. (2008) 'No Margin for Error and Its Implications for Future Research', *The Annals of the American Academy of Political and Social Science*, 620, 295–298.

Morawska, E.T. (1996) *Insecure Prosperity: Small-town Jews in Industrial America, 1890–1940* (Princeton, NJ/Chichester: Princeton University Press).

Morawska, E.T. (2001) 'Structuring Migration: The Case of Polish Income-Seeking Travellers to the West', *Theory and Society*, 30(1), 47–80.

Morawska, E.T. (2009) *The Sociology of Immigration: (Re)making Multifaceted America* (Basingstoke: Palgrave Macmillan).

Morokvasic, M. (1984) 'Birds of Passage are also Women', *International Migration Review*, 18(4), 886–907.

Mouzelis, N. (1991) *Back to Sociological Theory* (London: Macmillan).

Okafor, E.E. (2009) 'The Use of Adolescents as Domestic Servants in Ibadan, Nigeria', *Journal of Adolescent Research*, 24(2), 169–193.

Oliver, C. and O'Reilly, K. (2010) 'A Bourdieusian Analysis of Class and Migration', *Sociology*, 44(1), 49–66.

O'Neill, M. (2010) *Asylum, Migration and Community* (Bristol: The Policy Press).

O'Reilly, K. (1999) 'Trading Intimacy for Liberty: British Women on the Costa del Sol', in F. Anthias and G. Lazaridis (eds) *Gender and Migration in Southern Europe* (Oxford: Berg) pp. 227–248.

O'Reilly, K. (2000) *The British on the Costa del Sol: Transnational Identities and Local Communities* (London: Routledge).

O'Reilly, K. (2003) 'When is a Tourist? The Articulation of Tourism and Migration in Spain's Costa del Sol', *Tourist Studies*, 3(3), 301–317.

O'Reilly, K. (2007) 'Intra-European Migration and the Mobility-Enclosure Dialectic', *Sociology*, 41(2), 277–293.

O'Reilly, K. (2009a) 'Hosts and Guests, Guests and Hosts: British Residential Tourism in the Costa del Sol', in P.O. Pons, M. Crang and P. Travlou (eds) *Cultures of Mass Tourism: Doing the Mediterranean in the Age of Banal Mobilities* (Farnham: Ashgate) pp. 129–142.

O'Reilly, K. (2009b) *Key Concepts in Ethnography* (London: SAGE).

O'Reilly, K. (2011) *Ethnographic Methods*, 2nd edn (London: Routledge).

Papastergiadis, N. (2000) *The Turbulence of Migration: Globalization, Deterritorialization, and Hybridity* (Cambridge: Polity Press).

Parreñas, R.S. (2001) *Servants of Globalization: Women, Migration, and Domestic Work* (Stanford, CA: Stanford University Press).

Parreñas, R.S. (2003) 'The Care Crisis in the Philippines: Children and Transnational Families in the New Global Economy', in B. Ehrenreich and A.R. Hochschild (eds) *Global Woman: Nannies, Maids and Sex Workers in the New Economy* (London: Granta Books) pp. 39–54.

Parreñas, R.S. (2005) *Children of Global Migration: Transnational Families and Gendered Woes* (Stanford, CA: Stanford University Press).

Parreñas, R.S. (2008) *The Force of Domesticity: Filipina Migrants and Globalization* (New York/London: New York University Press).

Perlmann, J. (2007) *Italians then, Mexicans Now: Immigrant Origins and Second-generation Progress, 1890 to 2000* (New York: Russell Sage Foundation and the Levy Institute).

Phizacklea, A. (2004) 'Migration Theory and Migratory Realities: A Gendered Perspective', in D. Joly (ed.) *International Migration in the New Millennium: Global Movement and Settlement* (Aldershot: Ashgate) pp. 121–143.

Polanyi, K. (2001) *The Great Transformation* (Boston: Beacon Press).

Portes, A., Escobar, C. and Walton Radford, A. (2007) 'Immigrant Transnational Organizations and Development: A Comparative Study', *International Migration Review*, 41(1), 242–281.

Portes, A., Escobar, C. and Arana, R. (2008) 'Bridging the Gap: Transnational and Ethnic Organizations in the Political Incorporation of Immigrants in the United States', *Ethnic and Racial Studies*, 31(6), 1056–1090.

Portes, A., Escobar, C. and Arana, R. (2009) 'Divided or Convergent Loyalties?: The Political Incorporation Process of Latin American Immigrants in the United States', *International Journal of Comparative Sociology*, 50(2), 103–136.

Portes, A. and Fernandez-Kelly, P. (2008) 'No Margin for Error: Educational and Occupational Achievement Among Disadvantaged Children of Immigrants', *The Annals of the American Academy of Political and Social Science*, 620, 12–36.

Portes, A., Guarnizo, L.E. and Landolt, P. (1999) 'The Study of Transnationalism: Pitfalls and Promise of an Emergent Research Field', *Ethnic and Racial Studies*, 22(2), 217–237.

Portes, A. and Rumbaut, R.G. (2006) *Immigrant America: A Portrait*, 3rd edn (Berkeley, CA/ London: University of California Press).

Portes, A. and Walton, J. (1981) *Labor, Class and the International System* (New York/London: Academic Press).

Portes, A. and Zhou, M. (1993) 'The New Second Generation: Segmented Assimilation and Its Variants', *The Annals of the American Academy of Political and Social Science*, 530, 74–96.

Portes, A. (2007) 'Migration, Development and Segmented Assimilation: A Conceptual Review of the Evidence', *The Annals of the American Academy of Political and Social Science*, 610, 73–97.

Portes, A. (2010) 'Migration and Social Change: Some Conceptual Reflections', *Journal of Ethnic and Migration Studies*, 36(10), 1537–1563.

Ravenstein, E.G. (1889) 'The Laws of Migration', *Journal of the Statistical Society*, 52, 214–301.

Ravenstein, E.G. (1976) *The Laws of Migration* (New York: Arno Press).

Reay, D., Crozier, G. and Clayton, J. (2009) ' "Strangers in Paradise"?: Working-class Students in Elite Universities', *Sociology*, 43(6), 1103–1121.

Reay, D. (2004) ' "It's All Becoming a Habitus": Beyond the Habitual Use of Habitus in Educational Research', *British Journal of Sociology of Education*, 25(4), 431–444.

Richardson, J.E. (2008) ' "Our England": Discourses of "Race" and Class in Party Election Leaflets', *Social Semiotics*, 18(3), 321–335.

Richmond, A.H. (1993) 'Reactive Migration: Sociological Perspectives on Refugee Movements', *Journal of Refugee Studies*, 6(1), 7–24.

Robertson, R. (1992) *Globalization: Social Theory and Global Culture* (London: Sage Publications).

Rodes, J. (2009) *Europeans Between Migration and Tourism. Mobility and Registration Patterns Among Senior Europeans in Murcia*, Universidad de Murcia.

Rodríguez, V., Casado Díaz, M. and Huber, A. (eds) (2005) *La Migración de Europeos Retiradas en España* (Madrid: Consejo Superior de Investigaciones Científicas).

Rodríguez, V., Fernández-Mayoralas, G., Rojo, F. and Abellán, A. (2005) 'Migración Internacional de Retirados: Los Jubilados Europeos en Andalucía', in V. Rodríguez, M. Casado Diaz and A. Huber, (eds) (2005) *La Migración de Europeos Retiradas en España* (Madrid: Consejo Superior de Investigaciones Científicas).

Rosenau, J.N. (1997) *Along the Domestic-foreign Frontier: Exploring Governance in a Turbulent World* (Cambridge: Cambridge University Press).

Rouse, R. (1995) 'Questions of Identity: Personhood and Collectivity in Transnational Migration to the United States', *Critique of Anthropology*, 15(4), 351–380.

Ruiz, V.L. and Tiano, S. (eds) (1987) *Women on the U.S.-Mexico Border: Responses to Change* (Hemel Hempstead: Unwin Hyman).

Ruiz, V.L. (1987) 'By the Day or the Week: Mexicana Domestic Workers in El Paso', in V.L. Ruiz and S. Tiano (eds) *Women on the U.S.-Mexico Border: Responses to Change* (Hemel Hempstead: Unwin Hyman) pp. 61–83.

Ruiz, V.L. (2008) *From Out of the Shadows: Mexican Women in Twentieth-century America*, 10th anniversary edn (Oxford: Oxford University Press).

Rutter, J. (2004) *Refugees: We Left Because We Had To*, 3rd edn (London: Refugee Council).

Rutter, J. (2006) *Refugee Children in the UK*, new edn (Maidenhead: Open University Press).

Sassen, S. and Smith, R. (1992) 'Post-industrial Growth and Economic Reorganisation: Their Impact on Immigrant Employment', in J.A. Bustamante, C.W. Reynolds and R. Hinojosa Ojeda (eds) *U.S.-Mexico Relations: Labor Market Interdependence* (Stanford, CA: Stanford University Press) pp. 372–393.

Sassen, S. (1988) *The Mobility of Labor and Capital: A Study in International Investment and Labor Flow* (Cambridge: Cambridge University Press).

Sassen, S. (1996) *Losing Control?: Sovereignty in an Age of Globalization* (New York/Chichester: Columbia University Press).

Schiller, N.G. and Caglar, A. (2009) 'Towards a Comparative Theory of Locality in Migration Studies: Migrant Incorporation and City Scale', *Journal of Ethnic and Migration Studies*, 35(2), 177–202.

Schutz, A. (1972) *The Phenomenology of the Social World*, trans. George Walsh and Frederick Lehnert; with an introduction by George Walsh (London: Heinemann Educational).

Scott, J.C. (1985) *Weapons of the Weak: Everyday Forms of Peasant Resistance* (New Haven/London: Yale University Press).

Sewell, W.H., JR. (1992) 'A Theory of Structure: Duality, Agency, and Transformation', *American Journal of Sociology*, 98(1), 1–29.

Sharpe, P. (2001) *Women, Gender, and Labour Migration: Historical and Global Perspectives* (London: Routledge).

Shaw, G. and Williams, A. (2002) Critical Issues in Tourism: A Geographical Perspective, 2nd edn (Oxford: Blackwell).

Silvey, R. (2004) 'Power, Difference and Mobility: Feminist Advances in Migration Studies', *Progress in Human Geography*, 28, 490–506.

Skeldon, R. (1997) *Migration and Development: A Global Perspective* (Harlow: Longman).

Skeldon, R. (2004) 'Migration, the Asian Financial Crisis and its Aftermath', in D. Joly (ed.) *International Migration in the New Millennium: Global Movement and Settlement* (Aldershot/Burlington, VT: Ashgate) pp. 57–74.

Smith, A.D. (1979) *Nationalism in the Twentieth Century* (Oxford: Martin Robertson).

Smith, A.D. (2009) *Ethno-symbolism and Nationalism: A Cultural Approach* (London: Routledge).

Smith, Z. (2001) *White Teeth* (London: Penguin).

Solóranzo-Torres, R. (1987) 'Female Mexican Immigrants in San Diego County', in V.L. Ruiz and S. Tiano (eds) *Women on the U.S.-Mexico Border: Responses to Change* (Hemel Hempstead: Unwin Hyman) pp. 41–60.

Song, M. (2010) What Happens After Segmented Assimilation? An Exploration of Intermarriage and "Mixed Race" Young People in Britain', *Ethnic and Racial Studies*, 33(7), 1194–1213.

Spener, D. and Staudt, K.A. (1998) The U.S.-Mexico Border: *Transcending Divisions, Contesting Identities* (Boulder, CO/London: Lynne Rienner).

Stepick, A. and Stepick, C.D. (2010) 'The Complexities and Confusions of Segmented Assimilation', *Ethnic and Racial Studies*, 33(7), 1149–1167.

Stones, R. (2005) *Structuration Theory* (Basingstoke: Palgrave Macmillan).

Stones, R. (2006) 'Action and Agency', in J. Scott, *Sociology: The Key Concepts* (London: Routledge).

Tam, V.C.W. (1999) 'Foreign Domestic Helpers in Hong Kong and their Role in Childcare Provision', in J.H. Momsen (ed.) *Gender, Migration and Domestic Service* (London: Routledge) pp. 259–272.

Thomas, W. and Znaniecki, F. (1927) *The Polish Peasant in Europe and America* (New York: Knopf).

Thompson, J.B. (1989) 'The Theory of Structuration', in D. Held and J.B. Thompson (eds) *Social Theory of Modern Societies: Anthony Giddens and His Critics* (Cambridge: Cambridge University Press) pp. 56–76.

Tiano, S. and Ruiz, V.L. (1987) 'Conclusion', in V.L. Ruiz and S. Tiano (eds) *Women on the U.S.-Mexico Border: Responses to Change* (Hemel Hempstead: Unwin Hyman) pp. 233–259.

Urry, J. (1990) *The Tourist Gaze: Leisure and Travel in Contemporary Societies* (London: Sage).

Urry, J. (2000) *Sociology Beyond Societies: Mobilities for the Twenty-first Century* (London: Routledge).

Urry, J. (2007) *Mobilities* (Cambridge: Polity).

Van Hear, N. (2010) 'Theories of Migration and Social Change', *Journal of Ethnic and Migration Studies*, 36(10), 1531–1536.

Vasquezy, J.M. (2010) 'Blurred Borders For Some But Not "Others": Racialization, "Flexible Ethnicity" Gender, And Third-Generation Mexican American Identity', *Sociological Perspectives*, 53(1), 45–71.

Vertovec, S. (1999) 'Conceiving and Researching Transnationalism', *Ethnic and Racial Studies*, 22(2), 447–462.

Vertovec, S. (2001) 'Transnationalism and Identity', *Journal of Ethnic and Migration Studies*, 27(4), 573–582.

Waldinger, R. (2007) 'Did Manufacturing Matter? The Experience of Yesterday's Second Generation: A Reassessment', *International Migration Review*, 41(1), 3–39.

Waldren, J. (1996) *Insiders and Outsiders: Paradise and Reality in Mallorca* (Providence, RI/Oxford: Berghahn Books).

Waldren, J. (2009) 'Lifestyle Afterthoughts', in M. Benson and K. O'Reilly (eds) *Lifestyle Migration: Expectations, Aspirations and Experiences* (Farnham: Ashgate) pp. 153–164.

Wallerstein, I.M. (1974) *The Modern World System* (New York/London: Academic Press).

Watters, C. (2008) *Refugee Children: Towards the Next Horizon* (London: Routledge).

Wenger, E. (1998) *Communities of Practice: Learning, Meaning, and Identity* (Cambridge: Cambridge University Press).

Wessendorf, S. (2007) ' "Roots Migrants": Transnationalism and "Return" among Second-Generation Italians in Switzerland', *Journal of Ethnic and Migration Studies*, 33(7), 1083–1102.

Williams, A., King, R. and Patterson, G. (2000) 'Tourism and International Retirement Migration: New Forms of an Old Relationship', *Tourism Geographies*, 21(1), 28–49.

Willis, P. (1983) *Learning to Labour: How Working Class Kids Get Working Class Jobs* (Aldershot: Gower).

Wimmer, A. and Glick Schiller, N. (2002a) 'Methodological Nationalism and Beyond: Nation-State Building, Migration and the Social Sciences', *Global Networks*, 2(4), 301–334.

Wimmer, A. and Glick Schiller, N. (2002b) 'Methodological Nationalism and the Study of Migration', *Archives Européennes de Sociologie*, 43(2), 217–240.

Winch, P. (1960) *The Idea of Social Science and its Relation to Philosophy* (London: Routledge and Kegan Paul).

Worsley, P. (1984) *The Three Worlds: Culture and World Development* (London: Weidenfeld and Nicolson).

Yuval-Davis, N. (1997) *Gender and Nation* (London: Sage).

Index